BI 3309867 0

Policing for a New South Africa

D1639137

The state police force of South Africa has acquired massive notoriety since its formation. Its officers have developed a reputation for routinely provoking violence and torturing suspects. As the key bastion of apartheid it is in urgent need of change.

In *Policing for a New South Africa* Mike Brogden and Clifford Shearing evaluate the options for change. They critically analyse orthodox policing ideas imported from the West and contrast them with the indigenous models of independent policing from the townships of South Africa itself. *Policing for a New South Africa* documents this network of local policing and judicial processes. Together they offer significant possibilities for the future within a dual policing system, of the State and civilians.

Importantly, the authors suggest that South Africans need not import ideas wholesale from the West when they have their own experience on which to draw. In fact, in the light of the relative failures of their own police systems, the West may have much to learn from South Africa.

Mike Brogden is Professor of Criminal Justice at Liverpool John Moores University, and was Visiting Professor at the University of Cape Town in 1991. **Clifford Shearing** is Professor of Criminology and Sociology at the University of Toronto, and has been Visiting Research Professor at the University of the Western Cape from 1991 to 1993.

Policing for a New South Africa

Mike Brogden and Clifford Shearing

London and New York

First published 1993
by Routledge
11 New Fetter Lane, London EC4P 4EE

Transferred to Digital Printing 2004

Simultaneously published in the USA and Canada
by Routledge
29 West 35th Street, New York, NY 10001

© 1993 Mike Brogden and Clifford Shearing

Typeset in Bembo by LaserScript, Mitcham, Surrey

British Library Cataloguing in Publication Data
A catalogue record for this book is available from the British Library

Library of Congress Cataloging in Publication Data
Brogden, Michael.
  Policing for a new South Africa/Mike Brogden and Clifford Shearing.
  p. cm.
  Simultaneously published in the USA and Canada.
  Includes bibliographical references.
  1. Police administration – South Africa. 2. Police – South Africa.
  3. South Africa – Social conditions – 1961–   I. Shearing, Clifford D.,
  1942– . II. Title.
  HV8272.A3B76 1993
  363.2'0968 – dc20
                                                        92-47078
                                                          CIP

ISBN 0–415–08321–4
    0–415–10027–5 (pbk)

To
Prince Mhlambi
whose life, and violent death at the hands of
unknown assailants in October 1992, symbolizes
the extraordinary struggle and sacrifices of so
many South Africans

Liberty is a practice. . . . The liberty of men is never assured by the institutions of laws that are intended to guarantee them. That is why almost all of these laws and institutions are capable of being turned around. Not because they are ambiguous, but simply because 'liberty' is what must be exercised. . . . I think it can never be inherent in the structure of things to guarantee the exercise of freedom. The guarantee of freedom is freedom.

(Foucault 1986: 245)

Contents

Foreword	viii
Acknowledgements	xi
1 Introduction: through the looking-glass	1

Part I Catharsis

2 Policing apartheid – violence within the rules	15
3 Police culture and the discourse of supremacy	41
4 Township policing – experiencing the SAP	59

Part II Pathways of reform

5 An orthodox solution – doing it the Western way	93
6 Processes of ordering in the townships	130
7 Towards a dual system of policing	166
Notes	192
Bibliography	211
Name index	227
Subject index	230

Foreword

It is widely accepted that the South African Police Force has to be deracialized. Yet, as the authors of this deeply thought-provoking book argue, this is not enough.

Clearly, the force has to be transformed from being an instrument of white domination, and regarded as such, into a protector of the peace and security of all South Africans, accepted as such. No longer can we have a racial caste in command of the police force. The policing talents and skills of members of all communities must be tapped, so that the force, from top to bottom, becomes as culturally dappled and humanly diverse as the society from which it is drawn. Citizens must feel that this is 'our' police force defending the rights of 'all of us', not 'their' police force protecting the interest of 'them'. Imperative, however, though a programme of affirmative action undoubtedly is to enable suitably qualified men and women of all backgrounds to advance rapidly through the ranks, something far more profound is required.

It is also generally acknowledged that the South African Police needs to be professionalized. Yet, the authors insist, if effective policing is to be achieved, this too is insufficient. Policemen and women from the United Kingdom and the Netherlands have pointed out the need for transforming the way the South African Police work. While the Force has continually increased its striking capacity and bought more and more equipment, its internal functioning, particularly in relation to the recording, control and utilization of information, has gone from reasonably efficient to bad to worse.

Public opinion also increasingly demands that the whole police culture be thoroughly humanized. There is growing insistence that something drastic be done to remedy the profound and routine lack of respect for human life and human dignity shown by a great many

policeman in a great many police stations. Honest police officers –
and there are very many of them too – who want to earn a decent
living by doing work of value to the community, watch in dismay
while their more callous colleagues violate all the internationally
accepted rules of proper police conduct. Deaths in detention were
the scandal of the seventies.

Assassinations were the scandal of the eighties. Deaths in custody
are the scandal of the nineties.

Yet, as the authors of this book point out, while deracializing the
police force, cleansing it, upgrading its efficiency, improving its
morale, and altering its internal culture are all necessary, they are far
from being enough.

What is needed in addition to deracializing, professionalizing and
humanizing the police force is communitarianizing it (an attractive
phrase that is mine alone and will not be used again in this introduction). A community-integrated police force is one that of course
is drawn from and reflects the community at large, and that naturally
pays special attention to maintaining good relations with the public.

The authors argue that a strong state police force must be located
within an equally strong self-policing civil society. Self-policing, that
is, policing from inside the community becomes as important as
external policing, that is, policing by the state force. Their research
is based on working closely both with police and with community
organizations. It is not their objective to serve the interests of any
particular political grouping or formation, nor to extoll the police
above the community or the community above the police. Rather,
their goal is to encourage a new way of looking at policing in
contemporary society.

The challenges they pose are disconcerting to everyone. Those of
us outside the police force who hoped that the country could get the
kind of policing it has been longing for simply by curing the defects
of the present police, are pulled up short. Those already in the police
force are compelled to face up to the fact that, to put it in popular
language, they must not only clean up their act, they must alter their
act. Police like operating according to rules that are certain, in a
context of goals that are specific. Now they are being called upon to
establish relationships with the public that are process – rather than
rule – based and that have broad rather than narrowly defined objectives. Instead of carrying on as the unique representatives of internal
sovereignty, they now will be expected to work within a framework
of dual power. Whatever criticisms we might have of power-sharing

as a constitutional principle, it seems that modern policing requires a form of integrated power-sharing between organs of the State and organs of the community. The community accordingly does not surrender its sovereignty to the organs of the State but rather shares in the exercise of sovereignty with them. Civil society desists from handing over its security holus bolus to the state police. Rather it takes a large measure of responsibility for protecting itself. In doing so it is careful not to allow force to be used in a way not authorized by the constitution.

Thus self-policing does not permit the establishment of vigilante-type organizations, kangaroo courts, warlords, nazi-style paramilitary groupings or rule by gangsters. Nor does it condone local tyranny by party machines or prominent local personalities. On the contrary, self-protection involves the empowerment of all people equally to exercise their constitutional rights.

This is a concept book rather than a practical guide. Hopefully the authors will follow it up with a further volume directed towards practical implementation, one which will be in a format and a language accessible both to police officers and community leaders.

The approach adopted by the writers encourages us to deepen our understanding of the term Rule of Law. This concept must mean more than requiring that there be legal authorization and correct legal proce-dures for all state action. In the context of constitutionalized policing, the police must derive their powers from and exercise their authority in terms of the constitution. Their basic function is to protect people's rights as guaranteed by the constitution.

In a country with so many private powers – on the farms, in factories, in the home – the Rule of Law in the context of a system of constitutional rights, presupposes protection of all people against abuses of these rights. Human and community-sensitive policing requires appropriate police involvement in the defence of funda-mental constitutional rights. It also necessitates effective action against crime. The right to personal security, to walk freely in the streets, to sleep safely in one's home and to enjoy without disturb-ance the use of one's possessions, is one of the most fundamental of all human rights.

ALBIE SACHS
South Africa Constitution Studies Centre, Community Law
Centre, University of the Western Cape

Acknowledgements

We would like to thank the many South Africans who have so generously shared their knowledge with us. In South Africa, we have been helped by many individuals – Beattie Hofmeyer, Saras Jagwanth, Etienne Marais, Laurie Nathan, Janine Rauch, Wilfried Scharf, Nico Steytler, Elrena van der Spuy and Dirk van Zyl Smit. Lovell Fernandez has provided positive support throughout. We are especially grateful for his expert commentary on the text. The larger contribution of those many South African researchers who have struggled in their own way, often under conditions that can hardly be imagined in the West, is recognized by the many references to their work. We also acknowledge the insightful and often courageous reporting of many journalists. John Perlman will stand as representative of his South African colleagues, and David Berelson and John Carlin's works represent the Western press's attempts to convey the reality of transitional South Africa.

Clifford Shearing is particularly indebted to his colleagues at the University of the Western Cape – Thozimile Botha, Renfrew Christie, Tony Loubser, Bridgette Mabandla, Mzwai Mzamane, Michelle Morris, Bulelani Ncgoka, Harold Wolpe and Annemarie Wolpe – for providing such a stimulating work environment. He is especially indebted to the support and encouragement of Dullah Omar, the Director of the Community Law Centre. In getting to know the policing arena, he has had the benefit of the guidance of (as well as the above) Fink Haysom, Tony Mathews and Jayandra Naidoo. As always, his thinking has benefited from the work of colleagues in Toronto as well as his lively exchanges with colleagues elsewhere. He would like to acknowledge the influence of David Bayley, John Braithwaite, Richard Ericson, Philip Pettit and Philip Stenning, whose thinking has contributed to the ideas presented here. The South African Police have throughout indicated their willingness to be of assistance. His involvement in the writing of this book has been made possible by the generous support he has received from a variety of sources. These include the Centre of Criminology at the University of Toronto, the South African Educational Trust Fund, the Canadian Department of External Affairs and International Trade, the Law Programme in the Research School of Social Sciences at the Australian National University, the University of the Western Cape and the University of Cape Town.

Mike Brogden was initially involved in this project through the crucial financial support of the Oppenheimer Trust. Especially instrumental in that development was the key figure of Wilfried Scharf. The Institute of Criminology of the University of Cape Town provided hospitality and facilities. The Institute for a Democratic Alternative in South Africa (IDASA) facilitated many contacts. Nico Steytler of the University of the Western Cape contributed both academic and physical (!) insights into the South African condition. He acknowledges the hospitality of Ben Smit and Chris Botha at UNISA. For larger reasons, he is particularly indebted to Joey and Marilyn Moses, and for the kindness of the Wilgespruit Centre in Roodeport and to Billy Mpheto and other friends in Soweto. The NICRO staff in Cape Town provided an insight into the real world as well as humanity, as did the sanctuary of John Cartwright's domain. In Cape Town and Liverpool, Preet Nijhar provided sustenance and research support. In the latter city, the construction of this text drew on the support of several Criminal Justice students, among whom were Bill Hesketh, Gary Rowlands, Kailash Sharma, Chris Reid, Tony Egan, Sue Smith, and Gill Stopp. More generally, he pays a tribute to three friends on whose work and support he has drawn in recent years and whose socio-legal contributions have led to particular insights in the production of *Policing for a New South Africa* – Peter Fitzpatrick, Robert Reiner and Mike McConville. Lorie Charlesworth, Bill Dunford, Dave Graham, Trevor Jones and Sandra Walklate are aware of their own contributions. Shirley Mashiane of both Liverpool and Atteridgeville played a significant part. He also recognizes the key influence of his elder brother, the late Bill Brogden, who first pointed him in childhood to the particular evils of the apartheid regime. Finally, Marcus and Sasha have, once again, contributed through their tolerance of their father's commitments.

The excerpt from the article by R. Abrahams (1987) 'Sungusungu Village vigilante groups in Tanzania' *African Affairs*, 86 (343), is quoted by permission of Oxford University Press. The quotation from J.E. Eck and D. Spelman (1987) 'Who Ya Gonna Call', *Crime and Delinquency* 33, 1, is by permission of Sage Publishers, and the quotations from J. Cock and L. Nathan (eds) (1989) *War and Society: The Militarisation of South Africa*, and D. Pinnock (1984) *The Brotherhoods: Street Gangs and State Control in Cape Town*, are by permission of David Phillips Publishers.

Chapter 1

Introduction: through the looking-glass

If Vlok thinks that by simply talking to his officers or using an expert from the Department of Information to do so, he can transform what the blacks see as a Gestapo mentality into one closer to that of a London bobby, he is simply not in touch with reality.

(*Financial Mail* 19 April 1991)[1]

South Africans are searching for a new society, a new way of ordering their lives, in a geographic wonderland that has been an escarpment of oppression. Their dream is to abandon the institutions of tyranny that have so devastated this strikingly beautiful country and to replace them with ones that provide for harmony and goodwill among its diverse populations. They are seeking to transcend their past and usher in a better tomorrow. This dream is grounded in a long, hard and bitter struggle that has brought the leaders of the liberation movement face-to-face with the leaders of the apartheid state.

There is hope and there is fear. Hope that South Africans will find the wisdom to move forward towards greater freedom, justice, equality, and prosperity for all. Fear that 'the negotiations' that the country has embarked on, are just another chapter in the history of oppression. Fear, for example, that what is being negotiated are the conditions for the expansion of a corporate colonialism that will be as oppressive as the colonialism of apartheid that has wrought such havoc and despair.

This dream of a new South Africa is a vision of liberty understood as an assurance of equality of life-chances that Braithwaite and Pettit (1990: 63) have termed 'dominion' to distinguish it from conceptions of liberty as no more than freedom from interference by others.[2]

Dominion emphasizes that what genuine liberty requires is institutionally guaranteed equality of access to 'liberty-assets' like education, employment and security. On this conception liberty is not [a] natural condition. . . . It becomes something more like a social status that someone has vis-a-vis her colleagues in society, given the conventions and common expectations of that society. Liberty on the conception in question comes to the sort of things that is variously described as being enfranchised in a society, enjoying the freedom of a society, being incorporated as a freeman of the society and so on. Freedom on this understanding of the concept is a civic asset, the asset of being known to enjoy that protection.

(Pettit 1990: 11–12)

Within this conception, the liberation of South Africans requires more than the dismantling of the institutions of apartheid. It requires the establishment of new forms of governance that will promote the 'liberty-assets' of those most susceptible to 'discrimination, manipulation, and exploitation by others' (Pettit 1990).

The institutions of policing, as David Bayley has observed with reference to Eastern Europe, are central to this conception of liberty as a civic asset.

No institution is more central to the success of democratic nation-building in formerly-Communist countries than the police. The Soviet K.G.B. is the primary instrument controlling the character of political life, as the dreaded history of the K.G.B. and the Stasi in East Germany clearly show. The police regulate the freedoms that are essential to democracy – immunity from arbitrary arrest, detention, and exile, the ability to speak, write, demonstrate, and form associations. Their clandestine surveillance can 'chill' the impulse to participate in politics. If these institutions are left unreconstructed they will support, even perhaps engineer, a return to a repressive past. . . . Hated, discredited and dangerous, the police of these countries must be rooted out and replaced with institutions that can maintain stable social order but do so in ways which are humane and democratic.

(Bayley 1991: 1)

This conception of policing as central to dominion and liberation may seem strange to those South Africans who have struggled long and hard against institutions of policing that have sought to deny dominion by promoting both formal and substantive inequality. There is, however, no escape from policing. What is at issue is not whether there will be policing in the new South Africa but the shape it will take, the ways of doing things it will promote and whom it will empower. If policing can undermine dominion, it can also promote it. The questions facing South Africans are what kind of policing dominion requires and how it can be realized? We need to return through the looking-glass from a world where policing has meant nothing but oppression to a world in which policing is a source of protection, empowerment and liberty.

There are no ready-made answers to these questions that South Africans can simply adopt. Police everywhere have failed fully to realize the social empowerment dominion requires. Indeed, as South Africans know only too well, it has as often as not been an impediment to it.

This is true both historically and in the present day. In the period of late colonialism, for example, police forces under imperial flags were a major instrument for the subjugation and rule of territories for the sake of merchant capital. In over a hundred territories – from the Sind to the Cape of Good Hope, from Nigeria to New Zealand[3] – British police institutions were instrumental in tying indigenous peoples to the imperial yoke (Brogden, Jefferson and Walklate 1988). As Van Heerden (now a senior member of the South African Police Staff College) wrote in a revealing paragraph ten years ago:

> the need for a police service . . . arose not so much from any disorder in White society as from the presence of an over-whelming number of natives with primitive attitudes. It was necessary to use organized military force against the barbaric native population, and to protect life, livestock and goods in times of ostensible peace.
>
> (Van Heerden 1982: 29)

'Civilizing' the natives, with domestic missionaries teaching the gospel according to Rowan and Mayne, (Storch 1975; Brogden 1987b), constructing them as social dependents, in institutions, in life-styles, and critically, in rights, is the legacy of colonialism. Historically, colonial policing has been about repression not empowerment.

State policing has often been a similar source of oppression even in the most tolerant of liberal democracies where the police have frequently been a source of degradation.[4] Evidence abounds of police and their partners in criminal justice subverting rather than enhancing the liberty-assets of ethnic and racial minorities, of women, of homosexuals, and so on (Brogden *et al*. 1988: chapter 6). Public recognition of this reality has provided platforms for infinite programmes of police reform.

STATE AND CIVIL POLICIES

Underlying these programmes is a remarkable convergence around an analysis – to be found in the knowledge of practice as in explicit expositions – that identifies the centralization of policing, as a state function, as a principal source of the problems that have confronted contemporary policing (Johnston 1992). State policing has become isolated from the people whose peace it is supposed to be promoting. Indeed, it has become so distant from those it should be protecting that caring for communities, through 'community policing', has become a central plank of the reform agenda for state police in many parts of the world. Nowhere has this isolation been deeper than in South Africa, where the state police have had little conception of the distance that separates them from the majority of South Africans, as the following remarkable statement by the Commissioner of the South African Police (SAP) illustrates.

> In summary, it thus can be said that the South African Police as a result of its contact with the public at grassroots level during the last 75 years, has developed a sensitivity towards the dynamic processes taking place in the South African community. Our records show that we have been exceptionally successful in the management of these processes and in promoting order.
>
> (De Witt 1988: 84)

This isolation of the state police from communities has given rise to two consequential changes in policing: one quiet, by stealth (Stenning and Shearing 1980), the other much noisier and more triumphal. The quieter of these developments has been the emergence of corporately organized private policing through which the middle and upper classes of society have taken direct responsibility for their policing. In reducing their reliance on the state as a guarantor of peace, they have taken control over the ways in which their worlds are secured. In sharp contrast, however, the poor, who have little if any access to corporate policing, have remained largely dependent on the state police for their security. This disjuncture has reduced rather than enhanced equality of access to the liberty-asset of security. Visible evidence of this is to be found in the contrast between the peaceful worlds of work and leisure that the affluent have come to enjoy and the starkly impoverished domains available to the homeless (Davis 1990).

Those who have access to the new domains of security made possible by the privatization[5] and corporatization of public space (Shearing and Stenning 1983) enjoy far more liberty-assets than those who are excluded from them. This is strikingly evident in South Africa, where whites rely heavily on private police forces to guarantee their safety, while blacks remain dependent on a public state police whose mission above all has been the guaranteeing of black submission to apartheid (Shearing 1986).

The reality of civil or private policing as a threat to dominion must be distinguished from its potential as a source of dominion. The shift of control over policing from the state directly into the hands of communities that private policing has facilitated, holds great promise for any programme of police reform that seeks to promote greater dominion provided that its present class bias can be eliminated. Dominion requires more, not less, local civil policing but it requires it to be equitably organized so that it promotes the liberty-assets of the financially disadvantaged as well as those of the financially advantaged. The community control over policing that privatization has afforded more privileged South Africans should be generalized to South Africans universally if dominion is to be promoted.

The second, and much noisier change in policing, is to be found in a range of initiatives being promoted for or by the state police under the rubric of 'community policing'. In myriad guises, and with remarkable audacity the concept of community has been appropriated by the state and returned to them in a format dictated by it (Balbus 1978). As a result, community policing has come to represent not the defence of communities, as the term implies, but a form of policing that permits the police to keep a better watch over the community (Brogden 1982; McConville and Shepherd 1992).

As with private policing, there is much about community policing that is a cause for concern. But like private policing, it also constitutes an opportunity for the enhancement of dominion. What is valuable and attractive about these community policing initiatives is both their concern with integrating community and state resources in the 'fight against crime' through an emphasis on 'problem-solving' (Goldstein 1979) and the extent to which they provide communities with an opportunity to 'watch the police' (McConville and Shepherd 1992).

What is questionable is their affirmation of the state police as the players who should give direction and meaning to this 'fight' as this constrains the extent to which either of these possibilities can be realized. These contradictory features mean that while the established conceptions of community policing do not provide the basis for a simple 'blue' print that South Africans should uncritically emulate, there is much about community policing that can be used to promote dominion.

The conclusion to be drawn from this analysis is that while the struggle for better ways of policing has produced instructive initiatives in many parts of the world, there are no packaged 'cures' that South Africans can simply embrace. As with other 'gifts' from the industrialized West, such initiatives require not so much acceptance or rejection as a sceptical evaluation. There are lessons to be garnered in analyses that carefully separate the wheat of dominion from the chaff of oppression. There are no established models that South Africans can simply adopt. As in other forms of 'development', there is no unilinear deterministic path of progress to a more humane social order. South Africans are not going to be able simply to ride piggyback on the work of others.

In policing, as in other areas of social life, there is no clean slate. We seldom − perhaps fortunately − have an opportunity to work from scratch. The task at hand is nearly always one of institutional transformation within a context of existing institutions and disagreement over what should be accomplished. This is certainly true within South Africa where any new order is unlikely to rise like the phoenix out of the ashes of the old but will have to reshape, transform and transcend the old. The rebirth of South Africa will require institutional renewal. It will mean working from within the looking-glass world of apartheid in which the core institutions have been devised to undermine dominion to create a world in which those institutions support and empower South Africans.

The dream of a new society that values equality has long unified those whom apartheid has repressed. But it has set them apart from apartheid's beneficiaries, both black and white. A dramatic change in this polarity was signalled by the referendum of 17 March 1992, when South African whites overwhelmingly supported their President's initiatives to enter into negotiations to provide a new institutional basis for South African society. If the white minority and the black majority are to work together to build a new South Africa, they are going to have to engage in a process of healing that will enable them to move beyond the hatred and mistrust that has characterized South African race relations.

TOWARDS A TRANSFORMATION THROUGH CATHARSIS

How is this to be accomplished? A starting point would be a shared recognition of the terrible pain and suffering that white privilege has meant for blacks, 'a public accounting of what was done' (Shearing and Mzamane 1992: 13) so that the past can be left behind. Archbishop Tutu acknowledged these cathartic requirements in his comments on:

> the pain and disappointment . . . experienced by many black South Africans concerning the referendum in which the white minority decided the future of reform.
>
> (*Los Angeles Times* 20 March 1992)

This pain would have been alleviated, he argued, if De Klerk's comments on the appropriateness of letting those who opened the book of apartheid, close it, had been 'accompanied by a word of contrition'.

The healing the Archbishop sought is not simply a luxury. It is a necessity. A new transformation of the old must begin with a recognition of what the old has meant to those who have suffered under its yoke. It is for this reason that we will turn our attention first, in Chapter Two, to an account of the reality of the SAP and its policing. A police institution that has regularly killed, injured and tortured so many South Africans – sometimes within the legal rules and sometimes without – requires denunciation if it is to be transcended. This exposition is not intended as a 'shock-horror' exercise in exposé criminology that seeks to demystify the legitimatory claims of the apartheid regime. Any claims that the old South African state has had to legitimacy have long been exploded. Apartheid has no legitimacy. We review the reality of South African policing because it must be recognized if the healing that a new South Africa requires is to take place. We scrutinize the brutality that has shocked people around the world because a purgative is necessary, an evacuation of the bowels of the SAP.

Apart from documenting and illustrating state policing practices, Chapter Two concentrates on demonstrating how the accountability procedures that have connected the state police of South Africa to the wider society have served to facilitate, not to prevent police violence. The rules, legal and political, that govern South African state policing are essentially enabling devices that permit the SAP to conduct whatever actions are appropriate to safeguard the State against the citizens, not the citizens against the incursions of the State. In South Africa, as elsewhere, state police officers regularly break the law in order to maintain a notional public order. But commonly, there is little need to break rules that are themselves intended to maintain a society of grotesque inequality. In recounting police violence in South Africa, the concern is as much to expose the nature of rule-bound policework in the defence of inequality, as to provide a 'public accounting' of what has gone before and what must be surmounted.

THE DISCOURSE OF POLICING

In Chapter Three, we turn from the practice of South African policing to the discourses that have sought to construct it as legitimate (Du Preez 1988: 52). These state discourses, principally the theocratic justifications of the apartheid state, serve to provide legitimation for the cultural practices and exigencies of the rank-and-file. This analysis is explored further in Chapter Four, where we consider the way in which the South African state has criminalized black struggle in a manner that has sought to define it as illegitimate. These discourses, we argue, are as essential to the policing of apartheid as the inhumane police practices to which they have given rise.

A critical feature of this talk about policing is the conventional definition of policing as a state monopoly.[6] In the words of one critical South African scholar:

> most commentators on the role of the police in South Africa share a common assumption: they take the existence of the police for granted. They assume that any modern society has to have a large and ever-present body of people whose job it is to coerce other people. The police are either seen as a necessary component in the growing complexity of modern urban society, or as the thin blue line between order and anarchy.
>
> (Pinnock 1984: 260)

This conventional understanding has been used in South Africa and elsewhere both to discredit alternative forms of policing that are not state-based and to insist that the reform of policing must be conceived of as a reform of the state police rather than of policing more generally. This flies in the face of the mounting evidence of the privatization of policing (South 1988; Johnston 1992) as well as the evidence that security in South Africa's black townships, to the extent that it exists, very often occurs despite not because of the efforts of the SAP. Just because entities like 'street committees' do not wear blue uniform, do not swear to uphold the values of Dutch Reformed South Africa, do not ceremoniously intone the SAP hymn at passing-out parades, is not to say that policing in such communities has been abandoned.

'THE WEST KNOWS BEST'

Before we outline this alternative reality, we consider in Chapter Five, the implications of the conventional view of policing reform as reform of 'the police' through an examination of the 'underdevelopment' remedy, namely, 'doing what the West has done'. This thesis assumes fundamentally that modern South African policing derives directly from Baden-Powell's rag-tag of Canadians, English and Irish who formed the South African Constabulary in 1902 (Brogden 1989). It is like saying that Van Riebeeck settled South Africa, thus ideologically ignoring the existence of the policing institutions of black South Africans. By defining policing in that sleight-of-hand way, it conveniently excludes policing by non-state agencies and de-legitimizes forms of policing that do not fall under the convenient rubric of the state police. It assumes a unilinear progression from the early 'white' police forces of the Cape and Transvaal to the SAP of the present day with the Western model within evolutionary grasp.

However, the evolutionary approach has obvious attractions. In Western democracies, the state police kill, injure and torture fewer civilians and the urban ghettoes are not patrolled from that submarine-on-wheels, the yellow Casspir, that has become such a symbolically charged feature of South African policing. Whatever its demerits, Western policing has no tradition of legally enforcing racism.

What possibilities are there of South African policing moving towards a Western model of policing? Is such movement in any case desirable, given the failings of Western policing? In answering these questions, we argue that although what the West has been doing is decidedly better than what the SAP have been doing, any programme of reform within South Africa must recognize that the conventional view of police reform is being widely questioned. It is this questioning and the alternatives it is prompting, rather than the conventional Western understandings of policing, that should provide the point of departure for social and institutional change within South Africa.

Recent South African literature has not been short of plans for reform towards a Western model.[7] But critically, they all assume that changes in the state institution of policing will suffice, conveniently ignoring a whole gamut of policing activities – from the self-policing of the townships to the private policing of the white suburbs.

DUAL POLICING AS EMPOWERING

This critique of the conventional conceptions of police reform is followed, in Chapter Six, by a critical examination of models of policing that the struggle against apartheid has promoted. Here, we argue that while there is much in these 'experiments' that is consistent with the dream of greater dominion, there is much that threatens it. We conclude that what is required is the promotion of self-policing but within a constitutional framework of restraint that restricts the use of force as a resource primarily to the state and its police. This conclusion furnishes the basis for our proposal for a conception of policing that advances a mix of self and state policing as the appropriate model for a new South Africa. This we argue is required because dominion is most secure when its beneficiaries play a central role in providing the guarantees on which it depends.

We develop this proposal for a 'dual policing' strategy in Chapter Seven, where we argue for a fluid conception of accountability that seeks to promote argument and debate between the state and local communities. It is only such a dialogue, we argue, that will provide for a form of policing that will enhance the dominion of South Africans (Ayers and Braithwaite 1992).

This conception of policing, as a network of intersecting regulatory mechanisms (Shearing 1992a), which makes policing 'everybody's business', promotes an essential openness about what is to be done and what is being done in the name of order maintenance. This vision contrasts with the dominant images of policing – from Anglo-American to the gendarmerie inheritance of Continental Europe – that view it as a specialized, state-monopolized occupation, and conceives of police reform as the reform of the attributes and activities of these specialists, whose activities will inevitably be hard to scrutinize. Thus, the argument we advance is not the conventional one that the policing specialists known as the South African Police need to be transformed, but that the very conception of policing that has left the job to them must be recast.

Any proposal that seeks to de-centre policing is not without its dangers as the brutality so often associated with 'popular' policing in South Africa and elsewhere makes clear. After all, the modern reliance on specialized state police was borne out of a sustained critique of the inadequacies that made policing a local responsibility (Brogden *et al.* 1988: chapter 4). It is in response to these critiques that we argue for a system of dual policing in which both state and local entities are required to play a role. What is needed is an integration of the advantages of both of these traditions of policing, not a choice between them. Central to these proposals is an argument for policing as the dual responsibility of central and local authorities within a shared system of oversight and review.

Our proposals recognize that the upper and middle social classes have already wrested much responsibility for and control of policing away from the state. They respond to these developments with recommendations that seek both to empower others to share in this autonomy and to limit the extent to which the policing this promotes can be used to undermine dominion. We relate these proposals to the widespread move within Western policing towards *problem-solving policing*[8] by arguing that this approach both arises out of, and requires, a decentralization of policing.

The policing of wonderland requires both a return through the looking-glass of apartheid as well as a conception of policing that challenges the conventional wisdom that has for so long guided police reform.

Part I

Catharsis

Chapter 2

Policing apartheid – violence within the rules

The Honourable Leader of the Opposition reproaches us for our successful actions and the provisions of our security legislation, but does he think we are playing parlour games wearing white gloves? On the contrary. We are involved in a struggle against Communist inspired revolutionary forces, and the honourable leader must not expect us to combat them with the pontifical and euphonious democratic platitudes which he and his philosophical friends may dictate to us. In this struggle which we are concerned about and against which we are taking steps, we shall hit our enemies as hard as we possibly can.

(Minister of Law and Order le Grange, 1982)[1]

INTRODUCTION

Apartheid needs little introduction. Its simple function has been to limit black South Africans' access to their country's resources while at the same time ensuring their labour was available to promote the interests of white South Africans. It is both a state of affairs and a mechanism. It is a way of doing things that at once promotes discrimination and is discriminatory. It is both an order and the policing that secures that order (Shearing 1986). Racial policing existed before apartheid and may well continue beyond its collapse. Apartheid has, however, been both especially cruel and effective.

Successive South African governments in the era of National Party rule have institutionalized practices that were latent during Dominion status. They have been spectacularly successful in promoting a highly privileged life-style for whites which gave them – a minority of approximately one-eighth of the total population – priority of access to the amenities of this beautiful and resource-rich country. Blacks by contrast have either been crowded into the 'Bantustans' of South Africa's least hospitable spaces or segregated into the crude townships surrounding the centres of white population. To the Western criminologist, reared on social disorganization theory, South Africa is a topsy-turvy, looking-glass land with the white suburbs downtown and the black ghettos of the townships being expelled to the desert periphery. Apartheid, to put it bluntly, has meant that whites – who have access to economic opportunities, to social benefits and to structures of decision-making – have been able to step all over blacks with impunity.[2]

Maintaining this extraordinary state of affairs has, not surprisingly, required the use of extraordinarily coercive measures. Ensuring that people stay down so that they can be stepped on has been a brutal business. As apartheid has given all the carrots to whites, the policing of blacks has been almost all stick. On the coercion–consent continuum of an imported European marxism, there has been no space for consent. This policing strategy was expressed to one of us by a senior Namibian and ex-South African police officer as one of 'maximum force applied immediately'. All policing maintains order and all policing involves access to physical coercion (Shearing 1992d). What sets South African policing apart from most other policing is the oppressive nature of the order promoted and the violence it has employed.

The effects of this strategy have been experienced by blacks across South Africa for decades both through the segregated order it has institutionalized and the coercion this has required. Such policing has ensured that sustained brutality has been a central feature of black South African experience. South African policing has not simply promoted an order that has devastated the lives of black South Africans but has been an essential part of that order.

This brutality, and the authoritarian social structure of which it was part, has not produced the docile compliance its authors intended (Steytler 1990). On the contrary, it has led not just to active opposition but also to the development of alternative structures of social life. Violent oppression has fostered active opposition.

The oppressive policing that has sustained apartheid, much of it carried out by black officers, has been accomplished partly through the ample legal and physical capacity to kill, to maim, to torture and to terrorize. Accountability of the SAP to the law, to the courts and to the society it has served has been characterized by rules that permit – indeed, encourage – rather than constrain, police violence. In the

succeeding chapter, we examine the 'cop culture' which has encouraged SAP officers to engage in those practices. This culture has been
related to the legal framework of accountability by a peculiar South
African discourse. Before explicating those structures of law, culture
and discourse, we review some of the main features of South African
policing through violence. Our purpose in this chapter is to provide
the reader with an understanding of this violence by canvassing
examples which illustrate both its unity and variety.

POLICING THROUGH VIOLENCE

Police violence in South Africa is well documented, despite the
secrecy surrounding it. This violence, often sanctioned by law,
extends back to the beginnings of the colonization of South Africa
by Europeans (Sachs 1973). Since the 1910 Union, which formed the
present South Africa and which gave birth to the SAP, police
violence has been commonplace.

As early as 1936, an official Commission of Enquiry into the
police made comments that would not be out of place today:

> the relations between natives and the police are marked by a
> suppressed hostility which excludes whole-hearted co-operation
> . . . . This is due partly to the odium incurred by the police in
> enforcing unpopular legislation, but is contributed to by the
> manner in which such enforcement is carried out and the general
> attitude of some policemen to the native population.
>
> (quoted in Cawthra 1992: 7)

With the birth of apartheid, however, police violence has escalated
dramatically. This escalation has been correlated with black resistance which the apartheid state has disingenuously labelled 'unrest' –
a discursive strategy that implicates anyone who accepts the term, in
the claim that apartheid constitutes a state of 'rest'. This Alice-in-
Wonderland talk about police violence has been the staple diet of
official reports on the SAP.

> The history of the Force shows that since the earlier times it has
> succeeded in successfully managing situations of conflict. In doing
> so, the SAP has, by using the minimum of force, time and again
> succeeded in changing the conditions of anarchy and unrest to a
> state of peace and order within South Africa.
>
> (De Witt 1988: 10)

Deliberate killings of mainly black people by officers of the SAP occur at a rate which give South Africa the trappings of a police state. Symbolically, the most significant have been the occasional mass slaughters which act as period markers in the history of South African state violence. In between there have been spasmodic individual killings. In these confrontations, the SAP has resorted to the type of weaponry characteristic of military rather than police action, often against essentially unarmed or retreating crowds. For this, there has rarely been effective judicial condemnation. Historically, the most notorious massacre was the mass slaughter of the Israelite sect in May 1921. Much of the post-war violence has been in response to demonstrations against apartheid. Whenever blacks have politically challenged their oppression, the police have reacted brutally.

As the SAP have been tasked with maintaining apartheid, resistance has inevitably brought down its scantily gloved iron fist harder. Most of this violence has been so routine that it is unremarkable. Every so often, however, especially tragic incidents (like the events in Soweto on 16 June, 1976 when hundreds of children fell dead and injured to police and military fire) take place that epitomize the brutality of South African policing. These events form the basis for a history of struggle and brutal repression that has established South Africa's emblematic status as a moral pariah.

The occurrence that sparked the beginning of the contemporary era of police violence was the 1960 killing of sixty-nine people at Sharpeville. In this incident, a crowd of black residents, marching in protest against the extension of the Pass Laws to a police station, were dispersed with gunfire (after harassment by low-flying Sabre jets and police baton charges). This fire continued as they ran away in panic so that most of those who where killed or injured were shot in the back (Lodge 1983). This iconic incident has been followed by others, most recently at Boipatong, that have come to symbolize the hostile and brutal relationship that exists between the SAP and the people.

During the 'State of Emergency' of the mid-1980s that granted the security forces even greater powers, some 851 people (according to official reports) were killed by them in 'unrest-related' incidents. In 1985 alone – according to official figures – a total of 512 African adults and 187 African juveniles were killed in police shootings, and a total of 2,312 were wounded (Budlender 1988). In 1980, at Elsies River, at least forty-four were killed. No enquiry was ordered or action taken against the police. At Uitenhage in 1985, as at Sharpeville, most demonstrators – thirteen of whom were between 11 and

17 years old – had been shot in the back or side. The Kannemeyer Commission, like its predecessor after Sharpeville, refused to censure the police, while noting that the police commander had eschewed lesser armoury in favour of heavy-calibre weapons (Budlender 1988: 121).[3]

Killings have generally, but not always, been the province of particular police units (Steytler 1990). For example, of ninety-seven people killed during the Cape Town boycotts, ninety-five were killed by the Riot Police (described by the then Minister of Police as 'mandate holders of God' – Pinnock 1982: 314). South African riot squads, however, have their own peculiar history of violence. In an extraordinary case from Grahamstown, according to a police witness, the Squad was accused of marauding in the Cradock township after a bizarre drunken ritual of blood brotherhood – killing one person by shooting, stabbing another and suffocating a third with a plastic bag and a fan belt (*Argus* 26 November 1987; *Eastern Province Herald* 22 October 1987). There have been several incidents of deliberate police provocation in order to obtain 'kills' – the 1985 Athlone Trojan Horse incident, recorded by television cameras, is the most notorious (Steytler 1987).[4]

Recorded deaths have increased both absolutely and relatively in relation to population and police establishment changes (Foster and Luyt 1986). While there are no reliable figures available on those who have been wounded by the security forces (injuries are rarely reported to official agencies because of possible further police action), one can assume that many more black people have been injured than killed. Outside the 'unrest' context, deaths of civilians have demonstrated either extraordinary imagination or remarkable incompetence. A detective sergeant in Parow described how he had seated and tied a farm worker to a tractor's towbar but failed to notice he had fallen off. The farmworker died from multiple injuries after apparently being dragged behind the tractor. The sergeant denied assaulting him with a 'heavy blunt weapon' (*Argus* 22 July 1987).

Casual brutality to black people has been the normal practice of South African policing in this abnormal society, commencing with street confrontation and continuing behind police station doors. Nearly half a century earlier, the South African Institute for Race Relations (IRR) commented:

> the normal police practice is to manhandle an African who is passive, to jostle one who is slow in responding to an order, barked out in a language often unintelligible to him, and to push

and cuff a prisoner who shows less than the usual degree of submissiveness. Members of the force claim that harshness is essential to protect themselves.

(South African Institute of Race Relations 1949: 76)

Beresford captured the intended effects of this on black expectations when he wrote recently:

when the sergeant had barked at him to get in the squad car, he instinctively moved . . . to climb into the boot.

(*Guardian* 7 March 1992)

The violence that begins on the street continues inside the police station. Torture is as much a mainstay of South African policing as mass carnage. It has been, and continues to be, a normal part of the custodial and interrogative practices of the SAP. The only difference between the mid-1930s reports of floggings, beatings to the soles of prisoners' feet and near drownings (Franklin 1935) and the contemporary tactics of standing tortures, suffocation devices and electric shocks (Foster, Davis and Sandler 1987) is imagination. The pain and terror is the same.

Evidence that this is all routine and ubiquitous abounds for both 'political' and 'criminal' suspects (Fernandez 1991). Recently a Cape judge claimed that every accused who had been held in custody by the Brixton Murder and Robbery Squad over an eight-year period, reported having been tortured. In Natal, a police officer in court stated that placing a wet bag over the head of a suspect is an 'everyday occurrence' and standard practice in his unit. A former detective sergeant in a long affidavit claimed that the riot police in the Eastern Cape townships tortured 50 per cent of all suspects (Fernandez 1991: 51).

The coercive ingenuity of the SAP is chillingly bizarre.[5] In his study of the torture of non-political detainees, Fernandez notes a variety of inventive techniques involving animals:

[the police] set a dog on her. It ripped off her clothes in full view of the public, and she was later charged with assault.

(1991: 32–4)

The study also cites a case where the suspect

claimed to have been stripped naked, blindfolded, laid down on his back and held down while two policemen forcibly held his legs apart. Cabbage or lettuce leaves were placed on his stomach and a tortoise was encouraged to eat them. During this process it occasionally nipped at his genitals, causing him severe anguish

(1991: 32–4)

Fernandez also documents the imaginative use of electric shocks. A former member of Cape Peninsula Gang Unit described the use of a hand-cranked shocking device. He alleged:

> it looked like the pencil sharpener used in primary schools. Two wires were attached to this device, one end attached to the handcuffs of the victim – who was being held on the floor on his back with his handcuffed hands underneath him by a policeman. The end of the other wire was attached to a key which was slipped down his back. He said that 'each time the handle of the device was wound, the body jerked and the deceased was terrified'
>
> (1991: 34)

The use of electric shocks is pervasive. A former Member of Parliament for the Democratic Party, Jan van Eck, who has monitored police violence for years, provides an account of the treatment of three youths on their way home from a meeting of the Institute for a Democratic Alternative in South Africa (IDASA), a legal organization.

> They were stopped by police who wanted to know where they got the brochures of IDASA's in their possession . . . [they were] too scared to tell the police . . . and were beaten with rifle butts and kicked. They were taken to Nyanga Police Station. A sack was put over their heads. Little metal rings were attached to their fingers and for four hours they were given electric shocks. . . . [One of the youths was assaulted for six hours.] When he would not tell them what they wanted to know, he was undressed and both his hands and feet handcuffed. Two tables were brought into the room and he was made to sit on his haunches. A broomstick was stuck through his legs and arms and he was hung from this broom. The broomstick was hung over the two tables with him suspended in the middle. A wet cloth was wrapped around his little fingers, his wrists and ankles. Electric wires were attached to all these areas and electric shock upon electric shock was sent through his body while they kept on asking him questions. His fingers, wrists, and ankles were swollen and he had a terrible headache. . . . he was prevented from seeing a doctor and the next day taken to Johannesburg for further interrogation.
>
> (*Weekly Mail* 1987)

Such brutal interrogation practices are regarded by some police as legitimate.[6] For instance:

> A policeman told Capetown Regional Court that he saw nothing wrong with a person being interrogated with a pillowcase over his head.
>
> (*Argus* 23 January 1990)

Not surprisingly, deaths in custody have been a regular occurrence. More recently, a Johannesburg pathologist, Dr Jonathan Gluckman, alleged that since 1986, 130 suspects have died in police custody in suspicious circumstances (*Cape Times* 12 September 1992). The official explanations for such deaths are well known and include such 'natural causes' as slipping in shower; heart trouble caused by fall down stairs; injury to neck after falling against chair; natural causes – extreme sympathetic nervous system; haemorrhage after hitting head against desk during interrogation (*Evening Post* 15 December 1990).[7]

It is possible to continue *ad infinitum* with nauseatingly similar accounts. South African police have responded with extraordinary brutality, choreographed into terrible orgies of violence, to those who have dared to resist white rule. Terror, designed to promote utter and complete submission, has been at the core of South African policing (Steytler 1989). It would be easy and grossly misleading simply to blame misguided individuals for this brutality. That aberrational view – laying responsibility directly at the feet of individual rank-and-file members – ignores the systemic character of police violence in South Africa.[8] Yet this is precisely what the state discourse has, in the tradition of police institutions universally, sought to do:

> We admit that in such a large basket there must be a few rotten apples. But it is an undisputed fact that the police have never failed to act against any wayward member. Many are brought to justice by fellow policemen . . . not only the criminal element tarnish our image. Some indiscreet policemen may also cause a distorted image of the force.
>
> (*Star* 24 October 1987)

According to former Prime Minister Vorster, police deviance is a universal phenomenon. Police officers make mistakes like other human beings 'We are all sinners and we all commit an offence' (quoted in Fernandez 1991: 54).[9] In reality, the source of this violence is to be found within the institutions of government and law whose establishments white South Africans have voted into office for generations.

The systematic violence the police have inflicted upon black South Africans has established them as an enemy of the people.

> We in the community are so negative about the police, both consciously and unconsciously. For example, when I asked my son of two what we should do about the Police, he said we should shoot them.
>
> (quoted in Shearing and Mzamane 1992: 6)

The police in South Africa are viewed by the disenfranchised majority as a source of insecurity not security. Instead of promoting peace, the SAP are a source of violence both directly and indirectly. Amnesty International (1992: 46) commented on this collusion between the police and 'black-on-black' violence:

> In Calusa on the second of two days of sustained onslaught by Inkatha forces, uniformed police arrived with the attackers and took no action against them while they looted and burned homes. When residents attempted to fight back, they opened fire and wounded three of them. According to one eye-witness, when some women went to help one of the wounded youths, a white police officer intervened and asked him to open his mouth. The police officer then allegedly put a gun in the boy's mouth and fired.
>
> (Amnesty International 1992)

In a similar review of police complicity with violence, this time in the Cape Town Taxi War that reached a climax in 1991, Collins reviews police action and inaction under the following headings:

> involvement in attacks and violence, presence before attacks took place, assault on members of the community, shooting at victims while their shacks burned, preventing the extinguishing of fires, taking sides and escorting members or vehicles of one party, refusal to take a statement about biased police action, forcing a person to change his statement, police presence at the scene of attacks, police inaction against the perpetrators of violence, police ignoring pleas for help.
>
> (Collins 1992)

In the looking-glass world of South Africa, the police are often a source of trouble, not a refuge from it. Nowhere is this clearer than in the events surrounding the Trust Feed community in Natal, where a police investigation by 'an honest cop', after an attempted cover-up', has revealed a pattern of the most extraordinary police involvement in the fostering of 'black–on–black' violence.

> On 2 December the police held what was ostensibly a 'crime prevention' exercise. This operation was lead by Capt. Jacobus van den Heever, of the Riot Unit at Hammarsdale and later one of the accused. Twenty youths were rounded up by the SAP, and the Inkatha and UDF [United Democratic Front] supporters were sjambokked [whipped] and then detained under the Emergency Regulations. Residents were also warned to stay indoors that night, because the police would be operating in the area. It later transpired that Mitchell [a police commander in the area] was expecting Inkatha to attack the UDF that night. Thus the real motivation behind the exercise was to deprive Trust Feed of any young UDF men who would be able to defend the settlement in the event of an Inkatha attack.
>
> (Coombe 1992)

The strategic implications of police involvement in directly and indirectly promoting violence was spelt out, as Cawthra notes, by the judge who presided at that trial.

> In what should at last, put an end to official denials of the security forces' instigation of violence, the presiding judge stressed that the massacre – including women and children at a religious meeting – was part of an overall political strategy to divide and violently disrupt communities. Under this strategy, supporters of popular organizations such as trade unions and the African National Congress were targeted, and ordinary residents subjected to brutal attacks. The intention of this was to 'deliver' control of the whole area to Chief Buthelezi's Inkatha Freedom Party. Long seen as a government ally, Inkatha's importance has increased with the prospect of elections in which President De Klerk seeks to ensure a blocking veto. The pattern of violence is not confined to Natal. Since Nelson Mandela was released from prison in early 1990, over 7,000 people have been killed, through targeted assassinations and attacks on train commuters and township residents. Much of the violence wracking the black communities was the direct result of the strategy the judge pinpointed in the Trust Feed finding. A growing catalogue of important evidence has confirmed past and continuing police and military involvement in

violence, a huge, secret police network orchestrating political violence,[10] and bases for training and operating hit squads.

(Cawthra 1992: 1–2)

In summary, what the SAP shares with state police elsewhere is its access to, and use of, coercion. What sets it apart is the systematic use of extreme and bizarre forms of terror-invoking violence to promote compliance through intimidation with an extraordinarily oppressive order. Like violence, intimidation is no stranger to policing. It always lurks in the background of attempts by police to promote respect for their authority, respect for 'the badge'. In South Africa, where the majority of people grant the police little, if any, legitimacy, authority rests mainly on brutal intimidation.

The SAP use of violence has its roots in the oppressive order of apartheid and with those who encourage them to use their imagination to exploit fully its coercive capacity. South African policing is a matter of doing whatever it takes to squash resistance to injustice (Cawthra 1992; Laurence 1990; Pauw 1991; Shearing 1986). President de Klerk recognized these features of South African policing obliquely when he spoke to 500 of South Africa's highest-ranking police officers early in 1990 and set out his agenda for police reform.

Up to now the police have been required to perform two types of functions. The one is to handle typical crime situations – murder, rape, theft, etc – the task of a police force all over the world. But you also had other tasks to fulfil, and that was a control function connected to a specific political party and the execution of laws. You will no longer be required to prevent people from gathering to canvass support for their views. This is the political arena and we want to take the police out of it. We don't want to use you any more as instruments of certain political goals. We as politicians must take full responsibility for politics. . . . This is the direction we are taking and I want you to make peace with this new line.

(cited in Cawthra 1992: 3)

These words have an increasingly hollow ring as evidence begins to mount that the practices used to intimidate and divide the Trust Feed community continue to be employed. Amnesty International commented on this contrast between word and deed as follows:

While acknowledging the difficulties inherent in transforming a police force which had become deeply partisan and implicated in

covert activities against those defined as enemies of the government, human rights organizations stressed that the difficulties
were compounded by a contradictory message from the government. On the one hand, officials speak about the need for neutral
and professional policing. On the other hand, these pronounce-
ments have been accompanied only very rarely by swift and
credible investigations and actions against members of the force
acting unlawfully or in a biased manner.

(Amnesty International 1992: 7)

ACCOUNTABILITY – AUTHORIZING POLICE VIOLENCE

Accountability as applied to policing has frequently been a 'cop-out'
term – an excuse for failing to make police institutions as democratically responsible as other structures of the state. In South Africa,
with particular respect to police violence, the term has even less
meaning than elsewhere. The primary functions of accountability
structures have been to permit rather than to prevent violence. Four
separate structures are evident – accountability to the legal rules, to
the courts and judiciary, to police command, and to the political
structures of the state.

The empirical evidence on police violence can be read in different
ways. In 1990 1,871 police officers were found guilty in the courts
of offences and a further 5,314 judged guilty in departmental hearings. Police convictions for violence alone equalled 0.5 per cent of
the overall establishment (Foster and Luyt 1986). These staggering
figures, apart from identifying the SAP as a fundamentally unlawful
force, suggest that the courts and disciplinary tribunals deal appro-
priately with police transgressions. This implication is reinforced by
reports such as the following:

Senior officers have stressed the fact that misconduct by members
will not be tolerated or condoned. This is impressed on all ranks.

(*Business Day* 22 January 1989)

In fact, the patchy evidence available on police discipline, and its
sanctioning of police deviance suggests a quite different picture.[11]
Not only is it difficult for members of the SAP to break the legal
rules because they permit so much but when they do, the penalties
are minimal.

The legal rules enabling police violence

The South African Police, like police elsewhere, operate within a legal framework that expresses the directions of the state.[12] It is law that connects the police to the state. Law mandates policing and the state police institution can only artificially be distinguished from that body of legal rules from which it derives its authority (Jefferson and Grimshaw 1984). The South African state, like other states, presents itself as governed by law. There is considerable truth to this claim. Much of what the South African state does through its officials falls within the ambit of law. What is extraordinary about the South African state and its policing is just how enabling its legal provisions are: that is, just how broad is the police licence. What is remarkable is what its laws permit through the explicit provisions of its statutes. Not only is much of what South African police do perfectly legal but what they do legally can be extraordinarily brutal.

For the most part, South African police officers who kill and maim obey the law because their law is not an exacting taskmaster.[13] The spirit of law governing SAP conduct is that it permits massively discretionary police action. The imprimatur of law empowers the police to use whatever weaponry it has to ensure the subordination of the policed. The police and their masters pride themselves that they operate, for the most part, within the rule of South African law; a law that has the effect of killing and maiming those it disenfranchises so that those it enfranchises may enjoy the good life that South Africa has to offer.

The right to kill within the rules

While there is no general power to kill within the law governing police powers, South African law does provide the basis for a variety of legal justifications for doing so (Haysom 1987). These provide the SAP with what Foster and Luyt (1986) have called a 'charter for street execution'. One provision within this charter is section 49(2) of Criminal Procedure Act 51 of 1977 which grants an officer the right to shoot and kill 'suspects' to ensure that they do not escape. The section constitutes an extraordinary enabling power. All that is required in using it to justify the use of deadly force is that the person be reasonably suspected of having committed a serious offence (not a difficult matter under a legal regime where petty theft is regarded as serious if it involves trespass). In this case, the legal test of 'reasonableness' in effect means little more than that a second police officer also regards the matter as 'reasonable'. In judicial rulings 'probable grounds' are defined as a series of circumstances and events that would convince an ordinary person that a crime had been committed, was in the process of being be committed, or was about to be committed. (For an 'ordinary person' read 'ordinary white South African'.) While the South African Appellate Division has described this power as 'extremely, even dangerously wide', the courts have said that the seriousness of offence does not matter and have in effect placed the onus on the accused to prove that they did not justify being killed.[14] This power to shoot a suspect is unusual. The domestic law of many states expressly requires that advance warnings be given of the intention to use life-endangering weapons. No such caveat exists in South Africa.

In addition to this wide power, a police officer can also justify killings on the basis of the private power available to ordinary people to protect themselves and their property. A person may, subject to certain conditions, be legally authorized to kill in defence of self or property. While the extension of this justification to police officers is legally questionable, it has regularly been accepted as a justification both by the Attorney-General in deciding against a prosecution and by the courts.[15] If a police officer wishes to justify killing by raising the private defence argument, he or she must merely adduce evidence that there was an unlawful attack upon someone's property or person (Haysom 1986a).

Most significant from the point of view of the mass killings that have characterized South African policing, the draconian Internal Security Act 1982 (s.4) allowed the use of firearms to disperse an unlawful gathering. What is critical about this authority is that it does not require prior warning nor is there a requirement to use minimum force. Most of the killings that took place during the 1980s' State of Emergency were legally defensible in terms of these provisions. Furthermore, while these deaths have been regretted by members of the judiciary, they have on occasion been recognized as 'necessary' (Rabine Commission 1980).

South African law effectively recognizes police killings as a legitimate form of summary execution. These examples of 'summary justice' operate well as specific deterrence that avoid the problems of reoffending while at the same time providing a very clear message about the fate of those who do not submit to apartheid. On a more administrative level, of course, street killings also avoid the hassles and relative uncertainties of the judicial process (Haysom 1987).

It is a misapprehension with regard to South African policing to concentrate on that institution's resort to apparently illegal violence. South African law formally absolves much police violence from legal rebuke. Magistrates, for example, are legally enjoined from making public statements prejudicial to another state department. A magistrate who ignores this injunction is liable to an enquiry by the executive arm of government for misconduct. The Indemnity Act of 1977 indemnifies the State and its officials (including the police) in respect to actions undertaken 'in good faith . . . to prevent or terminate internal disorder.' The State and its functionaries are arbiters of what constitutes 'good faith'.

Monitoring interrogation and detention

Two inheritances from English practice frame the entry of a suspect into the South African criminal justice process – the euphemism of 'helping with enquiries' and the Judges Rules.[16] The former is an enabling measure by which the SAP can avoid bringing into play any legal rights for the suspect. The pressures that can be exerted during the interrogation process are governed by that curious English legacy, the Judges Rules. The latter are purely administrative directives without any force of law. The South African courts have emasculated these rules to the extent that non-compliance with their provisions may have no effect on the admissibility of a confession (Kahanovitz 1988). Formally, a confession made to a police officer below the rank of lieutenant is not admissible in evidence unless it is confirmed in writing in the presence of magistrate or justice of the peace. But this police problem can be circumvented – as it has been by the Brixton Murder and Robbery Squad – by using a justice who is a senior police officer, often belonging to the same unit (Fernandez 1991: 69).

Apart from the pressures that can be exerted during the interrogation process, two forms of violence are involved in the detention process. Forcible isolation without physical harassment constitutes a peculiar form of violence in its own right (Lawyers for Human Rights [LHR] 2 June 1983). Solitary confinement for repeated periods of ninety days during the Emergency had serious mental and physiological effects on many of those detained. Second, as we have seen, some of the grossest acts of police violence occur within the privacy of the police stations. The SAP has used detention as a form of incapacitation to remove persons from the struggle. Under detention, they could be exposed to prolonged police violence in the interests of intelligence gathering.

Detention has been as a response to demonstrations. Time in the cells, ranging from a night or two to months and even years, is used as a further form of summary sanctioning that is provided for by law. Section 29 of the Internal Security Act (ISA), which has now been amended, authorized senior police officers to detain indefinitely persons suspected of being about to commit a terrorist act or other. acts of resistance such as withholding information about terrorism. This provision was used in the 1980s as the principle 'Ways and Means Act' to justify the detention without a court appearance of thousands of persons. For example, in one of the less coercive uses of these powers:

> on 12th September, 1985, the police arrested 745 members of the Hlengiwe High School, in Soweto, and detained them for a day and night at Johannesburg's Diepkloof Prison, before releasing them without charge, following an application to the Supreme Court for their release.
>
> (*Sowetan*, September 1985)

Against such 'police justice', there is little legal defence. It also reverses traditional due process notions – guilt is assumed until innocence is proven (Brogden 1984). Children have been especially susceptible to incarceration. During the Emergency, some two thousand children were detained, some as young as eleven years (*Weekly Mail* 3 April 1986). Out of a sample of forty children giving evidence to an investigating committee, twenty-four claimed that they had been assaulted by kicking, sjambokking, the use of fists, caning and slapping during their detention (*Weekly Mail* 28 August 1986). At Middleburg an eight-year old was refused bail after a charge of intimidation (*Weekly Mail* 13 February 1986).

Many South Africans, as is well known, were detained by police without trial for much more extended periods. This could be accomplished through a variety of devices including setting bail at a prohibitive sum – something that is not difficult where most of the population live in the most abominable poverty. This, as Bindman has observed, can be used to ensure that:

> people are kept out of circulation without proving a case against them, or without detaining them under the state of emergency.
>
> (Bindman 1988: 117)

But for most detainees, however, the procedures followed have been more formal.

The 1982 ISA, as we have already noted, did not require such delicate ruses. While this power required ministerial approval, if the detention was to last more than thirty days, the Minister was not required to justify his decision to any other authority. This discretion was made even more absolute by a provision that permitted the police to say nothing about who had been detained and to deny detainees access to medical care. For example, section 7 of the ISA states that:

> the police shall inform the next-of-kin of a detainee of his detention – unless this will hinder an investigation or endanger the security of the State.

Similarly a new Detention Code introduced in 1982, which appeared to provide certain rights for detainees, was subject to significant caveats. For example, scrutiny by magistrates was subject to major restrictions on access. The Code could be suspended for the duration of a State of Emergency. Thus in 1985 and 1986, attempts to demonstrate police violations of the Detainee Code were not legally enforceable.

In addition to the ISA, there were a variety of other legal provisions that could be drawn upon to justify detections. Under the Criminal Procedure Act (CPA) of 1977 the police have had the power of short-term detention – being able to detain for 48 hours with magistrate-approved extensions beyond that period. No review is provided for. Together, the laws of South Africa have provided a network of justifications for police detention that require little imagination to employ. One example of such use is the combination of the provisions of the two Acts to avoid even the token rights granted under the ISA. For example, the Security Police could arrest suspects under section 50 of the CPA and then hold them under the infamous section 29 of the ISA. The CPA provides for less scrutiny of the person's health while in custody than the ISA but its powers with respect to the length of detention are cumbersome. Used together, they grant the space for early physical abuse as well as long-term detention – a useful combination for the maintenance of police terror.[17]

The effect of South Africa's legal regime, as the above examples illustrate, is police empowerment that makes even the most enabling laws in Western democracies seem enormously restrictive. As

Mathews (1986) has noted, the legal resources available to the SAP make the position of detainees one of complete powerlessness and vulnerability. Like 'summary justice' through police killings, the regulation of policing detention practices is there to provide for abuse not for supervision (McConville, Sanders and Leng 1991).

The South African judiciary has rarely concerned itself with monitoring police interrogation and detention practices. The 'Judges Rules' are even more misnamed in South Africa than they were in England and Wales. One of the few notable cases of judicial intervention was Justice Harms's criticism of the detention of potential witnesses to his commission by the Commissioner of Police (1990). Detention powers, like those relating to police killings, are characterized by flexibility and permissiveness in which caveats ensure that the police actions cannot be effectively legally challenged.[18]

The judicial context

The history of court decisions, as we have already suggested, indicates that South African courts have not consistently sought to ensure that even the few limits that the legislation does impose on the police use of coercive capacity are applied. South African courts, like courts elsewhere, repeatedly give the police the benefit of doubt. Magistrates and the judiciary regularly interpret the law in the most permissive fashion.[19] The view taken by the courts was neatly summed up by a Cape magistrate who, in response to a death resulting from a brutal police interrogation, excused the police with the statement that:

> members of the community are prepared to accept that mistakes do happen in the heat of the struggle.
>
> (quoted in Fernandez 1991)

A not untypical verdict by a coroner's inquest, as the Biko inquiry demonstrated, is the conclusion that no-one is responsible. A more recent example is the case of 16-year-old Mbuyeiselo 'Nixon' Phiri, who, police acknowledged, died during interrogation at Weleverdiend police station. An inquest held in private ruled that no-one could be held responsible for his death (Amnesty International 1992: 84–8).

Even in those very rare cases where police officers are found guilty by the courts for killing or injuring people, sentences are often commuted. Charges in any case are commonly reduced. A Western Transvaal policeman who beat a man to death for urinating in public was back with the police force after being convicted on a lesser charge of common assault and fined R100 by the Potchefstroom Regional Court (*City Press* 16 June 1990). Even where inquests find the police at fault, there are rarely prosecutions (Haysom 1987).

In Cape Town, two police officers found guilty of suffocating a suspect, were given a R3,000 fine (Fernandez 1991). In the same city, a former policeman was fined R500 with four months' suspended custody for indecently assaulting a woman in a police cell. More typical are mild rebukes in response to evidence of the most outrageous violence on the part of the police. An assault with plastic pipes on three street children during which they were thrown into a reservoir and tear-gassed in the police van, was justified by the magistrate because such children were accustomed to running around the streets late at night and were not like normal children (Fernandez 1991: 77). He imposed a fine of R50 on the sergeant responsible.

In the case of the prosecution of police officers, discrimination works as elsewhere against black people. Black police are more likely to be prosecuted because they cannot draw on the same organizational loyalty as can whites in the SAP (Brewer *et al.* 1988).

Organizationally sanctioned violence

The police organization itself is a further possible form of control and accountability over police practice. Formally, such organizational controls are extensive – including reprimands, demotions, unfavourable postings and dismissals. The command staff of the SAP potentially have considerable powers of internal accountability. As an institution with a quasi-military structure, its disciplinary profile contains many of the formal sanctions of highly centralized military organizations. Yet like the legal framework, it seldom operates to control police violence. It too seems to encourage and facilitate the patterns of brutality that characterize South African policing. This takes place through leaving the detail of violent action to be determined locally, through an acceptance of that brutality as an inevitable price to be paid for maintaining the apartheid order, and through sanctions within the force against those who refuse acquiesce with it.

An example of the latter is the case of Lieutenant Rockman, who protested against the actions by the Riot Squad in response to an event that he was responsible for policing near Cape Town. He was given a 'disciplinary' transfer and eventually resigned from the police. Generally, however, internal sanctions are irrelevant because superiors know intentionally little of the detailed practices of local commanders where security matters are concerned. According to one former senior officer of the Security Branch, the SAP maintains a 'need-to-know' policy where brutal actions are contemplated. Problems are passed down the chain of command to be resolved by the local commander:

> He's left to do the job and if he's an arrogant sort, he takes all the decisions. The police only feed up the line problems they can't cope with. They could have someone killed locally – the phrase is . . . something like 'permanently removed from society' – and the only thing which reaches (the higher levels) is a note to say that the problem has been solved. They don't explain anything so that the people at the top can always say they never knew.
>
> (Lieut. Col. John Horak
> quoted in the *Independent* 24 June 1992)

Where exposure of police violence occurs, sanctions are often designed to remove the individual from public gaze, not to punish. Colonel Pieter Goosen, named during the 1977 inquest as the man who ordered Steve Biko to be kept chained, was transferred after the 1978 death of another detainee. Goosen later received promotions in the SAP. Case after case demonstrate that officers who have ill-treated detainees have not only escaped punishment but been promoted in spite of their records (Foster and Luyt 1986). Captain Ockert van Schalkwyk as commander of the Bellville Unrest Unit, was censured by Acting Judge Viljoen for using 'unreasonable force' when he shot a 14-year-old in the back. Schalkwyck and a subordinate had the 'preconceived idea' of using an R1 rifle 'to bring down people' who ran from them. The year before he had detained an entire church congregation of some 225 people at Elsies River, some for two weeks, claiming it was an illegal gathering. He was further criticized by Judge Rose-Innes for high-handed and unacceptable harassment of a Cape Town printer and for lying under oath. The only effect of the court rebukes appears to have been his transfer and an investigation – not into his conduct – but into the effect of the judge's criticism on the image of the police force (*Weekly Mail* 10 July 1987).

The difficulties of providing a picture of the organizational influences on police conduct are more severe than is the case with the courts for here evidence is even more inaccessible. Foster and Luyt's unique study (1986) furnishes some evidence of police disciplinary practices, estimating that only 10 per cent of convicted police officers are discharged. Furthermore, the authors report that repeated convictions do not seem to have a detrimental effect on careers. In the face of this evidence, they conclude, with appropriate under-statement, that the police are not too diligent in policing themselves nor in dealing in any serious fashion with their own infringements of the law (Foster and Luyt 1986: 305).

In other words, even in those few cases in which the judiciary find against members of the SAP, the organization itself condones illegal violence by it members. Even when Commissions of Inquiry report on misconduct, there seems to be minimal organizational reaction to the wrongdoing identified. This even seems to be true following Inquiries specifically into police conduct. Thus when the Kanneymeyer Commission found that police had been provocative, and deliberately used heavy weapons and had then lied to the Commission about the events, no actions appear to have been taken by the police in response.

It is clear that in many cases of convictions, police officers may be temporarily suspended only to be reinstated and transferred to other geographical regions or sections of the force. Even where torture practices have been acknowledged in the courts and where the officers have been found guilty, there is no evidence of dismissals for that calculated violence. Deaths during interrogation have rarely led to disciplinary action (Foster and Luyt 1986).

Internal SAP regulations similarly have little constraining power.[20] The internal rules lack the status of law and are not issued as part of any enabling statute (LHR 2 June 1983). They are simply internal departmental directives and will not be enforced by the courts or by any independent body. Police regulations leave the police to police themselves.

Certain enhanced disciplinary measures were proposed in the Police Second Amendment Bill of 1992. These include increasing the penalty for misconduct from R300 to R2,000 or six months' imprisonment. Provision was made for demotions in rank and salary and, for the first time, a breach of the double jeopardy principle, with members potentially subject to internal hearings as well as to the courts (*Argus* 22 February 1992). But the history of organizational sanctions within the SAP suggests a dubious precedent for any internal regulative devices. Organizational controls in the SAP, like legal rules, seem to be devised to facilitate rather than to control the brutal style of South African policing.

Accountability – political restraints

Discussions about the political accountability of the South African Police have until recently largely remained outside the public domain, beyond 'legitimate' public concern. The line between discussing critically the SAP, and subverting the 'national interest' has been a very thin one (Frankel 1980). The state–police relation has been defined by an ossified security mentality, reinforced during the 1970s and 1980s, in which every aspect of policework has been deemed to be a state secret, unless the Minister declared otherwise. This mentality is reflected in the way the issue of political accountability has been handled by the governing elite. The following statement by Smit,[21] in which the question of democratic accountability is glossed, is typical:

> Control over police behaviour is exerted by mechanisms located from inside and outside the police. The judicial review and overview constitutes formal external control; inspection and discipline within the organisation are, inter alia, examples of internal controls. The police's informal accountability to the public is another form of control.
>
> (Smit 1988: 16)

Externally, the SAP has been closely identified with the executive branch of the government, an instrument of National Party partisanship. Political accountability remains minimal. There is none at all of course to the majority black population. But even for white society, accountability is very limited. The governing National Party has some notional accountability authority, through its right to appoint the Minister for Law and Order and in turn through his right to appoint the Commissioner of Police. But questions about policing in Parliament are regularly deflected being 'little more than a rubber-stamp for executive decisions' (Weitzer and Repetti n.d.: 32). The Minister, as in the case of Adriaan Vlok, regularly answers that it is not in the interests of public safety or in the public interest to furnish this information. The Minister is never in practice called to account. Indeed, he wins praise in the white Parliament by emphasizing coercion as illustrative of the effectiveness of the SAP. The Minister himself may well be often misinformed about police activities – for example, about the numbers of people held in detention during the State of Emergency. During the Emergency period, the SAP was only really accountable to the State Security Council, which included non-elected personnel from the military and from business (as mirrored locally in the Regional Services Councils). There is some evidence that the Minister himself is rarely in touch with, and unable to significantly influence, the internal decision-making process of the SAP.[22]

Governmental Commissions of Inquiry into particular policing matters appear more likely to be appointed now than previously but, like the Harms Commission, 1990, they rarely challenge the veracity of police accounts. Local accountability of the sort that characterizes the majority of Western democratic police is completely absent.

Accountability – the redress process

Formally, there are three methods of redress against the SAP – criminal and civil actions, and the formal complaint procedure. Criminal prosecutions may be brought against police officers. The Attorney-General may conduct such a prosecution or permit a civil action (there are few recent examples[23]). In any case, criminal charges against the police are extremely difficult to prove, witnesses are reluctant to come forward, and identification is difficult.[24] Civil actions are possible but subject to similar and critical limitations, such as lack of knowledge of legal rights on the part of the victim, lack of access to qualified lawyers (especially in the rural areas), the absence of financial assistance, and a six months' statute of limitations[25] (Selvan 1984). Section 3(2) of Police Act 7 1958 states that any civil action against the police must occur within six months (a major problem for township residents without legal and financial resources and lacking clear information). Other legal devices hamper potential complainants. For example, the Police Act of 1958, s.27(b) limits publication of materials about the police and (as we have seen) Act 64 of 1979 places an onus on the person to prove his/her allegations against the police. Both forms of redress are so rare as to make formal complaints almost impossible for the typical victim of police violence (Bindman 1988).

Problems with the police complaints procedure are hardly unique to the SAP. There is the usual litany of problems – especially those of the police investigating, prosecuting, and judging themselves (see Chapter 5). Few rational South Africans would indulge in pursuing the improbability of a complaint against the police. As the Le Roux Report stated, complaints of assaults were not investigated at a sufficiently high level, nor quickly and independently enough, and often by junior and incompetent personnel. Paradoxically, however, the South African government has shown itself willing to accept the *de facto* validity of complaints by paying out considerable sums to complainants. Some of these sums have been extraordinary – for example, R1.2 million to fifty-one victims of the Langa shootings.

Linguistic practices hinder complainants. Given the predominance of Afrikaner officers in key positions in the force, many rural Africans without access to that particular tongue, are being policed by persons with an alien culture and an alien tongue. Especially in the legal discourse of the court appearance, the black person without immediate command of Afrikaans (despite the possible presence of an interpreter) is, even more than defendants traditionally hampered by legal discourse when there is a common language, prevented from articulating a justified complaint.

One attempt to follow up the complaint process (Perlman *Weekly Mail* 15 May 1991) suggests that police claims of a rigorous internal investigation are absurd. Perlman investigated thirty complaints. Most of these were about allegations of police violence and two concerned fatalities. None of these complaints resulted in criminal proceedings against a police officer.

The difficulties involved in laying a complaint against the police with the police were summarized by a respondent in a study by Shearing and Mzamane as follows:

> the Minister says if you have complaints about the Police please feel free to lay a charge with the Police. But not only will the Police not accept a charge but they intimidate you for laying it.
>
> (1992: 9)

Just how difficult and dangerous it can be to lay a charge is made clear by the following case reported by Amnesty International.

> Despite fear of reprisals and a lack of faith in any likelihood of serious investigation, some of the victims of police assault and other human rights violations lodged complaints against the police. In one such case, 21-year-old 'Whitey' Mabitsa lodged a formal complaint of assault against three police officers on 26 April 1991. He had been accused at his home 12 days earlier the police who had accused him of hiding weapons for the 'comrades'. They also demanded to know the whereabouts of his brother, Johannes. The police first took him to Carltonville police station. Nine hours later he was transferred to Khutsong police

station where, according to his testimony, he was assaulted and tortured by the police, three of whom he was able to identify. He says they beat and kicked him all over his body and partially suffocated him with plastic sheeting. Then, after shackling his hands and feet together, the police administered electric shocks to different parts of his body, while continuing to interrogate him until he lost consciousness. On 17 April 1991 Whitey Mabitsa was released uncharged after a brief court appearance. He required medical treatment as a consequence of the assaults. With the assistance of a human rights monitoring organization, he lodged a complaint of assault against three police officers at Carletonville police station on 26 April 1991. Ten days later about eight police officers arrived outside his home in a vehicle with no registration plates. Three police officers, including one of those against whom he had laid a charge, questioned him and his father regarding the whereabouts of Johannes Mabitsa. Failing to get any information, the police then left. Later that day, Whitey Mabitsa was warned that he should not walk in the streets alone as one of the police officers against whom he had laid a charge of assault had threatened to kill him.

(Amnesty International 1992: 89–90).

The problems with redress against police actions and inactions since President de Klerk's promise of police reform are summed up by Amnesty as follows:

> The inherent difficulties in the police force mounting an impartial investigation into unlawful activities by its own members are even greater where the police are accused of serious crimes against part of the population for so long regarded by them as their enemy. The effectiveness of investigations into police abuse has also been hampered by what can only be described as the general passivity of the Attorney General's office.
>
> (Amnesty International 1992: 94)

The recently signed Peace Accord provides for complaint procedures that provide for some degree of external input. These procedures however still do not provide for external investigations or for comprehensive external review (Marais and Rauch 1991). The announcement by the Minister for Law and Order, Kriel, of the establishment of procedures for responding to complaints against the police that embody external elements and the statement by the

Goldstone Commission that it was establishing an investigatory arm
– to be monitored by United Nations observers – that will, among
other things, investigate allegations of police complicity in political
violence, are also encouraging.

CONCLUSION

The crux of the 'accountability' of the South African Police lies in
two problems. First, where formal rules governing police action exist
– legal and organizational – they are flexible. They can be bent at
will. Second, there has been no process of political accountability
that can be used to move behind the rules to control the police. The
brutal policing we briefly reviewed at the beginning of this chapter
is not simply a product of a misguided police culture or a few
misguided 'hotheads.' The violence of South African policing is
facilitated and enabled at legal, organizational and political levels. To
the extent that police culture, and the discourses on which it draws,
motivate police officers to do whatever it takes to sustain apartheid,
it does so with the full and unambiguous support of more formal
structures.

Chapter 3

Police culture and the discourse of supremacy

> It is so that the all-knowing God thought fit to exercise His authority on earth using the service of people, parents, officials of the Government. Therefore the wearers of the fine uniforms of the police are also the mandate-holders of God.
>
> (Minister Kruger quoted in *Argus* 1977)

POLICE CULTURE AND THE STATE

Police violence in South Africa is linked directly with two enabling structures – the rules formally governing policework (the imperatives of the white state) and, second, the normative expectations and practices of the rank-and-file (the police culture). We argued in Chapter Two, that the government, the courts and the police managers work in concert to provide for a system of incentives that encourage coercion as the mainstay of South African policing. South African state policing is not unrestrained. It is carefully choreographed and structured. The South African Police is not a force out of control. It is very much in control and it is this control, co-ordinated through the discourses of apartheid, that promotes and shapes the use of violence. The rules of law and of accountability provide a stamp of approval, for a policing process that seeks to fulfil the demands for the maintenance of white hegemony.

The military structure of the SAP guides and controls a wide discretion that rewards those who use the coercive capacity available to its members creatively in responding to resistance to the practice and institutions of white supremacy. This discretion in turn is guided by a police culture of enormous brutality that establishes the sensibility that constructs the ways of seeing and feeling that motivate police action (Ericson and Shearing 1991). State–police discourse, the language of a theocratic racism, connects the key state objective with the imperatives of the police culture. It ensures that state objectives fit with the goals of officers on the ground.

Thus police culture works hand in hand with the law and internal regulation, as guided by that discourse, to fine tune the choreography of violence that has characterized South African policing for decades. The culture itself operates as a 'subterranean process' of guidance (Shearing 1981a) ensuring that officers in the field, the rank-and-file, will respond firmly to the challenges of those who resist apartheid. These responses produce a style of policing that seeks to intimidate through violence all who dare to challenge the order it seeks to guarantee (Steytler 1989).

It is in this culture that the agency that controls and directs police activity in South Africa is to be found. It is here that the directions that constitute police management coalesce and crystallize through the discourses of the state to produce the potent force of repression that is South African state policing. In this, the SAP is no different from police elsewhere (Reiner 1985). Police culture is everywhere the primary source of the sensibility that shapes police actions. What differentiates the SAP is the brutality of its culture and the way it fits with the particular legitimating discourse of white hegemony. Together, the law, managerial resolution and the police culture, all mediated by the discourse of the 'Volk' (people), constitute a remarkably effective source of direction that has moulded a police force, half of whom are black, into a potent weapon for the maintenance of white supremacy.

The South African police culture, like police cultures everywhere, has often been blamed for police violence. For example, in the 1930s, when the force's composition was quite different, the solidarity fostered by the police culture was blamed for rank-and-file brutality to black people and the failure to testify in response to it. Lansdown comments as follows:

A difficulty with which complainants who have been harshly treated have confronted, is the disposition of some members of the police who have witnessed irregularities to stand by their guilty comrades and to suppress or distort the truth rather than to get them into trouble. This mistaken notion of esprit de corps often prevails among large bodies of men, who, when serious consequences threaten some of their members allow their sympathies to obscure the common interest.

(Landsdown 1937: 71)

More recently, now that some of the command staff have displayed an apparent readiness to accept the realities of the new South Africa, rank-and-file culture has been a useful fall guy to conceal upper echelon resistance to substantive change. Thus, a Deputy Commissioner, Van den Eyck, commenting on possible opposition to De Klerk's proposals' argued that:

the investigation should concentrate on opposition in the middle and lower ranks of the police.

(*Daily Dispatch* 15 February 1990)

Conventional Western approaches to the transformation of the SAP have, as we will argue in Chapter Five, generally concurred with this analysis of resistance to change. This focus, as we have already argued and will continue to argue below, distracts attention from the way the culture of the SAP is embedded in a more general system of repression. It is not autonomous.

South African police culture

The SAP police culture contains all the elements universally found among rank-and-file police – a sense of 'mission' (maintaining the 'thin blue line' that separates order and anarchy), a combination of suspicion and paranoia (a Hobbesian view of society as all-threatening), the isolation of the police as a community-within-a-community (solidarity with police colleagues is the only secure guarantee in a menacing world), conservatism (social change is threatening to the 'established way of doing things' and to law-and-order), a gender-based chauvinism (where masculine force is the key police problem-solving device), stereotypical assumptions about race, and qualities of realism and pragmatism (policing practice requires the bending of rules). The SAP Commissioner General Van der Merwe noted some aspects of this culture in a speech to conscripts entering the force:

Beware of boastful and cheap talk which could place young and inexperience boys on the road to violence. It is easy to create a false impression of bravery which in essence constitutes common crime, sometimes ending with the people in prison or even the death cell.

(*Citizen* 17 March 1990)

In South Africa, the extremes of police culture are accentuated by the social heritage of white police, shaped by their upbringing, family, friends and fellow police, who are taught that their special mission is to safeguard white (and especially Afrikaner) civilization against 'Die Swart Gevaar' (The Black Danger). White recruitment since the 1920s and 1930s has been mainly from that conservative segment most threatened by aspiring black people, often from rural backgrounds where they have been isolated from national changes and steeped in the culture of 'Christian Nationalism'. It was a culture that was shaped by deliberate intervention. For example, many middle- and senior-ranking Afrikaner police officers were recruited to the SAP through the Patrys Speurklub – a child police force in which potential recruits to the SAP were heavily indoctrinated into the practices of police racism.[1]

This culture is reinforced in the intimacy of the police canteen, the work-group, and the patrolling Casspir. It is most evident in the policing of the rural areas, where the structures of apartheid have been most resistant to change. Here police:

> are still steeped in the 'Baas' [boss] culture of the hinterland. Many are still besieged by a 'skop, skiet, and donder' [kick, shoot and hammer] mentality which brooks no cheekiness from Blacks. For those police who have spent most of their service posted on the Platteland [literally, flatland] nothing seems to have changed.
>
> (Fernandez 1991: 48)

Black members of the SAP share many of the key attributes of this culture. Accordingly,

> African police . . . , taking their cue from their European superiors, are especially inclined to assault Africans before and after arrest.
>
> (South African Institute of Race Relations 1949)

Goodhew (1991) notes similar historical evidence of the willingness of black officers to perform as black *SAP* rather than as *black* police. One of Shearing and Mzamane's respondents recently commented on this cultural constitution of black police as 'racists' as follows:

> There is a racist Police culture that even black policemen take on. A black policeman tells jokes like an Afrikaner and speaks like an

Afrikaner. He speaks and writes like them. There is a culture within which these people are trapped. We need a deep understanding of what these people are ensnared into. They tell jokes about Boesak and Tutu. These things overlap with religion. The police go for Conservative religion. It is a conservative culture.

(Shearing and Mzamane 1992: 7)

This police culture is not, as we have already argued, antithetical to legal rules.[2] It flourishes in an enabling legal framework. Permissive rules and a protective legal system furnish the fertile ground in which the police culture obtains immunity from wider scrutiny. Encompassing the formal rules of the legal frame and the informality of the police culture is a wider state discourse which integrates them.

LINKING NATIONAL IMPERATIVES TO THE CULTURAL EXIGENCIES

South African policework is sustained and legitimated by a circular ideology, a constellation of values rooted in the Christian-Nationalist conception of the 'Volk'. That belief system provides the discursive framework that justifies police violence and the criminalization of black people. It bridges the gap between state and the rank-and-file member of the SAP. It operates as a host culture that sustains the police culture. This wider culture has its roots in the key folk values of 'Afrikanerdom' that spawned apartheid. It is this wider culture of ethnic self-preservation that pervades and informs South African police culture. This wider culture has created strategies of survival that have charted the Afrikaner triumph over the English, despite their Anglo–Boer war defeat, and has guided them for generations in their struggles with the native peoples of South Africa.

Afrikaner culture has been given spectacular expression in the massive Voortrekker Monument outside of Pretoria, which stands as a constant reminder to the 'Volk' of their mission and the consciousness that gives it life. The narrative of this monument, written in its architecture and the friezes that cover so much of it, is one of white adversity in the face of black treachery, sustained by a Calvinist fundamentalism that identifies Afrikaners as a chosen people. This 'Afrikaner' consciousness provides the root meanings that the police culture mobilizes to justify the practices we have reviewed. It informs the way officers see the world. It provides the parameters of understanding within which they act (Ericson and Shearing 1991; White 1984).

At the heart of this narrative of legitimation are several related discourses. First, a religious discourse which represents state policing as part of a 'mission' bedrocked on the family unit. Second, a political discourse that constructs police persons as the defenders of an endangered 'civilization'. These twin themes are backed by a further discourse which seeks to define South African police practices as essentially no different from police tactics elsewhere. This third theme is used to claim that police conduct in South Africa is justified because it is legally right, because it is professionally correct, and increasingly, because it is technically and scientifically the correct way to proceed. To these has been added a discourse of black-on-black violence – the claim that black people are ethnically predisposed to settle conflicts by force. These meanings connect and unify the functionaries at all levels of the state from President all the way down to the rank-and-file police member. As one of the chroniclers of Afrikanerdom, the policeman and police historian Dipennaar, clearly understands it, it 'fortunately' permits 'men of vision like Vorster' (a Minister of Law and Order and later Prime Minister) to 'connect with police sub-culture'[3] (cited in Van der Spuy 1990). In this history 'written from the belly of the beast itself' (Van der Spuy 1990: 86) the meanings that define the Volk and its mission are identified as constituting a united crusade to maintain white supremacy.

Religion, state and police culture

The Calvinist discourse that sustains Afrikanerdom and apartheid finds its expression in a host of figuratively charged events that include parade ceremonies, inspiring speeches and the essays in the police house journal, *Servamus* (Shearing 1992c). The target of this sustained discursive barrage, that starts in training and continues thereafter, is the 'soul' of the member for the 'soul' as Foucault (1979) has argued is the 'seat of habits'. Police culture contributes to the maintenance of apartheid by 'governing the soul' (Rose 1989) of those who must maintain its order.

Policing, recruits are taught, is not simply an occupation but a sacred mission, a religious calling, in the life and survival of the Volk. The police mission is to guard over the lesser peoples of South Africa whose resistance to what God has proclaimed must be broken. As Rauch (1992a) points out, many police forces incorporate elements of religion into their formal codes and practices. What makes the

SAP different from many other police forces is the degree to which this message sustains and shapes the practice of the SAP. While religious references in police codes of practice elsewhere typically take the form of anachronistic references to fading symbols of legitimacy in South Africa, they give expression to the entrepreneurial zeal of a Calvinist theology that has provided a central justification for the 'apartness' of apartheid and the white dominance it has institutionalized (Van der Spuy 1990).

This network of meanings simultaneously drives and legitimates South African policing by assuring its police that they are to do their job, in the words of a SAP chaplain talking to a group of riot police, 'as children of God'.[4] A core medium in articulating this message has been the Afrikaans Cultural Association, established in 1955:

> because policemen felt a general need to express their Christian-National sentiments more fully within their own ranks and so foster a feeling of solidarity.
>
> (cited in Van der Spuy 1989)

The Association, with a membership of some 12,000, has as its symbol the Voortrekker Monument. While comprising only about 10 per cent of the total complement of the SAP, the Association's members operate as 'culture-holders' who work at cultural maintenance and reproduction both within and outside the force.

Working with white youth groups, the Association promotes a cultural synthesis between state and church that has the police as its centre. Its commitment to the Afrikaner search for ethnic autonomy is expressed in its motto, 'The trek continues' – an emotionally powerful reference to the history of Afrikaner struggle for survival and independence. This commitment is expressed repeatedly throughout the myriads of symbolically loaded mini-ceremonies that punctuate every feature of police life (Manning 1977; Shearing 1992c). Central players in these symbolic dramas are chaplains whose presence and words of inspiration are to be found everywhere from station parades to graduations. Their messages give expression to the 'eternal symbols of the Force', namely the 'flag, banner and creed' (*Annual Report* 1985: 35).

Of particular importance is the creed which gives discursive expression to the icons of flag and banner. This creed, expressed in the South African Police Code of Honour, is quite remarkable and worth citing:

> As a member of the SAP that serves a nation with a Christian National Foundation, a nation that in its meetings at the highest

level, acknowledges the honour and sovereignty of God above all else and therefore believes in an upright and honest way of life, I educate myself in the service of God and my country.

What the phrase 'a Christian National Foundation' references is the peculiar Afrikaner notion that South Africa is made up of genetically distinct groups whom God has ordained should develop separately under the wise but firm guidance of the evolutionary most advanced, the whites, who are duty-bound to ensure that they themselves remain pure and distinct so that they will be fit to bear their sacred burden.

This view of race and racial differences is explicitly spelt out for police in their training. This is set out in the police Ethics course as follows:

race can be described as that above-personal historically determined grouping of people that came into being under the presiding hand of God, and is associated with each other through spiritual–physical; hereditary qualities that enable us to distinguish one group from another.

(*Police Ethics* Training Manual 1991: 64)

This conception of 'lower races' who are unable to recognize the link between law and God, gives meaning to the role of the police as the bulwark of civilized order who must resist those who are unable to comprehend that 'law and order are not separate concepts. Law is order' (Van Heerden 1982: 12).[4] Police are Christian soldiers. Within this frame of meaning police are defined as persons chosen by God to fulfil a sacred mission. 'Police work is a calling, like the work of a minister or a teacher' (Commissioner Van der Merwe, *Daily Mail* 29 June 1991). Police are secular ministers.

This calling requires police to promote the order of racial segregation – a divine order that is right and good even though only the chosen few have the wit to understand this. This lack of understanding leads to resistance that makes policing difficult and regrettably coercive.

These conceptual linkages that constitute the will to act brutally were spelt out by former Prime Minister Vorster:

Had our country been inhabited by a homogeneous population subscribing to a uniform political philosophy with a traditional appreciation of the norms of civilized society, and a thorough knowledge of and strict adherence to the laws of the country, the task of the Police would have been far more pleasant. However, as we do not live in such a country, the task of the Police is more difficult. The multi-racial composition of our population should be borne in mind. This results in the Police having to persuade people who fundamentally differ from each other and who respect their own distinct norms, to obey laws they do not understand and maintain a kind of order which is foreign to their nature.

(quoted in Dippenaar 1988)

This discourse draws on the justifications central to the Afrikaner culture of which it is part to make police violence a sacred mission – far from being a source of humiliation and degradation it is a source of pride and an act of sacrifice. Police officers have been chosen by God to perform the difficult task to maintain God's order. They are chosen people within a chosen people – an elite within an elite.

Thus, in the midst of the repression of the State of Emergency that characterized South Africa in the 1980s, the Police Yearbook of the period reminded those officers who were suffering the hardships of violent policing that they did so on behalf of 'the King of Law and Order – Jesus Christ' (1985 Yearbook). For the South African Police, the 'thin blue line' is a line drawn by God in Deuteronomy and defended by God's workers.

This conception is developed and given 'academic' legitimacy in courses offered by the University of South Africa (UNISA). In one of its texts, students, among whom are members of the SAP, are encouraged to see themselves as part of a struggle in which many institutions work together to 'counteract criminalism.' Central among these is 'the church,' 'the prime bastion against criminalism' which works to harness 'man's innate religious elements in the struggle against disorderliness and criminalism' (UNISA 1983: 98). The implicit link between the police and the church established by this text is explicitly identified in *Servamus*, where police are identified as:

ministers of God . . . the front line of defence against the total breakdown of law and order. Police the world over must uphold their stance against this encroaching, patient evil.

(M. Botha, *Communism and the Police*, May 1991)

The fact that in this fight the police are often forced to use violence is a tribulation that they must face with courage. Strength is to be found in God and it is for this reason that religious ceremonies such as the church service that accompanies police parades are so important: 'God must keep us. We must work together to be brave' (quoted in Tanzer 1988). God and country are united because the laws of the state are by definition, laws of God. To obey the state is to obey God. To resist the state is to resist God and those who work to overcome this resistance must, as children and ministers of God, use the means at their disposal to uphold God's sovereignty.

> Evil and permissive force are almost unstoppably at work in the process of destroying authority in nearly every sphere [but] timeous and responsible action has, fortunately, always controlled this degeneration of life.
>
> (Minister of Law and Order Kruger, the *Argus* 6 August 1977)

The family is moulded into service with religion in the constitution of an environment of meaning that will sustain police officers called on to stem the tide of revolt and resistance. Police-wives are exhorted to sustain their men. The critical role of the police-wife was outlined in *Servamus* as follows:

> Do you realize just how important you, as the wife of a member of the SAP, really are? . . . Through the ages, the cornerstone of the inner strength of the family as the unit which the nation has been built has been the mother. Behind every successful man you will most certainly find, not merely a woman, but a woman with strength of character and determination of purpose. It is true that your husband may be in the front line of our ordered society, in the heat of the battle, but you must be that quiet, unseen source of his strength for that battle, from you must flow the strength that he needs to come out of that battle unscathed and victorious. . . . If she is a sour and disgruntled wife, it will not be long before her husband will also find his work a burden and a bore. . . . If she is constantly grumbling about the way in which the policeman is providing for his family, she will make him disgruntled and dissatisfied with his job. . . . The policeman has a high and sacred calling – but so has the wife of a policeman. He may be the wheel that has to turn to keep our slightly mad society from falling apart – but then she ought to be the 'nut' which keeps that wheel functional and in its place. . . . fulfil that high calling to which you, as the wife of a policeman, have been called.
>
> (*Servamus* August 1990)

Family and church combine as the natural units on which the South African police officer can rely when in distress. The 'wife' is fundamentally important to comfort her husband and to relieve him from the toils and pressures of his calling. She furnishes the unity and bedrock of the family and, in turn, the family is the core unit of the police organization.

Religion also plays an important part in Satanizing opposition. Resistance to SAP practices is not just evil but also transformed into Satanic practice in the work of one eccentric officer (who is however treated with some authority by *Servamus*):

> As Christian policemen we have a double authority to educate the public. We can show them the methods by which Satan slowly entraps our children. . . . I have the blood of Jesus over me . . . without this nobody can hope to wage war for Christ against the enemy.
>
> (*Servamus* May 1991)

As clerics in uniform, police officers undergo the trials of danger and vilification of a Satanic-driven opposition, with the fortitude of the calling. More secular forms of organization are irrelevant to such a priesthood. The white state has a theocratic base which incorporates its servants within one creed. The fundamentalism of the Dutch Reformed Church is not so much a civil religion as an Afrikaner ideology justifying apartheid (Ngcokvane 1989). Church and state are tightly intertwined in personnel through the National Party and through a theocratic ideology that sanctifies the separation of races. The religious discourse that connects state with the police culture is of central importance to the SAP – not merely because it provides for solace in times of danger but also because it connects the key concerns and practices of the police culture with the larger imperatives of the white state.

Political discourse

The Christian fundamentalism that constructs the will required to maintain apartheid's repressive order is embrocated with a selective remembering that highlights the treachery of the Other (the British and the blacks) in the face of an heroic Afrikaner determination to free the Volk from the yoke of repression. These themes are brought together in the symbolism of the 'great trek' from British rule, the Anglo–Boer wars, and the righteous wars against black barbarism and treachery (Worrall 1972). The historical discourses that create this Christian Nationalism weave together three dominant political themes – the communist enemy, ethnic authority (or what Van der Spuy (1990: 102) following Van den Berg calls a 'Herrenvolk Democracy'), and service to the community – with the religious themes we have already identified. The logic of this integration is nicely spelt out in a recent White Paper:

> traditionally [the SAP have been] regarded as an organisation which renders service. This 'service' is regarded as a very important prerequisite for successful policing, as it not only promotes good attitudes and close co-operation, but also projects the image of the Force as a body of the authority of the State.
>
> (1990: 7)

In the post-war years, the spectre of communism has been welded with the historical themes to mobilize the police to stand firm against resistance to apartheid (Van der Spuy 1990). It was not difficult to use communism's hostility to religion to represent it as the devil incarnate and the principal source of black resistance. Black opposition was a communist-inspired plot (deduced from the alignment of the South African Communist Party with the ANC) that it was the duty of the Police, as champions of Christian-nationalism, to resist.

This conception of communism and its implications for policing is outlined in the UNISA's 1983 Criminology course guide.

> Communism today is a Marx inspired, Moscow directed, international criminal conspiracy against civilization, based on a God-denying philosophy of life, sustained by faith in the dialectic, backed by the devotion of its fanatical believers and to no uncertain extent by the armed might of the Red Armies. The RSA is today experiencing an armed and an ideological onslaught from the communist ranks. South Africans who have been indoctrinated with this ideology have adopted the fundamental relations as interpreted by communism and justify the violation of accepted South African fundamental relations on these grounds.
>
> (UNISA 1983: 97)

During the Emergency period, the police were the first line of defence against communist-inspired 'unrest' and were required to crush it in the name of the peculiar conception of ethnic democracy that the farcical notion of internal self-governing states made possible.

> The Police swiftly identified the methods used by the subversive elements. . . . [resisting] the attempted undermining of the demo-

cratic state by denigrating it and assailing its power bases and presenting them as corrupt – a tried revolutionary method in which the foreign media, in particular, participate. They placed the SAP. in the forefront of international criticism, and accusations of police brutality were spread in an unscrupulous manner.

(*Annual Report* 1985)

The police as the upholders of democratic principles had to bear the cost of international vilification during the Emergency.

The Government of the Republic, which had been democratically elected by the inhabitants of the country, decided to stand by its decision, despite the fact that this would inevitably lead to international isolation. . . . The S.A. Police understood and supported the government.

(Dipennaar 1988: 734. Cited in Van der Spuy 1990: 99)

Similarly, state and police rhetoric have promoted a conception of police service that is breathtaking in its disingenuous naivety:

policing in the Republic has indeed developed into a community service which at present forms the corner stone of an orderly society. . . . Its activities are aimed at the lessening of conflicts and latent threats . . . to the orderly community: the informal pacifying of conflict by mutual relationships and the rendering of a variety of community services. . . . the community determines the roles and continually evaluates it in order to bring it in harmony with the changed structure. From the point of view of the Police, the person who accepts the role of maintaining law and order, that is the police officials, must in the executing of that role adapt his behaviour and the structure to the expectations of the community.

(Minister of Law and Order, Adrian Vlok. White Paper 1990)

Community, police social service, together with the notion of South Africa as a democratic defence against a defiling communism, are the key concepts in a political discourse that links the manifesto of the white state with conception of the police as a Christian bulwark against evil. Criticisms are delegitimated by pathologizing their source. For example, where the police have a bad reputation in the townships it is because communist-infiltrated agencies such as Radio Freedom incite the black population to violence. Criticism is a communist-inspired 'smear' tactic to discredit the police; 'troublemakers', 'agitators', 'ringleaders' (*Annual Report* 1980: 7), 'terrorists' and 'radicals' conspire to undermine law and order (De Witt 1988) by intimidating those 'ordinary persons who do not want to submit themselves to their authority (*ibid*: 33). 'Unrest' at school is due to the presence of 'trained guerillas' (*Annual Report* 1980) while the police killings at places like Sebokeng and Viljoenskroon are seen as activities 'forced on [the police] by mischievous, radical, agitators' (*Annual Report* 1988).

In this interpretive framework in which protest is individualized and pathologized (Van der Spuy 1990) law, order, and democracy are juxtaposed against the godless, Communist forces of anarchy or more simply any point of view that is not conservative.

In every society there is constant polarization of forces which tend to violate the fundamental relations and those which tend to maintain them. Crime will tend to decline to the extent to which philosophies and values which seek to preserve the fundamental relations predominate. Should less conservative philosophies prevail, crime will tend to increase.

(UNISA 1983: 95)

In Dipennaar's panegyric history of the SAP, the entire history of black politics is dismissed as a product of the whims of international communism and imperialism. By the 1970s, according to Dipennaar, South Africa is besieged by a multi-dimensional onslaught, orchestrated by communist imperialist powers and enacted by terrorist organization. The aim of this onslaught is the violent overthrow of the South African democratic state, and the destruction of its Christian values (Van der Spuy 1990). This 'academic' rhetoric, together with the wider Christian discourses with which it articulates, have sought to drain political legitimacy from black struggle at the same time as they have legitimated the SAP's paranoid search for the enemies of the Volk.

Subsidiary discourses

Political and religious discourses are, as we have already hinted, supported by a variety of other subsidiary discourses. One such discourse – as our analysis of accountability in the last chapter makes clear – is law. Another is science and technology (Ericson and Shearing 1986; Ericson 1992). As Posel has argued,

Large areas of state control are depoliticised by being depicted in technical terms which disclaim their political contestability. The legitimation of such policies then devolves upon 'proving' their effectiveness, rather than demonstrating their 'democratic' basis.

(Posel 1984: 2)

What increasingly characterizes the discourses of the SAP in the 1990s is an attempt to validate conduct by reference to a variety of scientific and technical devices. By assembling an array of both technical equipment, a technical service division, and a variety of technical 'testing' devices, the SAP is attempting to define crucial areas of its decision-making as governed by science (Ericson and Shearing 1986).

For example, arguments over the access black people have to careers in the police institution – for instance the debates surrounding Affirmative Action – are reconstructed as technical matters to be solved by a variety of scientific testing devices (Shearing 1992b). Similarly the discourse of scientific problem-solving is a recurrent theme in the contemporary SAP literature. This discourse constructs the police as experts and professionals rather than as actors advancing political agendas. SAP documentation waxes lyrically about 'scientific' innovations – for example, the first use of a 'sneeze' machine to control 'riots' in Soweto (*Yearbook* 1976). 'Fingerprint science' is exalted as an apolitical technical exercise. A police register of fingerprints of all black persons over 16 years was justified

because so many Blacks, unlike Whites, Coloureds and Indians, cannot be identified by name alone and, furthermore, do not reside at permanent addresses for long continuous periods, with the result that identification by means of fingerprints is the only infallible method that can be used.

(From Report for the Department of Cooperation and Development 1978–9. Quoted in Prior 1988)

UNISA's Police Science degree remains the major academic avenue through which SAP members can raise their promotional aspirations through formal qualifications. In the courses of this degree policing is constructed as the 'science' of criminalistics.

Where problems occur between white police officers and black people, resolution is sought through scientific devices. Criticism of police handling of 'riots' is responded to by having members of riot squads psychometrically evaluated by clinical and industrial psychologists at the Institute of Behavioural Sciences (*Annual Report* 1990: 52). Similarly problems of recruit entry are dealt with by 'scientifically screening' all applicants (*Annual Report* 1980). Through this 'scientification of police work' (Ericson and Shearing 1986) policing becomes just another 'expert system' requiring 'expert knowledge' (Ericson 1992) rather than a realm of political values and conflicts. Political conflict is denied and reduced to scientific questions of 'personality' or 'crowd psychology'.

Technicism as a discourse has had four primary functions for the SAP. First, it provides the police with an aura of professionalism that carries with it notions of service, self-sacrifice, and specialized knowledge to be placed at the disposal of the 'community'. This also lends legitimacy to the police culture by defining it as a 'professional' subculture that sets police personnel apart from the lack of expertise of their lay critics who know nothing of the practical realities of policework.

Second, scientism legitimates SAP activities that might otherwise be considered controversial. Fingerprint science, for example, appears to reduce to a simple technical matter, the mass fingerprinting of black people and subsequent record-keeping across the country. Third, as scientists are by implication, objective, and value-free, SAP members are portrayed as para-scientists whose judgements are based on objective scientific criteria. A recent example of the use of the rhetoric of social science to legitimate the carrying of weapons in demonstrations has been the defence offered for the carrying of weapons symbols by Inkatha supporters. When the government accepted a definition of spears, sticks and shields as 'cultural weapons,' rather than simply as weapons, they joined Inkatha in mobilizing a 'scientific' anthropological reference to justify this practice.

Fourthly, there has been an attempt to pathologize blacks as violent beings through the 'black-on-black' violence theme. The internecine conflicts in the black townships, often provoked and promoted by the SAP and the SADF, has been used by the SAP to promote an image of itself as a vital buffer between warring, primitive, black tribes. This 'black-on-black' theme has been used to promote the thin-blue-line thesis of the SAP as the bulwark of civilized values that will prevent South Africa collapsing under chaos that majority rule will introduce:

> to date the police have managed to save the lives of thousands of people in many unrest situations through their fearless and sensitive conduct, and therefore fulfil their task with distinction.
>
> (Minister Vlok, *Daily Dispatch* 27 January 1990)

This discursive strategy is used to define the SAP as mediators and peacekeepers caught in the middle of inter-tribal conflicts between primitive groups. The police role is to do whatever they can to keep these primitive inclinations and the activities they promote within bounds.

> Faction fights have always been a part of the Zulu life-style. The reasons for the feuds are lost in antiquity, but it is considered an honourable tradition to carry on a vendetta from one generation to the next. Faction fights have no political connotations. They start without warning as a result of some provocative action or remark.
>
> (*Yearbook* 1991: 83)

As Rauch points out, no-one refers to the Second World War, as 'white-on-white' tribal violence (Rauch 1992a). Nor is the terrible violence taking place in Europe as we write between Croats and the Serbians defined as either tribal or white-on-white violence. The black-on-black theme serves to blame blacks, rather than apartheid and its white authors, for the terrifying experience of township life at the same time as it elevates the SAP to the position of neutral referee arbitrating between uncivilized peoples before a shocked world audience.

CONCLUSION

The religious, political and most recently the scientific discourses of white rule in South Africa have been embedded in the police culture through a combination of selection and continuing cultural indoctrination. From the moment the National Party took power in South Africa in 1948, its politicians have worked with great skill and initiative to shape the ethos of the civil service into a mechanism that would enthusiastically promote its policies. The strategic recruitment and promotion of persons schooled in the values of the Volk (generally in the civil service since the late 1940s but in the SAP since the 1930s) has been successfully employed to command the loyal support of state officials. Although Afrikaners no longer dominate the South African police numerically, they continue to be its culture-holders. The police culture for both black and white police is the culture of Afrikanerdom. It is this culture, and the reward systems that support it that has enabled the SAP to place black police in the front lines of South African policing in this looking glass reality in which oppressed blacks have policed oppressed blacks. The practice of state policing is not a consequence of 'sub-standard human material' which 'results in poorer service' (Van Heerden 1982: 148). It is a product of a network of intersecting discourses that have shaped the ways of being and seeing that the maintenance of the South African order requires.

The discourses allow the culture to criminalize black resistance and to denote the 'ordinary' crime of the black townships as due, not to the pressure cooker of communities artificially constructed and legally and socially debased by apartheid, but as innate to black tradition. It is to this township experience that we now turn in seeking to demonstrate the effects, in practice, of the congruence between state discourses and police culture.

Chapter 4

Township policing – experiencing the SAP

I think that the South African Police will make an exceptional contribution to Soweto, as peacemakers, as social workers, and as friends of the community. For when I compare us, the SA Police looks like the winning team.

(An SAP General launching a police community initiative in Soweto. Quoted in *Servamus* 1991)

INTRODUCTION – POLICING THE TOWNSHIPS

It is in the policing of the townships that the consequences of the conjunction between state imperatives and police cultural exigencies have been most manifest. Within the overcrowded extra-urban ghettoes in which the major part of South Africa's black population has been legally segregated, state policing has been at it most intense. In these cockpits normal policing in South Africa has meant brutal control.

A wider coverage of South African state policing would give some space to other experiences. In the rural areas, state policing remains trapped in a feudal structure where the white police sergeant is lord of all he surveys (Fernandez 1991). Here, where the critical media or monitoring groups like Lawyers for Human Rights have little access to communities, major obstacles prevent the articulation of black experience of state policing. In the 'Bantustans', there is varying evidence of brutality.[1] Similarly state policing in the white suburbs is largely unexplored – there being no tradition of academic research on 'social service' policing in South Africa. Members of the SAP doubtless deal with barking dogs and guide schoolchildren across the road like their contemporaries elsewhere. Such police service is not, however, a germane field in documenting the key practices of state policing in South Africa.[2]

The day-to-day experience of state policing in the townships is not the spectacular stuff of headlines. The Security and Riot Police may have been notorious and their activities iconic but their sorties, fortunately, have been relatively rare. The same is true of the 'crime-fighting' efforts of units such as the all-white, Rambo-style Soweto Murder and Robbery Squad.[3] Encounters with such bodies by township residents, despite their emblematic significance, remain unusual. More routine and ubiquitous – and the focus of this chapter – is the black-on-black policing of municipal police, special constables, police assistants and the like. It is here, in the 'normal' experience of state policing, that the criminalization so central to black experience of apartheid is to be found.[4] It is here in the routine of everyday life that attitudes to the SAP are crystallized. The potential for transforming state policing, as required by the new South Africa, is determined daily in encounters on the township streets.

A DISCOURSE OF CRIMINALIZATION

Police-black relations are based on a fundamental historical precept. The rule of law enshrines inequality of condition. South African criminal and administrative laws have embodied the notion that rights routinely enjoyed by whites are to be provided only occasionally to blacks and then as a licensed privilege. Taken-for-granted practices, customary norms, for white people, may involve criminal sanctions when exercised by black people.

Long before the apartheid structure institutionalized legal inequality, black people were subject to legal police criminalization. That criminalization was not invented by apartheid but is embedded in the history of the South African state. At its formation, Cecil Rhodes had declared:

> this native question. Either you have to received them on an equal footing as citizens or to call them a subject race . . . there must be class legislation . . . Pass Laws and Peace Preservation Acts . . . we have to treat the Natives where they are in a state of barbarism, in a different way to ourselves. . . . The Native is to be treated as a child and denied the Franchise.
>
> (quoted in Mnguni 1988)

As we have argued earlier, the problem with state policing in South Africa is not so much police law-breaking, but the laws impartially enforced. Partisan laws implemented by a neutral police force damage and antagonize. Long before the enactment of the principal apartheid legislation, the Lansdown Commission had spelt out the consequences of legislative inequality for the policed:

> The differential legislation which has imposed upon natives restrictions peculiar to themselves, and has . . . placed in the hands of the police very comprehensive powers and entrusted them in some matters with a very wide discretion. Thus . . . a native in an urban area is required to carry a copy of his service contract, and failure to produce it on demand by a policeman constitutes an offence for which he may be arrested summarily. He is further required between certain hours of the night to carry a special pass as well . . . and if he is found in a public place and fails to show both of these documents, he is guilty of an offence and liable to arrest. So also under the Native Taxation and Development Act, a native . . . is liable to be arrested without warrant if he fails to produce his current tax receipt for examination by a European policeman. The provisions of the Liquor Act, 1928, while imposing drastic restrictions upon natives, give the police wide powers to enter and inspect any premises in which it is reasonable to suspect that any liquor is kept in contravention of the Act. This Act also makes it an offence to be drunk or semi-drunk in a public place, and as the question whether a native is drunk and should be arrested often fails to be decided according to the opinion of the policeman, there is a great probability of resistance. The comprehensive powers of the policeman, which can so easily be abused, tend to beget in him a spirit of arrogance towards the native, while the submissiveness imposed upon the latter and the reflection that he is targeted differently from others, induces in him a sullen and resentful attitude.
>
> (Lansdown 1937: 72)

Community hostility has recently been acknowledged by the SAP as they have begun to ponder the implications of a new South Africa for them.

> All these years we were black sheep in people's eyes because we had to enforce unpopular measures like the Pass laws and the Prohibition of the Mixed Marriages Act.
>
> (quoted in *Natal Mercury* 5 February 1990)

The rule of law in South Africa over the last century has involved the institutionalization of legal inequality. Black people conducting activities reserved for whites were criminals until proven otherwise. A conception of 'law and order' informed by dominant South African values prevailed over other considerations of legal and social justice. In this conception, the authority of the white official, the policeman, the master, the employer and the property owner ranked very highly (Mott 1979). In Haysom's words

> the laws against blacks are enforced with extreme vigour on the one hand, and on the other, the protection that the law is supposed to offer is ephemeral.
>
> (1986: 52)

Inequality in justice is apparent both in the courts and in the specific legislation:

> Had the evidence been given by Europeans it might well have prevailed against the single evidence of Warrant Officer de Beer. . . . But the native in giving evidence, is so prone to exaggeration that it is often impossible to distinguish the truth from the fiction.
>
> (From the judgment in *S v Xhego*, 1964. Quoted by Fernandez 1991)

Again Lansdown is instructive:

> This position is caused by restrictive enactments carrying criminal sanctions which affect them alone. It is the last of these factors that which mainly brings the police and natives into frequent conflict resulting in an attitude of mutual distrust, suspicion and dislike. The majority of natives who gave evidence before us . . . testified . . . that natives regard the police as enemies and persecutors rather than as protectors and friends.
>
> (Lansdown 1937: 69)

Racial legislation is the historical root of state policing in the townships. Whatever aberrational features characterize the practice of South African policing, the fundamental source is systemic – the structure of racial ordinances, as part of a wider network of domination, enforced by police functionaries. Reform of the relationship between the SAP and black residents finds itself stranded on an historical rock of criminalization. The new legitimizing discourses of police-black relations that are being mobilized to reform state policing seek, via a discursive sleight of hand, to sweep aside the concrete historical basis for township hostility to the SAP. History, memory of legal police oppression, is a central feature of the South African mosaic that cannot simply be washed away.

The depth of this police induced trauma can be seen in findings of research on the dreams of black children where police raids on the townships have been the central motif:[5]

> the knocks at the back and front doors and windows were raining loud and furiously, incessantly violent . . . torchlights were making angry shafts in the little rooms, the passageway, flashing through the curtains as if to tear them apart with their beams. Those strong torches flashing in the middle of the night or morning can be frightening in the ghettos of South Africa.
>
> (Pheto 1983: 13)

In opinion research surveys, the functionaries of the law – from Magistrates to the SAP – are generally seen as the dispensers of injustice rather than justice (Davis 1986). The institutions of the white 'justice' are seen as linked in a monolith of repression.

Two sets of laws are central to the historical systemic antagonism between SAP and black people: (a) those regulating the 'influx' of blacks into urban areas (the so-called 'Pass' Laws) and (b) those regulating their behaviour within such areas (the liquor laws, tax laws, and the infamous Master and Servants Laws governing indentured employees). Before 1945, the criminal and administrative laws affecting blacks only were enacted and enforced to establish white control of the economy and government. Since 1945, there has been an extension of criminal laws designed specifically to consolidate white privilege. 'Law and order' at whatever cost has been exalted to a cardinal principle of government (Fernandez 1991).

The history of the Pass Laws is well documented and needs little recounting here (see, for example, Hindson 1987). Criminalization through Pass devices was common from the outset of the South African experience. In the Cape, at the turn of the nineteenth century, they were used against the native black population – 'vagrancy'[6] was the legal euphemism for being Pass-less. They became a central feature of South African social institutions in the nineteenth century. The Voortrekkers took a Pass system with them to Natal and Transvaal. Early policing units such as the Natal Rijdende Dienstmacht included among their major functions the task of issuing Passes to non-whites. Later, mining interests encouraged the development of criminalization through the Pass Laws as a means of retaining labour. The Transvaal government introduced a series of Police Passes, to control 'incomers'. In Natal, indentured labour was tied by a Pass system.[7]

The early twentieth century saw a stream of Pass-related criminalization measures – for example, the Native Labour Regulation Act 15 of 1911 placed Africans under the Department of Native Affairs which was to be 'policed' by special Pass Officers. A string of related Pass legislation followed - Lansdown noted that

> a 'native' might have to carry as many as nine different Passes and evidence presented to his Commission protested vehemently at criminalisation through Pass-harassment by the police.
>
> (Lansdown 1937: 105)

Some 300,000 Pass-related offences were recorded yearly by 1942 in the Transvaal alone. In the late 1940s, Pass offenders had the Hobson's choice of prison or farm-work. In practice, the latter was almost obligatory and its consequences were seen when evidence in court revealed the presence of the corpses of these involuntary workers being buried on farms (Hindson 1988). White critics of the system, like white critics of apartheid generally, were regarded as 'unpatriotic' (Randall 1972: 56).

Later extension of the Pass system simply made the large mass of the African population susceptible to normal police harassment and criminalization – especially by Act 67 of 1952, which made it compulsory for African males over 16 to carry passes on their person at all times, powers which were later extended to include women. The Pass Book had become a major device for police control, containing all the criminalistic record-keeping paraphernalia of the white South African state. By the time of abolition, some fifteen million fingerprints were held centrally in Pretoria with computerized access to local police stations.

Township experience involved a continued process of degradation at the hands of the police with women often bearing the brunt of repression:

> no husband can ever be sure any day that his wife is his wife; nor can he be sure that his child may not be taken away from him and sold to farmers under the pretext of failing to comply with the pass regulation . . . how can any decent home, be built for the proper upbringing of the children. . . . A man has only to come into any home or stop a woman on the street and say he is a policeman or detective and the law of the country empowers him to take away

that woman and to touch any part of her body as they can do with men under the pretext that they are searching for a pass. Even in the days of slavery there was nothing like this. This is the basest method of humiliating people and destroying the honour of womanhood.[8]

(ANC leaflet, quoted in Lodge 1983)

The mass actions staged by blacks to protest their rejection of criminalizing Pass Laws, usually attracted violent police reaction – for example, the August 1956 march by some 10,000 women and the challenges that culminated in the Sharpeville massacre by the SAP in 1960. These protests and related actions in defiance of the criminalizing process contributed to banning and political outlawing of the ANC and of the Pan African Congress (PAC).

The repeal of the Pass Laws in 1986 was undoubtedly an important concession. But at the same time, the government announced stricter anti-squatting measures. Trespass charges provide a substitute form of harassment and criminalization to the defunct Pass system.[9]

Pass criminalization was bound up with enforced racial segregation of residential areas. Initial separative policies were, to a large extent, dictated by an economic imperative. An example is the marginalization of Indian traders during the 1880s. During the early years of the Dominion, a succession of attempts followed the 1924 Lange Commission in attempting to criminalize these entrepreneurs. White shopkeepers and property owners complained that they were losing trade to the influx of Asian and Muslim traders, especially in the black townships. The result was the Asiatic Land Tenure and Indian Representation Act of 1946 (known as the Ghetto Act) which restricted Indian occupational and business rights in Natal.

Simultaneously, there had been pressure to criminalize black people under the early and related 'influx control' legislation. In 1923, the Native Urban Areas Act was passed to expel 'unwanted, nuisance elements' from the cities. A 1937 Bill aimed at 'establishing once and for all the policy that natives should only be in the towns so far as their presence is demanded by the white population.' An early key measure was the Black Urban Areas Consolidation Act 25, of 1945. This legislation was tightened with the passing of the Group Areas Act 1950 and related legislation.[10]

Together, Pass and segregative legislation has been instrumental in defining African and Indian experience of state police. Such legislation was historically buttressed by taxation measures directed specifically at black people, designed both to raise local revenue and to extend state control over them. These latter devices, constructed as apparently apolitical revenue devices, operated in reality as criminalizing mechanisms. Numerical accounts of Africans subject to policing, as we have already suggested, through such legislation draw attention to the normality of that experience. For example, between 1948 and 1981, there were twelve and a half million prosecutions under the Pass Laws (*Argus* 3 April 1981). In 1972, it was calculated that one out of four Africans was arrested each year by the police for some 'technical' offence or which did not apply to whites (Randall 1972). One court in the Cape dealing with influx control heard 14,000 cases in 1981 alone and imposed some 684 years in prison, as well as several thousand deportations to the Transkei and Ciskei. Nationally, during that previous decade, some 33,000 people were jailed monthly for influx control offences (*Argus* 30 May 1981). In 1984, some 238,000 Africans were arrested for Pass and other technical violations (Amnesty International 1986).

Criminalization under 'administrative' legislation was augmented by measures under the several security Acts. Between 1970 and 1978, Parliament passed sixty-two Acts dealing with the control of blacks with the Police Act itself being reinforced eight times (Turk 1981). Legislation designed to criminalize black protest was a key feature of black experience. As early as 1953, the Public Order Safety Act, allowed for a state of emergency to be declared and for most laws providing for civil rights to be suspended.

During the 1980s, the most significant practices of black criminalization occurred under the state security legislation. The definition of crime could be stretched to include any opposition to white rule. For example, counter-state violence in South Africa was described as 'a method applied by a group or groups to eliminate the existing order in the country by means of non-Parliamentary conduct' (Du Preez 1982). This definition conveniently glossed the lack of legitimate non-violent democratic means of opposition available to most of South Africa's people. Showcase trials on such political occasions afforded the state the opportunity both to legally remove key activists by imprisoning or killing them as well as to make political gains through the criminalization of oppositional politics.

The principal security laws permitted people to be banned and detained without trial, for meetings to be prohibited and for organizations to be declared unlawful. Under the Prohibition of Information Act 1982, the State President could declare any area a forbidden place. Unauthorized entry into such an area could be visited with a penalty of up to twenty years imprisonment. Similarly, the Intimidation Act of 1982 prohibited most forms of protest available to blacks. Likewise the Emergency powers criminalized a broad spectrum of dissent – with the onus being placed on the accused to prove innocence and with severe penalties attached. The police and security forces generally were mandated with broad, permissive powers. Any state officer of whatever rank could use these powers, with indemnification against alleged abuse. The concept of 'disorder' was permissive to say the least – its scope was determined by the judgement of the state functionary.

Belated judicial criticism of the segregative and control legislation[11] was of some symbolic significance but it did little to alter the oppressive legal regime. The laws themselves were a necessary feature of the maintenance of white supremacy. Because the South African legal form was essentially racially discriminatory and oppressive for so long the police were inexorably embroiled in institutionalized racist practice. Police raids and the mass arrest of hundreds of Africans at a time for 'screening' were methods of policing that could be used only against a people who have no civil rights, and they are also the natural consequence of a system in which the penal law was the chief instrument of public administration and social control (South African Institute of Race Relations 1949: 76).

The administrative and security legislation directed against black people was peculiar in that, unlike the vast body of normal criminal legislation, they had a proactive character. Such legislation required no civilian intermediary, no rapporteur, to translate action into offence. Criminalization through the racist laws of South Africa involved a direct nexus between legal intent and cultural support – police officers armed with such ubiquitous powers, and guided by the occupational culture, could actively seek out those they wished to criminalize.

The systemic nature of legal oppression in the townships

Irrespective of the repeal of the various forms of administrative criminalization and of major features of the Internal Security Act in June 1991, the residue remains. The recent amendment to the law does not, and could not, produce an instant change in the role of the police in the continuation of black oppression. This is prohibited by the variety of discourses, discussed in Chapter Two, that have so successfully embedded the practice of oppression deep within the SAP. Black experience of the SAP – whether through harassment under the variety of technical legislation or under the security powers – seals the relationships in the policing of the townships.

The violence involved in these encounters has several meanings. At the personal level, it sustains a subjective antagonism between the two parties. 'Policing by consent' in Western mythology involves an attitude change on behalf of the two parties. Abolish the legislation, retrain the police, and Bingo! – community consent to policing is achieved.

But to analyse the relationship at that level is to pathologize it and to ignore key interlinked factors. Most violence committed by the SAP towards black people in the townships and elsewhere, was legally sanctified within a wider structure of domination. South African law structured and determined that violence but within an omnibus range of economic, political and spatial controls. Focusing on the individuality of police violence in the townships and the oppressive laws being enforced – the fault of bad police or bad laws – is to see it as aberrational or as simply as a function of legislative provisions. The SAP hierarchy blames the law. State politicians scapegoat individual police officers. In either case it is something that can be rectified relatively simply. Sachs sums up the alternative position – namely that the violence, the nature of the SAP as presently constituted, is systemic:

> to confine inquiries to whether the law, the judges, or the prisons, or the lawyers are getting 'better' or 'worse' is to avoid the more crucial long-term questions of how decisive the coercive apparatus is in maintaining domination.

> (Sachs 1975: 224)

'Better-trained' police officers, 'high standards of recruitment', 'more equable laws' are largely irrelevant. Since the repeal of the major forms of control legislation, individual harassment appears to have decreased. But suspicion that the police are promoting disorder and violence has increased. The police are viewed with as much or more suspicion as ever. This distrust arises in large part out of a recognition that the central discourses and values we reviewed in the last chapter, that inform and sustain police culture, remain intact. Reform of the SAP requires an unscrambling and reconstruction of the very meaning of policing.

The reality of township policing has been historically formed. Police practices cannot be divorced from the cultural legacy of SAP or from the apartheid structures through which black existence was criminalized.

POLICING THE TOWNSHIPS – THE EXPANSION OF BLACK POLICING

In the early days of the state police – the era of the South African Constabulary (SAC) – policing was commonly white-on-black. The values and norms of white police officers directly impinged on the daily lives of black people. In the last two decades, an alternative source of police manpower has been vigorously sought. Embedded white objections to the notion of black police officers under arms have been surmounted.

A variety of reasons have been offered by the state for an increased reliance on black police officers. These include the claims that South Africa has a shortage of police officers compared with Western countries, that white officers have been siphoned off to higher-paid private security work, that the traumas of the last decade have kept morale low and resignations high.

These arguments that there are simply not enough whites willing and able to take on the job of policing South Africa obviously have some validity. Perhaps more telling, however, have been the image problems associated with white-on-black policing both within South Africa and abroad. The use of black police to oppress blacks has been an essential part of a game-plan designed to confuse and conceal the reality of everyday policing in South Africa from both local and international audiences.[12]

The quandary of police manpower

Central to the increase in the number of black officers has been the expansion in the size of the SAP. This increase in establishment has been justified on the basis of need. South Africa, it has been argued, is a crime-ridden society and as such it requires more police to police it. This symbiotic representation – more police required to deal with more crime – has linked orthodox commentaries, such as Minister Le Grange's despairing search for more white police manpower in 1981:

> we're undermanned and using the schoolboys for help seemed like a good plan. It also gave them some idea of what a policeman is about . . . we really need them
>
> (*Work in Progress* 20 March 1981: 23)

with more radical proposals (Baynham 1990) for police reform. The 'more crime more police' thesis has seen both critics and community groups support proposals that have led to a continuing expansion of the SAP.[13]

Crime in South Africa is undoubtedly rampant.[14] Cape Town, for instance, has reputedly the highest recorded homicide rate in the world (1,600 for 1990–1 or 65 per 100,000) which is approximately five times the rate for New York City. One estimate,[15] records the South African homicide rate as 49 per 100,000 population per year compared with 9 per 100,000 in the United States. According to the National Institute for the Care and Resettlement of Offenders (NICRO) survey evidence, 95 per cent of rapes are unreported. On that estimate, in 1991, some 418,000 women were raped in South Africa, approximately 3 per cent of the female population. Assuming consistency of the rate over time, the 'average' South African woman can be expected to be raped twice in her life! Inevitably, the number of rapes and other forms of sexual abuse is disproportionately skewed towards young, black, township women.

While the lack of public scrutiny of the way crime reports are compiled by the SAP[16] makes assertions about the level of crime open to question (*Sunday Times* 7 April 1991), there appears no doubt that the crime problem in South Africa is of dramatic proportions and escalating. If one uses the changes in the homicide rate (a relatively tangible figure) as an index of the increase in violent crime (unrecorded as well as recorded), the last decade has seen an increase of over 30 per cent. In the black townships, crime runs at approximately six times the USA figure (Shank 1991).

But police expansion is likely to have little effect. Overwhelming evidence from other societies demonstrates that increases in police establishments have minimal effects on the recorded crime rate.[17] Apart from the primacy of public order – as opposed to crime control – functions in all state police forces, new officers are in any case invariably drafted in to duties with little relation to crime. Claims in South Africa that the dramatic crime rate is a function of police shortage is so much humbug – its source is to be found in the fundamental conditions of existence that characterize South African society. The proposers of an increase in police resources need look little further than the conditions created in the townships for one major source of interpersonal violence.

In any case, the relatively small SAP has been reinforced by many other agencies of legal and social control, both public and private.

The policing-shortage rhetoric (Sachs 1975) ignores the link between the several agents of state domination. First, there is the system of apartheid itself which functions both as an order and as a source of that order. Historically, devices such as the Pass Laws, segregative township devices, and the mass fingerprinting of black people minimized the number of police officers that would be required by an authoritarian state policing a more spatially mixed population. The modest size of the SAP was more than compensated for by the institutionalization of racial segregation policies.

Second, the SAP has always been able to rely on a variety of auxiliary battalions, such as the 12,000 part-timers of the Reserve Police Force[18] and some 35,000 in the Police Reserve (retired members), and ancillary bodies such as the intelligence services' vast network of informers (Brewer *et al.* 1988). During the Emergency, and today, the SAP has been regularly supplemented by units from the SADF. The latter claims to be able to mobilize some half-million soldiers and civilians with regard to both external and internal activities. White 'military' conscripts have been directed to fill up vacancies in the SAP. Employers were incorporated in the policing of black work-forces, being legally liable to keep records of black people's movement and registration under the Influx Control legislation.

The major 'hidden' supplement to the state police, however, lies in the expanding world of private security. In 1987, the then Minister of Defence, General Magnus Malan, gave the opening address to a conference entitled 'Security – A National Strategy: The Integration of Security in the Public and Private Sector. Malan argued for a shared will to 'resist destructive forces' through a 'joining of forces and efforts and optimum use of human and financial resources'.

Civil policing as a complement to the state police

South Africa has historically been developed through a massive private security industry. Its origins lie in the practices of mining employers exercising totalitarian control over compound migrant labour (Ramahapu 1981). In recent years, private security expansion owes much to the crime panic of the white suburbs. Certain police-work has been formally privatized – such as the guarding of important establishments under National Key Points Act 1980, which required that a significant portion of the costs of such security should be shouldered by the employer (Schalkwyk 1987). Similarly, the privatization of the railway police in 1987 placed vast areas of public domain under the policing agency of private security (Scharf 1989). In 1986–7, approximately 300,000 to 400,000 people (Grant 1989: 98) were employed as security guards. This compares with an 'actual establishment of the South African Police at the end of 1987 [of] 60,390' or 'about five times as many persons' (Grant 1989: 98). This contrasts dramatically with the situation in other countries for which figures are available where the number of police and private security personnel are more or less equal (Shearing and Stenning 1983).

Formal recognition of the burgeoning private sector was provided by the Security Officers Act of 1987.[19] This legislation serves a dual purpose. On the one hand it seeks to ensure higher standards in private security. On the other it provides a framework for the extension of the network of a state–corporate 'partnership' policing further into civil society. This partnership, as Brig. Muller indicated in his address to the 'Security – A National Strategy' conference (referred to above), requires 'the highest degree of goodwill and unison between the public and private sectors' as what is required by this partnership:

> is an integrated action in which both the public and private sector play an indispensable role towards achieving the common goal, namely survival of the total population of our country.
>
> (Muller 1987: 30)

Certainly, at the present time, the South African private security industry is remarkable for its variation in standards and equipment, and in the level of force at its disposal. Sometimes private security in South Africa, like that elsewhere, is ramshackle with operatives at times shockingly under-trained. For example, a security guard, accused of killing an innocent civilian, had received no training in legal powers or in the use of weaponry (*Cape Times* 2 February 1991). This, however is only one side of the picture.

Many security firms have adopted a high profile in imitating the equipment and patrol techniques of the SAP. Mine security utilize identical equipment, including Casspirs (*Weekly Mail* 28 August 1987) and, according to one account, possess 'the largest private army in the world' (Philips 1989: 214). In the white suburbs of Johannesburg, for example, some private security firms present their personnel as 'super Cops':

> The logo, in lipstick red on glossy black, reads simply 'Super Cops – Attitude'. One of the publicity brochures shows a beefy guy with upper arms looking like a topographical map. He is wearing

a uniform suspiciously like those of Californian police. . . . 'We're different' says Rykaart. 'I employ only ex-policemen – trained professionals. We drive around in black cars with tinted windscreens. Our guys are good-looking, people you can trust'.

(*Weekly Mail* 26 May 1989)

Private security is similar in other ways to the SAP with practices of unauthorized entry to blacks' houses, beatings, and the conveyance of black suspects in car boots (*Weekly Mail* 26 May 1989). The larger security companies claim a faster reaction time than the state police and have assumed much of the day-to-day policing of the white suburbs.[20]

The SAP has recognized its dependence on the private security industry (*Annual Report* 1985) with calls for closer cooperation, (Commissioner Van der Merwe, *Agenda* 8 October 1992) in a relationship that has been historically sanctified (as early as the 1930s Lansdown had noted the 'utility' of the exchange of fingerprints between the mines' police and the SAP). The SAP has traditionally collaborated with private security in defeating strikes.[21] Policing integration between the SAP and the private security industry occurs not just in 'unrest' situations but includes the routine reliance on the extensive surveillance activities conducted by private security (Philips 1989).

There is a contradictory relationship between the SAP and the private security sector. On one hand, the latter provides policing services at private expense that save publicly funded state police resources. The private security industry recognizes this and boasts of its 'complementarity' to the state police (Grant 1989). On the other hand, SAP Commissioners have complained of what they regard as the 'poaching' of officers by private security (*Annual Report* 1980). A continuing justification for the shortage of white police – with the concomitant resort to an increased black presence – is this 'leakage' to private security. In the eyes of the policed, however, the difference between state police and private police is more nominal than real. In black districts, private police 'have taken on the role and powers of the state in the eyes of the workers' (Philips 1989: 216).

White police morale – pay, promotion and families

The resort to black state police was in part a function of the conditions that encouraged that drift to private security employment. In recent years, work conditions and poor salaries have encouraged mass resignations. At the end of 1989, according to the *Sunday Times*, twelve police officers were resigning each day with National Servicemen being drafted as replacements. The problem of maintaining a white life style, in an occupation that was relatively underpaid, came to a head in the late 1980s. The problem was expressed by one policeman as follows:

> We are expected to work day and night, and on our days off and we are sick and tired of it. Improved perks are nice but you cannot use them to feed your family.

> (*Pretoria News* 25 April 1990)

Claims of under-payment were exacerbated by the effects on morale of the Emergency operations in the unwinnable 'battleground' of the townships. Social life was strained and the military structure of the SAP appeared impervious to career ambitions. One such officer summed up his reasons for resigning in the following terms:

> Being a cop in the field and working long hours I had to sacrifice time I normally would have spent with my family to study and improve myself. After four years, I obtained a BA Police Science through UNISA so as to be able to climb the promotional ladder. But my colleagues who did not study were promoted with me as there was a policy change for free promotion. . . . While doing duty on the detective unit, instead of a 40 hour week, I gave you a 76 hour week without grumbling or moaning as it was 'part of being a detective'. And when finances were tight and a shortage of new police vehicles occurred, I and others did our bit to look after resources at our disposal. On weekends, public holidays and days off, we did not hesitate to report for special duties when ordered to do so at the very last minute as this was also part of the job. Earlier this year I attended an officers' training course in Pretoria and after three months of intensive management training I was transferred to Kempton Park even though there were three vacancies for a detective lieutenant in my area, George. Over 300 of us stood at the end of the training course and listened while we were transferred throughout the country without regard to our personal circumstances, family or financial commitments. I went through all the channels as we are required to do and requested the Commissioner to reconsider the transfer as it would cause me financial as well as other hardships, due to family commitments

but was informed by letter to report to Kempton Park. It is obvious that no one cared. . . . all I can say is yesterday I was an officer in the SAP and today I sit without a career and without employment.

(*Argus* 3 February 1990)

These career strains were of course not just a function of the Emergency. The maintenance of a military-style organization, with its concomitant commitment to arbitrary unquestioning, unthinking obedience, did not sit well with pretensions to a postulated goal of Western-style state policing. Nor did the organization's demands meet the state's formal commitment to upholding the family and family values. The following account of family life by the wife of a Riot Squad policeman provides a sense of the frustrations and strains of police family life occasioned by the State's crackdown on black resistance in the 1980s:

now he leaves at odd times, and is constantly on stand-by. Once he came in late and a little more than an hour afterwards – we had just got into bed – he was called out and did not return until the next morning. The children who used to sit at the breakfast table with him, sometimes only see him as they prepare for school early in the morning. . . . I don't keep food warm for him any more, because he is too tired to eat a proper meal when he comes home in the early hours of the morning. My biggest concern is his safety . . . he could be knifed or overpowered by the crowds at any time and never come home at all. My personal relationship with him is under stress. I hear myself saying things to him that I do not mean. . . . I have been thinking of giving up work but we cannot afford it.

(*Cape Times* 16 October 1985)

Losses in white manpower due to problems of pay, of organizational strains, and of the effects on family life of the strains of imposing white control on the townships, led inexorably to the state searching for a substitute. That latter had to be cheap and relatively acceptable to a sensitive international audience. But the central reason for police shortage was created by enforcing the discriminatory criminal and administrative law to maintain the institutional inferiority of black people.

Policing the townships – black-on-black policing

One way of enlarging the SAP in the face of supposed shortages was to draw upon the female reservoir. There have always been token women police officers in the SAP. It was not until 1972, however, that the SAP commenced a deliberate recruitment of women, first white women and then later in the early 1980s women from other ethnic categories. Women police are now, according to the SAP, used in all contexts of policing apart from riot and counter-insurgency (De Witt 1988: 23) although according to Rauch (1992b) sexism permeates training.[22]

The primary solution, however, has been the recruitment of more black males (Cawthra 1986) to be the public face of the SAP in the townships. After the Soweto uprising of the mid-1970s, police publicists were sensitized to the implications of media pictures of white police clubbing black protesters for the country's image. Black police would play an important ideological role. They could be used to counteract criticism of police methods, allowing part of the policing of apartheid to be conducted by the victims themselves (Grundy 1983). They would be cheaper. Fears of the torn loyalties of black police defending the white state had historically proved to have little weight (Frankel 1980).

But there were major contradictions in recruiting black police. There have always been a minority of 'non-white' police in South Africa, although normally in ancillary roles. Early British rule in the Cape included reliance on armed Khoi-Khoi in the first paid police (Sachs 1973). Chinese and Indian police (Brogden 1989) had been recruited to control indentured ethnic labour in the late nineteenth century. There was spasmodic resort to formations of black police forces in the early history of the Dominion – by 1910, for example, there were some seven hundred black police in the Transkei alone (Sachs 1973). No training for black police, however, was provided until the late 1930s – police knowledge was 'acquired experience mainly while on duty' (Sachs 1973: 227). In the 1930s, Lansdown, had recognized that inequality of black people at large was being reproduced with similar discrimination inside the SAP. Racist views of the presumed different capacities of black police were evident throughout SAP history – for example, over detective training. Lansdown had emphasized the 'natural' affinity of black officers for the policing of the rural areas. Black recruits were not expected to be literate (institutionalizing career inferiority), could not arrest whites, and were able to enforce the law only within specific racial parameters.

'Coloured' police were separated in training from black recruits 'owing to cultural differences' in 1960. Until 1953, there were only two career rungs for 'non-whites' – the ranks of first and second class sergeant – with the first Asian station officers being appointed in the late 1960s. Only in the last fifteen years have black police been allowed to wear the same uniforms as white. Not until 1980 was the first black officer given authority over white police, with the first black station commander being appointed in 1980. At the time, black police officers earned approximately two-thirds the pay of their white contemporaries.

By the late 1980s, there was rough parity in numbers between 'white' police and 'black' police. However, this simple quantitative comparison fails to recognize the major distortions illustrated above by Sachs – that some four-fifths of black police officers were of constable rank only, as compared with less than half of whites. The higher the SAP office, the more stark the disparity. A career structure was available only for whites. With the onset of the Emergency, the SAP responded by creating a token representation of other races in the lower echelons of the more senior ranks.

Cop culture, black police – unity and dissent

But the increased dependence on black police highlighted a contradictory situation. In the long run, gross inequality and institutionalized discrimination within the SAP were clearly not compatible with the coercive needs of the racial state (Cawthra 1986). Internal discrimination was a time bomb. A degree of unity was created partly through accident and partly through structural relations. The grosser forms of discrimination inside the force were removed (including one Indian, one 'coloured' and one black officer being appointed to the 'General Staff'). Furthermore the structural source of police culture ensured that there was a certain cultural empathy between black and white police. Many of the features which sponsored a unified police culture were also evident for the black police – a rigorous indoctrination in the new training colleges was combined with social ostracism in local communities and in the townships where black SAP members, despite hopes to the contrary, were even more unpopular than white police (Grundy 1983), as their propensity to resort to violence made them little different from their white peers.[23] Stories of brutality by black police are widespread.

Black police isolation has been enhanced by postings far from their own communities. As they became targets for guerrilla attacks during the 1970s and 1980s, their local alienation was institutionalized. The economic discipline of the police wage (as well as fringe benefits such as free medical care), together with harsh internal discipline, has promoted an instrumental loyalty to the SAP.

There appears to have been no shortage of recruits among black people, especially among black women (although female Indian recruits were notable only by their relative absence). The paradox of a black woman joining the racist and sexist SAP may also be explained to some extent by factors other than that of economic conscription. While there is no systematic evidence available on this issue, anecdotal evidence is suggestive. Constable Smangele Mtambo, for example, reported that it was an experience while in high school with a man who assaulted her and nearly abducted her that steered her to the job:

> I would feel very angry each time I read about rape and sexual abuse and saw women being assaulted or bearing scars of assault. I vowed after I was attacked by a man on my way from school that I would follow a career that would help me prevent crimes against women.
>
> (*Sowetan* 27 June 1990)

Vlok, the then Minister of Law and Order, had claimed in 1990 that 40 per cent of the next 10,000 recruits would be female (*Daily Dispatch* 13 June 1990) although *Cape Times* enquiries produced evidence of no vacancies for 'coloured' women recruits (*Cape Times* 16 June 1990). In practice, the vast majority of black state police were, and continue to be, male.

Despite the forced unity with the white police culture, there is some evidence of unease in the black SAP ranks over their role as the instruments of black oppression (Grundy 1983: 148). Recently this resistance has found expression in attempts to develop a Police and Prison Officers Civil Rights Union (POPCRU), in the wake of the celebrated 'Rockman affair'. POPCRU's creed contradicts the basic mandate of the SAP.

> The reason for joining POPCRU is not because we are undisciplined or irresponsible. Our reason is to change the image of the force and to become true helpers and protectors of the people as defined in Clause 5 of the Freedom Charter.
>
> (*Daily Dispatch* 1 April 1990)

Other POPCRU members have phrased their dissent more succinctly:

> We know we have blood on our hands. But we won't wash it off in the bathroom. We will wash it off in public.
>
> (*New Nation* 3 March 1990)

State reaction to the fledgling police and prison union has been severe. POPCRU public meetings were tear-gassed and attacked with batons and dogs by white SAP members. Rockman, an early police organizer, resigned, and nearly a hundred black and 'coloured' SAP members have been sacked. These dismissals have meant virtual destitution with the loss of family housing and medical rights.[24]

The black police dissent that emerged has tended to be wage-related. In 1986, nearly two-thirds of the Municipal Police in Soweto who had previously been involved in breaking a boycott by residents of municipal facilities, went on strike, joining other employees in rejecting orders to collect rent and to evict residents as ordered by the local council. Similarly, Municipal Police in the East London township of Duncan Village went on rent strike over living conditions:

> Our houses have no electricity, ceiling, the floors become damp at night, there is normally leaks from the roof during rainy days and rooms are without doors – we do everything in the same small rooms, cooking, putting every thing we have in the rooms in which we sleep.
>
> (*Weekly Mail* 19 November 1987)

Municipal Police at the Lekoa township in Vaal mutinied over low pay and conditions of work. About a hundred of them, armed but in civilian clothes refused the command for an Inspection. They were prevented from conducting a protest march by riot police in Casspirs who beat them with sjamboks, tear-gassed them, and exchanged fire. Strikes by Municipal Police have included incidents in Katlehong (where 115 were arrested by members of the SAP) and by approximately a hundred others in Kagiso in the West Rand. Violent confrontations between black and white police have been reported in townships near Sebokeng, where a black police captain and alleged leader of the 'mutiny' was reportedly seriously injured by members of the SAP.[25]

Evidence of competing political loyalties is rare but there has been some evidence of black police demonstrating overt sympathy with the ANC. In 1986, two black Security Police appeared in Court accused of helping the ANC. Earlier, in May 1979, the death of a police officer in Soweto in an ANC attack, suggested active support from at least one ex-member of the force.[26]

Racism within the SAP has also been a factor in generating conflicts within the force. One black police sergeant explained that its effects caused him to resign and to join the ANC:

> As a bodyguard, I used to travel a lot. In some of these places we visited, I had to sleep in a tent while the white policemen lived it up in hotels and expected blacks 'to jump at their command'.
>
> (*South* 2 March 1990)

The case of Indian Constable Kevin Moodley is illustrative. That officer quit the SAP in 1990 after he was humiliated for using a shower and toilet reserved for whites at the police headquarters in Durban (*Sunday Times* 7 April 1991). Inter-racial violence within the force has been alleged. After an incident at Jeppe police station in Johannesburg, a young black constable died in hospital from injuries allegedly sustained in a brutal assault on him by three white superiors (*Sunday Times* 14 January 1990). In large part, SAP facilities are still segregated apart from 'training, prayers, and having a drink' (*Cape Times* 30 June 1990; Rauch 1992).

Despite these problems the State appears to have achieved a certain cultural affinity, a shared appreciation of the enemy if not a common loyalty, between white and black police.[27] This unity, however, is decidedly fragile and may well disintegrate as the political character of the country changes (Shearing and Mzamane 1992).

Surrogate policing – the municipal police

The key strategy for furnishing ideologically acceptable state policing for the black townships was to remove the SAP from day-to-day patrols. Members of the SAP were to be only involved in township work at the supervisory level or on occasions of 'disorder':

> much of the immediate responsibility for crushing anti-governmental organisations and reasserting control over the townships has been devolved onto the black municipal police.
>
> (*Weekly Mail* 20 March 1987)

The first attempt to develop a surrogate black police force nationally was the decision to permit the illegitimate black municipal authorities to appoint their own Municipal Police in 1984. Under the Black Local Authority Act, the Municipal Police (also known as Community Guards) possessed wide powers of order-maintenance, including enforcing Council by-laws. General factotum institutions, the Municipal Police became the bodyguards of the unpopular black councils. They had a restricted geographical mandate and were also subordinated to the local SAP commander, such as in dispersing 'illegal gatherings'. Like the SAP, they had the authority to use force and there were severe penalties for resisting or suborning them. In the words of De Witt:

> [they] are chiefly utilized in black residential areas to bring about and maintain stability in these areas. They carry out this task excellently.
>
> (1988: 42)

There were several public rationales for their inception – such as the claim that they were part of a 'bobby-on-the-beat' initiative and the argument that their formation would help create more local employment opportunities. Largely recruited from rural areas, they had little sympathy for the black townsfolk whose interests they supposedly served in enforcing unpopular council writs (*Weekly Mail* 7 November 1986). Minimal educational requirements were deemed necessary. Before the SAP assumed formal responsibility for them, they could be placed on guard duty with slight legal knowledge and meagre firearm training. They were, in comparison with the cost of white police, very inexpensive – in the Eastern Cape, for instance, they received only some R225 a month. In comparison with other waged jobs in small townships, however, they earned a considerable sum. Their task of 'implementing council decisions' became a catch-all term that permitted them to work as hatchet-men and bodyguards for the survival of the unrepresentative councils. Their role was expansive and included such activities as, for example, sjambokking children who were late or who boycotted school, as in the Tumahole township of Parys (*Weekly Mail* 21 August 1987). There have been remarkably contradictory accounts of their 'effectiveness' and there have been wildly differing claims and counter-claims. For instance, a Transvaal township Mayor claimed that they were 'doing a fantastic job' at the same time that a Council of Churches report documented random beatings and harassment by the same Municipal Police force (*Weekly Mail* 27 March 1987). The Heidelburg police commandant contended that such reports were 'absolute nonsense'. Reports of beatings of curfew-breakers with sjamboks by Municipal Police were denied by Warrant Officer Wolmarans of Duncan Village Township Guards – he had heard of neither a curfew nor of any assaults and had received no complaints.

These police soon earned themselves pejorative labels in townships, where they were called variously 'greenflies' (a reference to the flies that buzz around faeces), Amstels (after the beer bottles), and 'sunlights' (after a soap commercial on TV2 'promising a faster response to your washing up problems'), magodolos (the opposers), magundawane (wild rats) and 'Zulu boys' (Fine 1989). They made few actual arrests, with interrogations normally being followed by the instant 'punishment' of a beating. Complaints against them were exceptionally difficult to lodge or sustain.[28] State functionaries knew when to give the 'Nelson touch' to the work of the black surrogates.

These police were an especial target of local black anger, being perceived directly as a political force. For example, between January and July 1990, twenty-eight of the Municipal Police were killed on duty (while themselves killing nearly two hundred civilians). There were twenty assaults on Municipal Police stations, 420 attacks on individual Municipal Police, and 145 on their homes. Between 1984 and 1990, 440 were killed on duty, and some 25,000 injured (Safro 1990). There are many accounts of the deaths of municipal police officers at the hands of local activists. (See, for example, *E.P. Herald* 18 April 1990; *City Press* 4 March 1990; *Argus* 9 April 1990.) They bore the brunt of local opposition to the white state and to its surrogate local councillors. They were often the victim of 'first-strikes' – their housing being relatively exposed and unprotected.

Under the Police Third Amendment Act 1989, the SAP was given full control over the Municipal Police, which were now to be organized in every African local authority area. The pious intention was to upgrade their standard of work. In reality, they were incorporated into the SAP, partly because of their embarrassing abuses and partly to bolster the numbers of SAP – constituting in 1990, one-in-eight of SAP numbers and one-fifth of all black police employees. They were also predominantly masculine – only one woman was among the 1,000 recruited in 1990.

In practice, they were simply 'forlorn hope' surrogates, cheap to train and to employ, and available to save white lives by taking the sting out of immediate township anger. As surrogates, they were used by the state as part of a larger authority structure to enforce the white state's order in any township where alternative structures were gaining strength and to persuade unrepresentative local councillors that they could count – distantly – on the firepower of the South African state. Together with those 'representatives', they supplied a buffer behind which the white power structure could be hidden. And of course, the SAP could distance itself from their abuses.

Surrogate policing – the kitskonstabels

During the 1980s, the SAP increasingly relied on a second shock absorber between township peoples and the white police. New SAP-financed Special Constables – kitskonstabels (so-called because of the 'instant' brief training period) were appointed in September 1986. A thousand black recruits were given basic police training for three weeks at Koeberg and then used as auxiliary police in the black townships. The Police Act allowed them to be used as temporary replacements in locations where the SAP was overstretched.

Recruits required no educational qualifications, and included many illiterates. Equipped with shotguns, and dressed in functional blue overalls, they were allocated the tasks of foot patrol and riot control. They were given (at the outset) considerable credit by the state:

> [they] contribute largely to the suppression of the revolutionary climate and maintenance of law and order in the black townships.
> (Brigadier Wandrag, quoted in the *Star* 22 September 1986)

They had other, less overt functions. Like the Municipal Police, their principal merit was that they were inexpensive. Not only did they save on training costs but they were legally defined as temporary employees who were paid hourly and therefore not entitled to regular SAP benefits such as medical aid, pensions or paid holidays. A Cape Town study reported the kitskonstabels as being promised R400 a month but in practice they received less that R330 gross (Tanzer 1988). There was no career structure.

To an even greater extent than the Municipal Police, during the Emergency period, they allowed the State to withdraw regular SAP and SADF from the townships, thereby permitting it to accede to the 'troops out' calls by the township Civics. By taking advantage of press censorship during the Emergency, the State could refer to the excesses of the kitskonstabels in the townships as merely further examples of 'black-on-black' violence, thereby obscuring its own role. For conventional white society, the violence of the kitskonstabels in the townships was filtered through the racist lenses of media controls. The strategy of relying on them was meant to remove the most obvious racial overtones, giving the impression that 'law-abiding, moderate' blacks supported the white regime (Fine 1989).

Often recruited from rural areas such as the 'Homelands', many kitskonstabels were forced into the job by the same kind of economic conscription as the Municipal Police – 'they didn't say what the job was, only that we would "get plenty of money"' (quoted in Tanzer 1988). Rarely does the nature of the job – acting as a miniature army of occupation in the townships to impose the state social order – seem to have been explained to the prospective recruits. Training was elementary in the extreme:

> we were told to shoot a suspect in the following situations: when the suspect runs away, in riot situations, when we were in danger. Major Z. told us to shoot to kill – without warning.
>
> (quoted in Tanzer 1988)

Discipline from white superiors was direct and violent:

> They hit us sometimes in the chest with a gun butt, kick our buttocks and in the stomachs . . . a certain Constable van der Walt shot one of the recruits in the back of his legs. Then we were forced to sign papers denying [his] responsibility.
>
> (Tanzer 1988)

Verbal abuse was more common. 'They sometimes called us "Kaffirs", "Hey you, you fucking black dog"' (Tanzer 1988). But resignation was complicated: 'Many were unhappy, but they said they needed the money . . . it's better than no money and no job at all' (Tanzer 1988).

The kitskonstabels rapidly became notorious for their violence towards local people. A University of Cape Town survey (Fine 1989) of Bhongelethu township (near Oudtschoorn) produced clear-cut views of kitskonstabel behaviour. Of some 500 residents over 18 years, 80 per cent felt they treated people badly, only 2 per cent well. Three-quarters of them had seen kitskonstabels drunk on duty and aggressive. Most of them had seen beatings by kitskonstabels and half had observed them pointing firearms at residents. The local SAP commander reported that he had received no such complaints – although the Incident Book at the township police station listed a number of such occurrences. In affidavits, local people described the kitskonstabels as 'de facto vigilantes officially licensed to terrorise anyone whose views differ from their own' (*Weekly Mail* January 1988). There is evidence of kitskonstabels continuing with such violence despite judicial condemnation. For example, injunctions against the kitskonstabels by Justice Kannemeyer in the Grahams-town townships appeared to have been largely ignored. It was a violence that was reciprocated. They were seen for what they were, a surrogate agency which concealed the apparatus of white state control: 'People call us "Botha's fucking dogs"' (Tanzer 1988).

By the 1990s, the violence of the special constables had been recognized by the state to be dysfunctional, creating too much of a backlash. Even their initiator, General Johan Coetzee, lamented his invention.[29] The resolution, however, was not to disband but to 'reform'. By 1991, ranks were to be open to all races on the basis of a Standard 6 education and recruits were to be given three months' training. Regret at their formation was not accompanied by a dim-inution in their significance. Increasingly, potential black recruits to the SAP were diverted to the kitskonstabels. In 1990, for example, 3,400 of them were trained as compared with only 1,000 black recruits to the SAP proper (Rauch 1992b).

The kitskonstabels, in their isolation – from both local township society and from the white cadres of the SAP – and in their behaviour reflected the cultural attributes of a besieged group, endowed with the legal imprimatur of access to random violence against outsiders. While attempts have been made to keep their identity separate from the SAP, they pose the same problem as the Municipal Constables and the regular SAP for the policing of a new South Africa.

Vigilantes – home-grown surrogates

A third form of surrogate social control in the townships is represented by the phenomenon of the vigilantes. In South Africa, that term has come to mean violent, organized and conservative groupings operating within black communities. Although they receive no official recognition, they have been politically directed in the sense that they have acted to neutralize individuals and groupings opposed to the apartheid state and its institutions (Haysom 1990). In this capacity they function as a further proxy for the SAP in attacking and suppressing elements of township society who oppose apartheid structures.

These forces arose as a consequence of the failure of the SAP to maintain order, in the form of ordinary crime control, within the townships in the mid-1980s (although outbreaks of vigilantism were evident in areas such as the Ciskei before that date). Their origins lay in practices little different from that of many municipal police patrols:

Under the guidance of council members, patrols were organised and inspired by the old axiom 'spare the rod and spoil the child'. All meetings of potential stone throwers and arsonists were broken up with no more violence than the energetic use of sjamboks.

(Haysom 1986)

But during the crisis of the mid-1980s, vigilante violence became more directed towards specific enemies. For example, Indian vigilantes in Queenstown developed out of what they perceived to be a threat to their own property. Once established, the vigilantes assumed the characteristics of a police reserve (Haysom 1986).

Vigilantes have several values to the SAP. They are better able to disrupt black opposition than the state police because they are less afraid of adverse publicity in carrying out brutal attacks. They are useful in controlling black areas because they need not worry about adverse legal considerations. They provide a cheap alternative to the Municipal Police (into which many were recruited [Haysom 1990]) for the local councils. Being indigenous, they could target activists more directly. Once they cowed opposition, they created a political vacuum into which the political surrogates of the National Party government could step. To the outside world, these vigilante attacks could be presented as merely another example of 'black-on-black' violence.

In Natal, vigilantes were used by local Inkatha-sponsored warlords to suppress not only township resistance but also political and trade union organization – a systematic campaign was initiated against the United Democratic Front (UDF) and affiliates of the Congress of South African Trade Unions (COSATU) (Sutcliffe 1988).

There have been many formal denials of SAP involvement with the vigilantes:

In general, the SAP opposes the operation of vigilantes, since they are unselected, untrained and prone to penetration by skollies [scoundrels].

(Minister Vlok, *Cape Times*, 14 June 1988)

But there is much evidence to the contrary. An attack on UDF members in Kwanobuhle in the Eastern Cape by a thousand vigilantes carrying knobkerries and similar weapons was described by police liaison officer Major Eddie Everson as 'just a group of concerned people' (*Weekly Mail* 9 January 1987). In the notorious vigilante attack, by 'witdoekker' (white-hats) on squatters at Crossroads near Cape Town, forty-five affidavits from squatters claimed that the police had supplied the witdoekker with arms and ammunition and had actively participated in burning houses:

> I watched as police Casspirs moved ahead of the vigilantes, firing tear-gas and bird-shot at KTC residents trying to defend their homes against the vigilantes milled around the Casspirs, and the police talked to them and cracked jokes.
>
> (quoted in *Weekly Mail* 5 June 1986)

The Crossroads incident left seventy dead and 80,000 people homeless. An ITN cameraman was allegedly killed by vigilantes within three metres of a police vehicle. There is similar video evidence of police collaboration with vigilantes in Zonkezizwe on the East Rand (*Daily Dispatch* 4 December 1990).

A self-confessed vigilante, Abraham Zwam, testified that he had been paid R120 by the police to throw bricks and a petrol bomb in the townships of Thokoza and Katlehong (accompanied by white and black SAP members (*Weekly Mail* 5 June 1986). At Tembisa, there was evidence of a vigilante group being established by an SAP major (*Weekly Mail* 19 June 1986) although normally, the SAP support appears to have been oblique rather than direct. This was possible because they were able to use local councillors as a front – for example, in Alexandra, police officers stood by while town councillors used Inkatha vigilantes to attack the Civic (*Weekly Mail* 1987). Violence has been the central vigilante technique.

> The council in this township has put together a group of vigilantes whose horrendous acts cry out for justice and retribution. That the authorities and others responsible should turn a blind eye to such deliberate acts by men who have been given authority through the Town Council to take the law into their lawless hands is just shocking . . . it is completely out of order for civil bodies to take the law into their own hands.
>
> (quote from *Sowetan* on Makgotla associated with Soweto Town Council)

The use of vigilantes by the local council to break alternative structures has been relatively common. Tembisa schoolchildren claimed they were hired by the township mayor (who also allegedly supplied them with guns) to join vigilantes in an attempt to eliminate ANC activists:

I was trained in the use of an R-1 rifle by policemen from the East Rand administration and given R10 (by the mayor).

(Weekly Mail 13 June 1986)

Similarly, a vigilante captured by residents in Katlehong claimed he was paid by the police to participate in attacks on black activists. He stated that he was forced to become an informer after being jailed for smoking dagga (marijuana). With thirteen other vigilantes, he allegedly accompanied two white and three black police in throwing bricks and petrol bombs at seven houses of known activists in Thokozxa and Katlehong (*Weekly Mail* 1986). Collaboration with local police was not unusual in those attacks. Development Board police, for instance, allegedly participated with local vigilantes in attempting to break a school boycott in Tumahole by assaulting schoolchildren (*Weekly Mail* 1986). Township residents were much more likely to die in vigilante violence than as a result of confrontations with the SAP – by October 1988, 90 per cent of township deaths were related to vigilante and counter-vigilante violence (Haysom 1990).

Haysom argues that the rise of mass vigilantism relates to several township phenomena – the surge of opposition to black councillors, economic cutbacks during the recession by community councils in the form of rent increases and the related school boycott. Faced with the potential collapse of local administrations, the first response by the state was a policing policy of maximum force. But the resistance was simply too great. Similarly, the alternative resort to the SADF had major drawbacks, resulting in major clashes and a mushrooming of protest. So what the state needed was a strategy of disorganization. Like the Municipal Police and the kitzconstabels, the vigilantes were black (encouraging the notion of black-on-black violence), inexpensive, and could combat popular organizations, by extreme violence in a way that the police could not. Vigilante action as exemplified by the Crossroads violence has been a largely successful technique:

> through its black proxies, the state appears to have been hugely successful in eliminating what for the past eight years has been a troublesome symbol of black resistance and defeat for governmental polices in the Western Cape.

(Weekly Mail June 1986)

They were also part of a larger strategy, encompassing not merely the other surrogate forces but as part of the larger SAP's, 'Winning the Hearts and Minds' campaign.[29]

CONCLUSION – BLACK-ON-BLACK POLICING IN THE TOWNSHIPS

Given the physical separation of communities within the apartheid structure, the major experience by black people of state policing in recent years has been through its proxies – Municipal Police, kitskonstabels, and vigilantes, and through black members of the SAP. Only occasionally in the present day are they likely to confront patrolling white SAP officers through the portholes of an armoured vehicle, though the renamed Riot Squad continues to make its presence felt as an occasional marauding visitor. Even rarer have been direct contacts with the Security Police (although its network of informers have reportedly indulged a voracious appetite for the trivia of township life). The limited evidence on the 'policing of the homelands' suggests strong comparisons with the policing of the townships. Although the position appears worst in Boputhatswana and KwaZulu (where the police force is closely associated with Inkatha), the general pattern is one of institutionalized surrogates providing the cover of black-on-black policing as part of the wider white supremacist strategy.

Inevitably, this tour of township policing has omitted many other aspects of the policing of South Africa. But in so far as township policing has been the key manifestation of majority black experience of the state police and of its surrogate agencies, it is critical to focus on that practice. Consequently, any concern for the reform of the state police in South Africa must give primacy to that context. In Part II, we outline two alternative strategies for creating policing institutions that seek to empower rather than to repress those township communities.

Part II

Pathways of reform

Chapter 5

An orthodox solution – doing it the Western way

I don't think that we should change the standards of law enforcement in this country because in every country in the world, if you lower your standards where law enforcement is concerned ... the result is catastrophe.

(General Jacobus Calitz of the SA Police Academy.
Quoted by David Beresford in the *Guardian*)

INTRODUCTION

The emerging approach to the reform of the SAP is founded on the claim that their practices are out of line with accepted 'international standards'. What is required to solve the problems of South African policing, it is argued, is a reform programme that will make the SAP more like the police in Western liberal democracies. The problem of reform is straightforward. Find a model of sound 'liberal-democratic policing' and then reshape the SAP so that it approximates it. The central feature of the policing models being offered to South Africans is that they all adhere to the two central principles of liberal-democratic policing. First, the models accept the liberal principle that policing should be constrained by a rights-based 'rule of law'. Second, they accept the democratic principle that the goals and strategies of policing should have the support of the people as a whole – 'policing by consent'.

These twin principles have considerable purchase within South Africa's liberation politics, where the ideal of liberal democracy has for decades provided a critical basis for the critique of the apartheid state, and where the 'demise of communism' has left the principles and practices of the West as virtually the only standards for reform. Within this framework, the critical issue becomes one of transforming the SAP in ways that will enable it to comply with the requirements of a new democratic South African polity.

An example of this approach has been the transformation of the old South West African Police, a SAP satellite force, into the present Namibian police force. The post-independence government invited a team of British police officers, under the direction of an Inspector of Constabulary, to develop a blueprint for remodelling the police force it had inherited. This team undertook a 'comprehensive study' of the pre-independence police structures and methods. It then evaluated them in terms of liberal-democratic norms and British police practices. On the basis of this study, the team proposed a programme of reform that is now being implemented under the watchful eye of three experienced British police officers who advise the Minister of Home Affairs, the Commissioner of Police and the officer-in-charge of training. The Royal Canadian Mounted Police (RCMP) are contributing to the reforms by providing the Namibian Police with advice – in a 'training the trainers' project – on how to transform their procedural manuals so that they are consistent with the principles of democratic policing as reflected in RCMP practices.

Acceptance of this approach is widespread and South Africa is being inundated with offers of advice from Western experts on how to reform the SAP. Experts from such countries as Britain, Canada, the United States and Holland are offering advice to South Africans through a variety of forums. A recent example is the multinational panel of experts that advised the Goldstone Commission[1] on the reform of the policing of demonstrations (Panel 1992). South Africans are being exposed to the equivalent of an international computer fair, featuring software packages for the creation of 'democratic policing'. National 'sales representatives' can be found marketing their country's model by talking at conferences, writing in newspapers, advising interested parties, lecturing at SAP training institutions and so on. According to these 'sales persons', all South Africans have to do is to decide which software program they want to adopt. The country that wins the 'contract' will then provide the 'service support' necessary for the model's installation. The speculation has it that Britain will be accorded this contract because South Africa is within its 'sphere of influence' and because of its historical links as a colonial power in Africa.

In this chapter, we consider the applicability of the sales products of Western (and particularly British) policing, as informed by research, by social and legal commentary, and by the changes in

British policing in the last decade. Here, the sales pitch can trade on major areas of salience. The British colonial origin of the original South African Constabulary is one. More important is the inheritance of English common law and criminal law procedures as a framework for South African state police practices. In a variety of ways, the legal position of the SAP reflects that of the situation in part of the UK in the early 1980s – procedures such as the 'Judges Rules' over the interrogation of suspects, the arguments over the 'office of constable', the phraseology of enabling public order charges in South African law, and the lack of serious discussion of the prosecutorial powers of the SAP all reflect the position of the police in England and Wales in the early 1980s. Many of the potential sites for transformation, at face value, in the market of police goods, seem to reflect the corner shop of the police High Street of the 1970s before it was transformed into the shopping mall of the 1990s. For example, when the Goldstone Commission wished to investigate the SAP shooting of unarmed demonstrators at Boipatong, it turned immediately to a British academic (and former police officer) who has advised the British Home Office on crowd-control procedures (Waddington 1991). A British police sales representative coming to South Africa would regard herself to be in a time warp – where the Police and Criminal Evidence Act, 1984 (PACE) has not yet been invoked.

Democratic policing is being marketed as one commodity among others in an international technological supermarket. The approach being adopted is consistent with the marketing of other products where what is on offer is the result of 'research and development' that has taken place elsewhere in the industrialized world. While policing itself is not a product which will generate direct profits, it is, like much foreign aid, a 'loss leader' that will facilitate future exports by establishing 'cultural links'. Business links between countries tend to be strongest where they share similar cultural sensibilities and where the rules of the game correspond.

Given an orthodox definition of policing – policing is what people in blue uniforms do – then the problem of transforming the South African Police is relatively straightforward. The solution is one of 'nudging' it up the evolutionary trajectory of Anglo-American models (or for that matter, the gendarmerie model of Continental Europe).

TRANSFORMING THE SAP – INFILTRATING AND CONSTRAINING COP CULTURE

British concerns with police transformation have focused on the occupational or 'cop' culture, whose importance we discussed in Chapter Three. That culture is perceived as one major impediment to police responsiveness to the wider community both by outside commentators and by senior police officers. In orthodox thinking, the problem of police practice has been reduced to one of manipulating the rank-and-file to act in ways more conducive to organizational demands. In South Africa, that police culture has been commonly depicted as the major impediment to SAP transformation, a key obstacle to policing in response to community demands. In the words of a former SAP lieutenant 'Years of indoctrination and brainwashing would make it difficult for policemen to change their attitude' (*Sunday Times* 7 April 1991).

There have traditionally been two approaches to changing police culture – to making the rank-and-file more socially responsive. One of these perspectives has emphasized *legalist* or *rule-making* devices. The second has been to meet the police culture head-on and to attempt to change it directly – *culturalist* devices. Legalist approaches to the perceived autonomous practices of police culture have suggested that the primary way of dealing with it is one of rule-making. Police failure to act according to desirable requirements is portrayed as resulting from the absence of appropriate directives. The solution therefore is either to impose rules where they do not exist – for example, in creating an 'exclusionary' rule with regard to confession evidence – or alternatively, to specify in more detail, where the general rules of policework do not cover adequately the specifics of particular situations.

Legalists acknowledge that rule-making on its own may have little effect on rank-and-file practice. Rules, when not congruent with police practice, are there to be ingeniously broken, rather than to be obeyed. The heterogeneity of police practice, the varied situations of policework as it has developed historically, has meant that ways round the rules are constantly found. New rules can never catch up with police practice. Attempts to transform police practice that have envisaged the problem as critically one of rule-making have failed to recognize that 'where there is a will there is a way'. The culture is resilient. Rule-making practices on their own are insufficient. Principally, rule-making devices have failed to recognize that you cannot

'crush' the culture. They must be complemented by more sociological culturalist approaches – seeking to change the culture from
inside. The ways of thinking and of acting by police officers are to
be changed by exposing them to more community-sensitive values
and norms. However, the latter are also insufficient on their own.
Attempting to change the culture – for example, by changes in the
patterns of recruitment or training – to alter the racism or sexism of
the police culture, ignores the overall rule-bound nature of policework. Legalist and culturalist devices are complementary.

These two devices draw on a biological analogy in suggesting how
that culture might be changed. Changing the character of the culture, the culturalist approach, and limiting the intake of particular
life-giving gases to that seedbed, rule-making approaches, are interrelated devices in tackling the police culture.

Cultural reproduction requires two critical elements – defences
against the infiltration of impurities, and life-giving oxygen.
Impervious barriers prevent the importation and implanting of
foreign strains. The more aseptic the atmosphere, the more likely
that a pure culture can be reproduced. Controlling police culture,
making rank-and-file police officers more receptive to social
demands, means breaching those protective barriers and substituting
more community-benign cells. Second, the culture requires oxygen
for the cells to propagate. It requires space, territory, in which to
survive and multiply. Constraining those survival and reproduction
processes requires closure techniques to diminish the supply of
oxygen, and to decrease the autonomous space of the culture.
Reforming the practices of the rank-and-file, affecting the sustaining
energy and the imperatives of police culture, constraining police
discretion, requires restrictions upon the space within which the
culture survives. Like a tube of toothpaste, the discretionary space
must be squeezed to minimize the area for independent action and
circulation while at the same time, altering its biological
composition.

The orthodox approach to transforming the SAP concentrates on
the work of both 'rule-makers' and of 'culturalists'. The problem of
transforming the SAP is conceptualized as primarily one of changing
the practices and community responsiveness of the rank-and-file, and
necessarily takes on board both rule-making approaches and culturalist experiments in relating the formal rules of law and organization to the potential impediment of the police culture. Generally,
the orthodox approach, as we shall argue, avoids the larger systemic

problems of police organization and of the political relationship of the police to the wider community.

Four separate orthodox techniques of transformation can be conceptualized – *cultural colonialism, incorporative devices, internal rule-changing*, and *external rule-making*. The first two of these are essentially sociological and seek to affect the composition of the culture, transforming the constituent elements – by modifying certain of the key values ('malign cells') and substituting ones ('benign cells') more communally acceptable. The latter are primarily legalist and attempt to interdict the supply of oxygen, restricting the space within which the culture can propagate – confining police discretion in the name of greater police reform.

CULTURAL COLONIALISM – TAKING THE POLICE TO THE COMMUNITY

Cultural colonialism as a technique for police reform has several elements, varying from selection and training devices to strategies of community involvement. It assumes a public mandate to change existing police values and norms and to substitute alternatives deemed more congruent with those of a wider public. In Western forces, colonizing cop culture through 'positive' selection and training has been given authoritative imprimaturs through police academies. These initiatives assume that police culture is an impediment to the professional performance of policework. They are premised on the assumption that directives of law and of police management are being subverted by the cop culture which is conceived of as alien to the host body. These techniques attempt to colonize the space occupied by the 'alien' culture. The central idea is to promote a culture which is more supportive of legal and organizational directives.

The thesis advanced from the orthodox position is that more representative and better trained police will be responsive to both communal requirements and democratic norms. This argument assumes that the principal source of the problems with policing is the predisposition of rank-and-file police, which are often incongruent with democratic values and norms.

According to this analysis, transforming cop culture requires the introduction of new selection devices coupled with a purging of culture-holders in positions of power within the SAP (Rauch 1991a). A related and complementary strategy involves rewarding people within the SAP who possess the appropriate characteristics but whose inclinations have been subverted by a hostile cop culture, to act in accord with their 'natural' predispositions.

Selection devices typically have two targets – personality factors and attitudinal characteristics – on the grounds that the police culture reflects the origin of police officers. Orthodox critics[2] assume that traditionally certain kinds of authoritarian individuals choose the police occupation to fit their personality or that police officers are actually selected from a more conservative and authoritarian section of the population. In South Africa, the evidence on such recruitment remains speculative. But the relatively low salary level of white officers (as compared to other white occupations) and historically (white officers were chosen from that stratum of the population that suffers from 'status frustration' [Goodhew 1991]) a fear of the encroaching social mobility of sections of the black population, suggest that police officers have generally been drawn from a more conservative milieu.

In South Africa, police selection procedures have been designed to recruit white officers who are especially sympathetic to the order of apartheid and black officers who are cooptable. Black police officers are often enlisted from lower social classes (as measured by literacy and origin) than that of many township dwellers. The elderly British colonial tradition of 'strangers policing strangers' has been followed.

According to the orthodox reform programme, the way to counteract the effects of the police culture lies in solutions that attract a different type of recruit. Such measures involve raising the social status of the occupation, especially with regard to levels of remuneration. Changing the culture in this context means changing predispositions of recruits and modifications in the economic and social profile of the force. Conduct is changed not through top-down supervision but through strategies that promote an intra-organizational dialogue by bringing more community-sensitive recruits into the police. Such a resolution assumes that a key obstacle to culture change lies in stratification-based (class, gender and race) predispositions. It assumes that a new type of recruit can resist more effectively the conservative influences of peer group police pressure. Affirmative action programmes are instances of this strategy.

Apart from the traditionalist Afrikaner source of police recruitment, arguments in favour of diverse recruitment as a strategy for transforming the SAP (as elsewhere) frequently point to the dominance of white males in the police. (We noted in Chapter Four the striking gender inequality that characterizes the force [Rauch 1991b][3] and the very small number of blacks who hold officer rank.) Increasing the proportion of women at all ranks and blacks at the officer rank would, it is argued, fundamentally alter the sensibilities that cop culture expresses and reproduces. Recruitment and the increased opportunity for the upward mobility of police officers other than white males is a priority for change.

Given these disparities, a direct road to SAP transformation would be to raise the socio-economic status of the SAP as an occupation, thus drawing on recruits from a less conservative and traditional background, and to increase the recruitment and career opportunities of black people and of women generally. Hence, it could be expected that the racist and sexist aspects of the SAP police culture would be diminished.

However, there is little evidence that changes in recruitment patterns ultimately produce a significantly different style of policing. Police culture appears to be largely resilient to changes in recruitment patterns in relation to stratification. The evidence from Western police forces suggests that unless significant numbers of personnel are recruited from other than the dominant groups, their inclusion is likely to have minimal effect on the prevailing culture. For example, research literature suggests that women police officers in a largely male force, tend to adopt either overtly POLICEwomen definitions (embracing the male culture as their own), or policeWOMEN (those who see themselves as fulfilling the more traditional expectations associated with the role of policewomen) the service role (Ehrlich-Martin 1980). The culture does not change significantly just because more women are recruited. Similarly, enhanced black recruitment in itself is unlikely to have more than a marginal effect. Cashmore (in a review of the recent American experience where there has been a dramatic increase in the number of black officers, at command as well as street level, in what were previously essentially 'white' police forces) comments that for some blacks, police employment is a way out of the under-class. But in accepting police employment, they assume a commitment to the institution and to the *status quo*, and absorb the 'working personality' of other officers:

> But what has been the effect on the rest of the black population? It has been to exact compliance, to stifle political activism, to facilitate physical control.
>
> (Cashmore 1991: 107)

The culture has a remarkable ability to reproduce itself, to re-socialize recruits. In South Africa, simple changes in recruitment practices with regard to race and gender are unlikely to have commensurate effects on the occupational culture. Dramatic changes in policy with regard to female and black recruitment are unlikely to significantly affect the day-to-day practice of policework unless accompanied by significant structural changes in the character of the police organization related to the normative handling of police-public encounters. Similarly, unless new patterns of local policing are followed, combined with less exclusive opportunities for promotion, any changes in recruitment patterns will have little benefit. Legally supported affirmative action programmes, in any case, seem to have little effect on the composition and culture of Western police forces.[4]

The second prong of the colonialism strategy is police education. Training is the major device traditionally used to combat the pervasive effects of police culture. Considerable research now exists on the impact of such training programmes.[5] The problem facing South Africa, as perceived in the orthodox proposals on transformation, in devising a training programme relevant to the new SAP, is essentially that of any force commander in the Western world concerned to instil in new officers a consciousness of community responsibility. Most Western forces have at some time in their evolution had to switch from a narrow interpretation of the police task, for which technical knowledge of the law is the primary prerequisite and military discipline the manner of its acquisition (Bittner 1980), to a much broader and socially aware interpretation of the role, especially with regard to policing skills. The problem facing the new SAP, from this perspective, is only different in degree from other police forces.

A central element of initial training in Anglo-American forces has been to tackle directly elements of racism and sexism within the culture, and to make police officers more socially aware of the experiences and expectations of particular social groups. Racism has been the main focus, encompassing both interactional skills and knowledge of the social context of the behavioural patterns of the second party, between white police officers and black (especially young) civilians. The general trend has been to make community and race relations education an integral part of training, and to view that training as career-long. The current schemes involve a combination of factual learning about the formal characteristics of policing as a form of work plus training designed to produce appropriate attitudes and effective behaviour. The recruit is to be equipped at the outset with wider social skills and knowledge to counteract the negativity of the culture, and to have those resources reinforced at later stages.

The argument developed here is that the sensibilities that govern policing do not simply reflect predispositions but have been actively developed and enhanced through training programmes. With respect to the SAP, for example, it is argued that training is used to deliberately create stereotypical images of blacks as dangerous and threatening barbarians who only respond to heavy-handed coercive policing and who seek to destroy the Christian order of apartheid (see Chapter Three). The solution proposed in response to this is the solution proposed all over the world, namely, training to provide police with a new way of seeing the world and acting in the world. As with the strategy of recruitment, here too the idea is to bring the community into the police by transforming cop culture so that it incorporates new sensibilities that reflect the community being policed.

However, much of the present training in the Western police forces has been subject to twin criticisms – that what are essentially psychologistic patterns of learning do not equip the new police officer with the understanding that forms of prejudice and racism are not simply predispositions but are produced by particular experiences as police officers (Jones and Joss 1985). It is not so much the attitudes that the police officer brings to the job that are important but rather – even where the officer does possess what are essentially non-racist views – that the practice of policework, in the company of fellow police officers, produces situations in which prejudiced attitudes are formed. For example, if the young officer learns early in his or her life that criminals regularly come from a particular stratum or ethnic group, the officer soon comes to stereotype all members of such groups according to that informal learning.

While the preliminary UK evidence of such training gives some positive indication in terms of the decreased level of complaints that have been levied against officers who have experienced it, the effects to date have been marginal (Bull and Horncastle 1986). In the case of racism, the evidence suggests that the culture is too resilient to be significantly modified in this way. Any initial impact of anti-racist training is lost soon after the trainee officer is placed 'on the street' as the culture, with its immediate relevance, resumes as the key practical teaching guide. In South Africa, such changes to date have been essentially cosmetic, *ad hoc*, and ignore the racism embedded in the institutions of training themselves (Rauch 1992a).

Strategies of cultural colonization have been criticized on the grounds that they do less in practice to incorporate community sensibilities into the police culture their advocates think. Cop culture, the evidence suggests, is remarkably resilient. It is accordingly the new sensibilities acquired through training that are most likely to be subverted by the old, not the old by the new. Recruitment and training makes a difference, but not as much of a difference as one would hope. The general lesson from cultural colonialist devices is that they have little impact in themselves. Recruitment of officers from a different background, a more heterogeneous intake, and specific forms of attitude and behaviour training can only make marginal inroads on the negative features of the police culture. There are only minor gains to be made through such orthodox selection and training solutions to the perceived cultural problem.

INCORPORATIVE DEVICES – BRINGING THE COMMUNITY TO THE POLICE

Incorporative devices represent more or less informal devices to construct unmediated links between the police and the notional community. From the orthodox perspective, if the police culture is subject to continuing encounters with community sensibilities, it is liable to undergo a positive modification. In the UK, as in many other Western countries, local police forces are encouraged to develop direct community relationships through devices such as Community Forums, Lay Visitor practices, and Neighbourhood Watch schemes. These structures permit direct local interaction outside the normative practice of state policework. Potentially, they allow direct community influence on day-to-day policing practices in the locality.

Community Forums (which exist under various rubrics in many Anglo-American police districts) generally possess three common characteristics. They involve regular, direct face-to-face meetings between police officers and members of the local community. They take as their agenda a joint discussion of the police priorities for the local area. At the meetings, police officers are required to explain what action they have taken in response to previous Community Forum requests. There is however, no communal sanction where dissatisfaction is minuted.

Community Forums can ideally influence the occupational culture by requiring police officers to confront directly local public perceptions of their function and of their degree of efficiency in meeting publicly determined goals. They provide an alternative reference group, away from the immediate work-group influence of police peers. In the UK, Community Forums were developed under PACE, to provide direct representations between community and local police. There is a precedent for exporting such devices to Southern Africa. The new Namibian Police drew directly on British advice in developing such structures (Nathan 1990). There have also been several South African initiatives in this direction,[6] including the Local and Regional Dispute Resolution Committees established under the Peace Accord.

These forums have been criticized in Britain for several reasons (Morgan 1987). Lacking an appropriate representational structure and continuing membership (on both police and community sides) and sanctioning powers, they have generally been atypical of local communities. Debate over critical policing issues has largely been absent, more trivial issues have dominated. Police officers (with a large organiational bureaucracy behind them) have increasingly set the forum agenda for meetings, so that their priorities have police concerns rather than communal ones. In some cases, they have been used by police chiefs to construct a surrogate form of accountability, avoiding serious issues of police responsibility to democratic structures.

> It is hard to see how middle-class, powerless, police-dominated committees are going to be able to produce effective policing for those 'dispossessed' minorities (the policed communities) who bear the brunt of it.
>
> (Brogden *et al.* 1988: 176)

Community Forums might be conceived of as an ideal way in which the culture could be influenced and made responsive by direct interaction between the relevant local police officers and representative members of the community. However, it appears that cultural attributes remain almost totally unaffected by such experiences. It may be that the British model (which arose from twin sources – the inner city conflicts of the 1980s, and a more general concern with the exponential increase in recorded crime) provides the wrong model of Community Forums. There is some evidence that where forums develop (as in parts of Canada[7]), out of consensus rather than conflict, from community initiative rather from police sponsorship, they may have some impact. But the South African social milieu hardly suggests Community Forums as an organic development able to affect police practice significantly.

Lay Visitor schemes draw on a tradition which, since the abolition of the jury system, is institutionally alien to South Africa – the practice of involving non-legal personnel in monitoring and adjudicating in the criminal justice process (although voluntary monitoring practices have a long existence – see later). Lay Visitor schemes aim to provide communal oversight of the detention of persons in police hands – the context where the practices encouraged by the police culture flourish without any public scrutiny. In the UK, under PACE, they developed both by statute (in the provinces) and informally (in the metropolitan area). Lay Visitors have the right (subject to particular restrictions) to inspect the position of detainees in local police stations at any time of day and night, subjecting the police culture's potential degradation and abuse of the detainee, to an element of external scrutiny. Sanctioning power is limited to reports by the Lay Visitor to the municipal authority. It is more the threat of the Lay Visitor's unexpected arrival that is meant to influence police conduct than his or her actual appearance.

The potential value of such a scheme in South Africa is self-evident. Some approximation to such an office is the ANC proposal for a Police Reporting Officer (envisaged as an independent lawyer[8]). Given the evidence of physical abuse of suspects, observation by community representatives of the previously closed police context, could have a salutary effect. The formal rights of suspects during the detention and interrogation processes could be realized. The power of the occupational culture to determine the features of the detainees' passage through police hands would be much inhibited.

In practice, as a check on cultural practices, Lay Visiting has only a marginal effect in the UK (Walklate 1986). It affects only one aspect of policing practice (albeit an important one). A general monitoring of detention does not allow for detailed observation of interrogation practices. Various legal caveats allow the UK police to conceal any significant misdemeanours.[9] Consequently, Lay Visiting, as practised in the UK, depends on an existing police commitment to the scrutiny process. Like the Community Forums, Lay Visiting in the UK rarely encompasses citizens who might perceive the police culture and police practices as problematic.

Generally, there are major problems in adapting such a British initiative to South Africa. Unlike in the UK where Magistrates and Prison Visitors are often lay people, South Africa (as we have noted) has no recent formal lay tradition and resistance is certain from

entrenched interests.[10] Without favourable reception of the scheme
by SAP rank-and-file, abuses in the police station can easily be
concealed. In the absence of an elected local Police Authority, the
lack of sanctions against malpractice remains a major problem. However, despite these reservations, some form of Lay Visiting Scheme
could – given the scale of customary police abuse of detainees – have
some significance, in allowing a measure of public overview of that
context in which the scope of potential police violations is greatest.

Third, in the 1980s a quite different type of incorporative strategy
blossomed in the form of Neighbourhood Watch Schemes (NWS).[11]
They were formally intended to promote a measure of self-policing
(Johnston 1992). The schemes are conceived of as providing the
police with assistance through the promotion of community crime
control. Senior officers in the UK have described NWS as one device
by which the police can become socially accountable. They can
ideally influence the culture by creating continuing contact between
police and citizenry. In the course of such dialogue, alternative
priorities to those dictated by police culture and police organization
may emerge.

In South Africa, Watch schemes are widespread in white areas
with an insignificant number in black districts. They first appeared in
Randburg in 1985 and by the end of 1986, were formally adopted by
the SAP, which required divisional commanders to promote the
concept with the emphasis upon police coordination of the schemes.
The 'whole success of the Watch hinges on liaison between the
Watch and the local police officials' (Department of Protection
Services 1987: 1). There is some indication that the Police Reserve
has been influential in organising and running the schemes (Rauch
1988). The accumulated evidence on NWS is that they are limited
and of transitory effectiveness with regard to crime prevention
although they may lessen the fear of crime by residents (Bennett
1989). In South Africa as in the UK, the schemes generally have
much more present on paper than in practice. Significantly, they
appear to have signally failed to influence police practices. The first
NWS were established in the United States as part of a much larger,
multi-strand attempt to increase crime detection and awareness and
to enhance local accountability, and grew organically out of local
communities (Kinsey, Lea and Young 1986). UK Watch Schemes
differed in two ways. The communities were more heterogeneous.
They were imposed from the top – from the police – not growing
from the grass roots of the community. The South African situation

would seem to accentuate the British criticisms, especially that where Watch schemes develop out of social schism – the fear of the neighbourhood being 'invaded' by elements already defined as undesirable – they accentuate social conflict (Davis 1990).[12] They are basically only concerned with a limited number of crimes that are easily observable and liable to be reported, thus leaving out of public scope a whole range of policework which is influenced by the police culture. They have grown most successfully in middle-class white communities where no active challenge to the culture is likely to be mounted. The crime-, street order-directed focus of the NWS means that they simply reinforce the cultural perspective of a schismatic society, building on, and exacerbating existing social divisions. The values and norms of the police culture may in effect simply reinforce the predispositions of the white suburbs by enhancing the fear of 'outsiders' especially of those many black people who 'service' the life-styles of the suburbs. As an element of pressure on the SAP to change its practices, they can only be effective if they are utilized as part of a much larger multi-racial community responsiveness strategy, if they develop out of organic community demand rather than through police initiative and if they are given some power to sanction any lack of commitment by the police organization. Critically, their one positive value within the orthodox model of policing change could be to reinforce the movement from security-consciousness on the part of the SAP to crime-consciousness.

INTERNAL-RULE MAKING

Cultural colonialist and incorporative strategies operate primarily through psychological and sociological techniques, seeking to change police culture by exposing it directly to community influences. Rule-making strategies seek to limit the space within which the occupational culture can grow. The strategies seek to constrain the opportunity for rank-and-file values, and the sensibilities associated with them, to shape the character of policework.

The principal and almost universal internal rule-making device has been that of police professionalism. Internal rule-making through professionalization of policing is perceived to be a solution to the political problem of creating an 'impartial' policing free of assumed partisan communal influences. By elevating policing practice to that of a high status occupation, independent of political influence, in the service of a public 'good', professionalism is intended to resolve both a political problem and also that of the malign influence of the police culture. Professionalism as an internal rule-making device offers an alternative set of goals, means, and values to those of the occupational culture. (A consultant to the Metropolitan Police, Diana Yach, has argued for detailed professional changes in the SAP.[13]) The idea here is that partisan influences can be forestalled if the police are orientated to an impartial professional ethic. Professionalism, it is argued, contributes to the development of dispassionate policing because it establishes standards and directions for police discretion that are independent of political partisan interest. Essentially what this means is that being accountable to the law and the law alone, in practice comes to mean being answerable to a professional sensibility that can be fostered through training.

The advocacy of professionalism as a device for limiting the influence of police culture has its roots in the managerial strategies advocated by the American police chief Vollmer. The features of this professionalization strategy have been identified by Niederhoffer (1967) as high admission standards, specialized knowledge and theory, a code of ethics, altruism and commitment to the ideal of service, long training period, regulation of membership, autonomous control, professional pride, and public status and prestige.[14]

In the UK, the major statutory manifestation of professionalism (as in PACE) focused directly on professional forms of control through developing a system of internal rule-making, and centred upon the notion of professional ethics and accountability. Specifically, it developed three Codes of Practice (on Stop and Search, on Search and Seizure, and on Detention and Questioning). Each Code was to be monitored by a senior officer. Officers who break the Codes are subject to internal disciplinary charges (not to criminal and civil proceedings) thus holding the police accountable to the police in a 'trust the police' approach to the problems of police culture.[15] Under this system, rank-and-file professionalism is monitored and enforced by professional superiors who act to limit the effects of the police culture by reducing the space in which it has to operate.

The central difficulty at the crux of the professional thesis is that it is the institution itself that determines the nature of the 'good', the service to be supplied to the client. There are also other problems as professional codes are, in practice, easy to evade in view of the tendency (as we noted in Chapter Two), for senior ranks to tacitly support deviations from professional codes (Shearing 1990a). In the

UK, senior officers appear to have become relatively blasé about monitoring the Codes established by PACE.

This strategy of controlling the police through professional ethics has been adopted in South Africa under the provisions of the National Peace Accord, which provide for a Police Code of Conduct. While it is too early to tell what its effects will be, early evidence suggests that it is likely to be no more effective in controlling police behaviour than Codes elsewhere. Rauch (1992b), for instance, notes that the Code appears to be little more than a 'political defence' for existing police conduct that may, in Benyon's and Bourn's words, encourage:

> the portrayal of policing as a separate and expert profession [which] may create a gulf between those who do it and the public. Professionalization as a device for constraining police culture is at best a long-term process that depends on a gradual establishment of a commitment to community protection backed by rigorous supervision.
>
> (Benyon and Bourn 1986)

More realistically, for professionalism to be effective as a device that will restrain police culture, it must resonate with rank-and-file experience and not be imposed from the top by a police elite. It must be connected to the operational reality of policing, be relevant to the specificity of policing, and experientially based.[16] Professionalism in policing should not be removed from the hurly-burly of rank-and-file work. Rather it should seek to elevate, in skill and commitment, the 'best practice' of ordinary police persons. Doing this, like so many things in police reform, is easier said than done.

Directly linked to professionalism as a device for internally constraining the police culture are the various record-keeping devices – whether on paper or by new technological recording devices. They have become a major means of increasing the transparency of police practice. One PACE Code, for instance, requires the recording of justifications for stop-and-searches and details of the detention process. These records are accessible to the public and must be produced on 'reasonable' demand. This insistence on records is intended to reduce the autonomy of the rank-and-file police and thereby the space in which the police culture has to operate. This strategy of transparency through the insistence on the creations of records of police activity is easier to formulate than they are to utilize. For example, in the case of stop-and-search records, the actual 'stop' may occur on little more than the patrol officer's intuition so that the *post-facto* justification may have little relation to what actually happened (Dixon, Coleman and Bottomley 1990). While this requirement to justify action in terms of a Code does influence action by 'formatting' it (Ericson 1992) this restraint is more limited that the use of Codes suggests. For example, as the records are produced by police, who can typically count on the support of colleagues, it is difficult to dispute their version of events. Indeed the existence of the paper record provides a 'proof' of what happened – the simple act of 'recording' legitimates police justifications (McConville *et al.* 1991).

The opportunities that paper trails provide for 'creative' recording have been countered in many Anglo-American jurisdictions through the introduction of audio- and video-recording devices, on the grounds that they directly capture what has happened. In some Canadian forces, for example, the processing of suspects from the time they enter the police station is video-recorded. More commonly only the interrogation process is subject to recording. The expressed intention of such practices is to safeguard the suspects constitutional rights by providing a 'true' record of what transpired for the court. Again the intention is to limit the scope of play of the police culture. As there is much that can still happen off-camera, and as the police become skilled at performing before the camera, these devices are in principle not very different to paper systems.

The use of technological devices to 'improve' police behaviour and to modify the cultural imperatives is in its infancy in South Africa. Pressures to use such devices will become intense during the transitionary period as critics of the police and the SAP themselves are exposed to precedents in Western policing and the attractions of technology solutions. Although initial rank-and-file resistance is common where such devices are introduced, opposition appears to be temporary, in part because of the gains police discover in their use both in terms of deflecting criticism and in terms of presenting evidence. Video- and audio-recordings of suspects as they appear in police custody often prove useful in challenging defence claims about the character of suspects and attempts by them to create a positive image in court by 'dressing up' accused persons in court. Video- and audio-recording, while it continues to provide the police with considerable control over depictions of 'what happened', limit the space in which they have to operate at the same time as they provide more space for creative accounting.[17]

As we have suggested, internal restraint practices suffer from what has become known as 'the technological fix'. They rely on the assumption that mechanistic, technological devices have an in-built objectivity that cannot easily be corrupted by agent intervention – 'pictures don't lie'. They imply a value-freedom in the monitoring of police behaviour that is unwarranted. All such techniques, whether written self-reports or the audio-visual 'capturing' of events provide space for human agency in the construction of the records. For the most part recording devices operate in the service of existing police goals. 'Objective' recording techniques are particularly useful to the police as 'arse covering' resources precisely because they do appear to be so 'fail-safe' – it is hard to appeal against the ultimate statement of the recorder (McConville *et al.* 1991).

A related problem with recording devices is that the invasion of privacy they permit extends beyond the privacy of the police they are intended to limit, to the privacy of suspects. For example the introduction of video devices into the cells of detainees (which would mean, *inter alia*, lighting cells for 24 hours a day) has been criticized by civil rights bodies as an invasion of privacy which would only increase the mental pressure on detainees. Thus, Haysom, for instance, in a review of both the American and South African experience, argues that:

> If anything the innovation perpetuated the deception that the high rate of detainee suicides is attributable to the pathological state of the detainee, and that accordingly detainees are guilty of their own suicides.
>
> (Haysom 1984: 102)

Video devices intended as a strategy to enhance the effectiveness of rules as a restraint on police culture may – like its predecessor, the peephole system – actually serve as a source of harassment. Technology is not a neutral device, but – like the female contraceptive pill – serves mainly the interests of those who introduce the device, not those who are exposed to it.

EXTERNAL RULE-MAKING

Like the previous category, external rule-making devices affect the space available within which the culture can grow. As we saw in Chapter Two, the external environment of rules can facilitate the expression of the values and sensibilities embodied in the police culture. But external rules, as a source of restraint, when backed by both positive and negative sanctions, can also limit the space within which the police culture can operate. Whereas the old orthodoxy emphasized the importance of the internal rules, later critics – in the UK as elsewhere – have argued that it is not police practice in itself that is the problem but rather the way the formal rules by their very vagueness and elasticity permit police officers to abide by the rules of the culture rather than by those norms of the community.

External rule-making devices operate in three ways. Generally, they are concerned to minimize the permissiveness of police practice by clarifying and rigidifying the formal rule structure of police work through explicit formal constraint – tightening the legal rules under which the police operate. They may be intended to minimize police influence over the totality of the criminal justice process. Or they may be rules enforceable by local community pressure or by independent external bodies. The focus on external rules represents one area where orthodox approaches to police reform have caught up with more critical explanations. Thus in the UK, the reforms represented in PACE, embodied not just internal attempts to constrain police culture but also a recognition that the external rules – of law and of police powers – were also problematic.

Conventional explanations of police deviance in common law legal cultures, saw it as in part produced by the failure of police officers to obey 'law-in-the-books'. 'Law-in-practice', it is argued, differs from law-in-the-books because legal personnel, including the police, break the law in order to achieve speedier processing of suspects, to gather evidence and so on (Shearing 1981). In this analysis, law itself was viewed as unproblematic. Police misconduct, deviations from the formal rights of the citizen, was a consequence of police failure to be bound by the law. As we indicated in Chapters Two and Three, a variety of socio-legal research has challenged this account and argued that police deviance as a cultural manifestation is enabled rather than constrained by law. Law-in-the-books, it is argued, far from preventing police aberrations, provides for police deviance by permitting police who deviate from the values of liberal democracy, to operate within the law. The law provides a legal space within which the police culture can thrive. Accordingly, the occupational culture does not deviate from the standards of legality but fits with the legal requirements. Occupational culture works in tandem with the law. The vagueness of much criminal law discourse allowed cultural determinants to operate within the law.

Within this understanding the focus of reform shifts away from the police culture itself to the law that enables it to operate. Restraining the police is accomplished through tightening the legal regime within which the police operate so as to reduce the discretionary space available. Police officers need not break the law when the law itself is adequately permissive for cultural practices to be the guide. In the UK, the mythical Ways and Means Act is often invoked to demonstrate the elasticity of police powers. Police officers need not break the law, when that discourse itself bestows on them permissive 'ways and means' of acting within the law to dominate a second party. There are always alternative charges available. Precise charges are often sufficiently vague to be used to cover different situations. Historically, South African criminal law assumed many of the vague categories of persons within the older common law tradition, and applied them generally to black people. For example, section 29 of the Bantu (Urban Areas) Consolidation Act permitted a police officer to arrest without warrant in an urban area any African who he 'has reason to believe' is 'an idle or undesirable person' and to bring him before a Bantu Affairs Commissioner who 'shall require such Bantu to give a good and satisfactory account of himself'. Such charges not merely gave the state police massive discretionary powers, they also reversed the assumptions of due process – placing the onus upon the person to prove innocence, not on the state to prove guilt.[18] A similar power, with the right of the state unilaterally to determine guilt, was inserted through a new clause in 1956 – the Bantu Affairs Board could order the removal of an African from an urban area if his presence was 'detrimental to the maintenance of peace and order in the area'. The individual was guilty as determined by the state police, even when born and domiciled in the area. No appeals were allowed. The cultural values informing police discretion, determined guilt.

Two existing powers from the Criminal Procedure Act 1955 provide a more specific exposition of the present discretionary space. Section 22(f) confers on the police officer the right to 'without warrant arrest . . . any person who obstructs him in the course of his duty.' In that section, nowhere is the term 'obstruction' defined. It is in effect for the white male member of the SAP to define obstruction subjectively according to his own cultural predispositions. Courts rarely challenge that police definition. But what may be obstruction to the police officer may, normatively, not be obstruction to the person arrested. The law in effect gives the more powerful party in the encounter the right to define what is an obstruction. Similarly, section 22 (b), (e) of the Act utilizes the term 'reasonably suspect'. The only clarification of the term offered by the authoritative *Swift's Law on Criminal Procedure* is circular:

> Where a policeman receiving advice from another that circumstances exist authorising a search . . . , it seems that unless there is a good reason to the contrary, the second police officer will generally have reasonable grounds for the belief.
>
> (Harcourt 1969)

In both cases, the law appears to clarify the powers of the officer but in practice permits the police occupational culture to determine what constitutes an offence. Thus law-in-the-books, far from preventing police aberrations, actually provides for police deviance – the autonomy of cultural practice – to operate within the law. In the vast majority of relatively petty cases that police officers bring before the South African courts, similar permissive euphemisms exist. The law is not watertight but actually provides for the culture, rather than specific concise, clear-cut, legal maxims, to operate as the police officer thinks appropriate. In such cases, the occupational culture does not appear to deviate from the standards of legality but actually fits within the agreed permissive legal discourse of the white legal system. The prejudices of the occupational culture of the SAP, often at odds with the cultures of different groups and communities, becomes the objective device for law enforcement.

There are a variety of problems associated with the implementation of a strategy designed to tighten such legal discourse. While it is possible to reduce the space the law makes available to the police culture, it is not possible to eliminate it entirely. Such legal rules cannot be formulated so precisely as to eliminate discretion (McConville *et al.* 1991). Discretion can none the less be reduced by establishing a legal regime that requires the police to justify their action within narrow bounds. In South Africa, where the legal regime has been extraordinarily wide, this would have a significant effect on police action.

A second external rule-making area in which recent British developments have pointed the way to mediating the effects of South African police culture lies in the context of police powers of prosecution. A peculiar and almost unique feature of the South African criminal justice process is in the combination of powers held by the SAP. Essentially, there are two separate police powers in

South Africa – the power to arrest and the separate power to prosecute (subdivided into the powers to bring or not to bring a charge, and the power to determine the level and nature of the charge to be brought). While in practice, actual police participation as prosecutors is confined to certain rural areas and state prosecutors exist as part of a separate state institution, the SAP retains considerable influence over the prosecution process. The problem is that both stages – the decision to arrest and the decision to prosecute – are in the majority of public order cases (roughly half of all cases appearing in the Magistrates' Court, where commonly the only prosecution evidence is provided by a police officer), and in more serious controversial contexts, highly influenced by the police culture. Where evidence is vague and disputed, the dominant party, the police, has the determining influence over those critical stages of the criminal justice process.[19]

This combination of powers in the hands of the SAP is highly unusual in a country which has developed its dominant legal discourse from a European ancestry. In countries with a Roman law inheritance, the second power – that of prosecution – is given to a different agency. In France, for example, the state police make an arrest but it is up to a second body, the *Police Judiciare*, (as requested by the Examining Magistrate, the *Juge d'Instruction*) to conduct the investigation and to determine the character of any subsequent charge. A different approach is taken in Scotland, where prosecution powers lie in the hands of the civil Procurator Fiscal and the police conduct the investigation – but under the administrative authority of a notary appointed by the Procurator's office. The rationale for this system is principally that the 'arresting police' are committed to a guilty finding and may necessarily bias the charge against a defendant if they also have a prosecuting power, whereas the Investigating Magistrate is only concerned to discover the 'facts' of the case – and operates, in effect, with no prior presumption of guilt. The Investigating Magistrate offers a check upon police commitment to convict by intervening between the process of arrest and the process of adjudication. His or her concern is not so much with questions of 'guilt' (the police predisposition) or 'innocence' but rather with searching out the 'facts' of the case.

The indivisibility of the two powers was primarily a feature of countries with a common law legal culture. Even in such countries, there are few cases of police forces possessing the combined powers of the SAP. In the English criminal justice process[20] until the development of the Crown Prosecution Service in 1986, the police had also primary responsibility for both decisions to arrest and to prosecute. However, countries such as the United States and Canada which also have a primarily adversarial process of law, have also recognized the autonomous realm of prosecution. Until 1986, England and Wales and South Africa were almost unique in permitting those twin powers to rest in one body. Now South Africa is the only major anomaly.

A key advantage of stripping the SAP of its influence over the prosecution process is that it reduces the culture's impact to the arrest situation alone, and prevents its having a directive influence on the nature and character of the prosecution process.

However, there are also problems in this transformation proposal. The existing prosecutorial system in South Africa is barely nearer the community than is the SAP. Subtracting police powers hardly guarantees community-sensitive prosecution practice. Where, as in the United States, the Investigating Magistrate (the District Attorney) may be an elected officer, there are some benefits directly accruing in sensitizing the office to communal demands. As a minimum, however, at best, all he or she can hope to do is to provide a check on police malpractice. At the present time, there are few instances of prosecutors publicly approaching police practices sceptically:

> prosecutors still tend to place a dangerous confidence in the infallibility of the police . . . despite the high incidence of police abuse of power, it is extremely rare that a prosecutor will take up the matter with the control prosecutor or the station commander of the police station where the accused alleges in court that he or she has been assaulted or tortured by the police whilst in custody.
> (Fernandez 1992: 16)

Although the recent development in England and Wales of a Crown Prosecution Service is not a good example of best practice, it does demonstrate how a country in which police prosecution powers have traditionally been inviolate, can come to terms with the necessity for transformation. In South Africa, the prosecution system has a relatively low public and institutional profile as compared with other criminal justice agencies (Fernandez 1992). It also has major problems with the recruitment of legally qualified staff (ibid). Utilizing the Public Prosecutors as a means of counterbalancing the cultural effects of the SAP requires a strong autonomous existence and career structure, an occupation confident of its own powers. This is not apparent in South Africa.

The evidence from other European countries is that simple factors of bureaucracy and excessive demand may result, in practice, in the police rather than the Investigating Magistrate assuming most of the prosecution work. The ideal requirement, as occurs formally in France with the *Police Judiciare*, for a separate investigating police, again involves what may be much duplication of activity and expansion of personnel numbers. In South Africa, the denial of police prosecution powers would require major legislative change and consequent opposition from several quarters. But the development would have the particular benefits of making the SAP fall in line with the criminal justice processes of other countries (where the issue has been debated intensely and conclusively) while at the same time confining the occupational culture to only one part (if the major one) of the process.

A third device for tightening the external rules over police practice exist through the medium of crime and victim surveys. A number of commentators in South Africa have called for increased measurement of community satisfaction with the police.[21] An essential feature of these arguments is the proposal for the establishment of an index of police effectiveness. One strategy that has been proposed for establishing such an index is victim surveys designed to measure the degree to which people in particular areas are insecure and the extent to which they feel secure. Such surveys, it has been argued, are a critical weapon in the struggle for more responsive policing and crime control (for example, Kinsey, Lea and Young 1986) and provide for feedback on police practice. This argument reflects a critique of the extent to which police performance has been assessed in terms of statistical data that is directly under the control of the police, in particular, statistics on clearance rates. Such indicators depend on police generated crime rates and police generated rates of their success in responding to crime – such as clearance rates.[22] Crime rates, it is argued, are an inappropriate base from which to assess police effectiveness as they measure people's willingness to report crime and the willingness of the police to record crimes. Similar problems exist with respect to clearance rates.

While this issue of rates has not been a subject of sustained critical debate within South Africa,[23] what evidence there is suggests both that many people are reluctant to report crimes and that when they do the police are often reluctant to record or respond to them. The following is a typical response given by black South Africans in response to questions about police responsiveness to local crime.

> No one lays charges any more with the Police. People have given up. If you try and lay a charge you are likely to get assaulted. The Police are often drunk on the weekend. One is scared to go to the Police. We want guarantees that we will not be harmed if we report crimes. If you report a crime you are likely to end up in prison. . . . When you are trying to lay a charge the officers intimidate you by playing with their guns.
>
> (quoted in Shearing and Mzamane 1992: 9)

Victim surveys seek to provide an independent measure of the security/insecurity and thus indirectly of the practices of policing within a given area. They are also utilized to assess the extent of unreported crime, the reasons for that non-reporting and the responsiveness of the police to community concerns. As a form of external-rule tightening, victim surveys offer a potentially useful device for shaping police action, but they have not been utilized in South Africa. This is due in no small measure – as Mathews (1991) suggests – to the enormous logistical problems in a country that has for many years been on the brink of civil war and where perhaps as many as half the population do not have a conventional address. The pioneering study of perceptions of policing by the Centre for Criminal Justice in Pietermaritzberg encountered considerable problems of security and access (Mathews 1991). Because they challenge the official control of information, victim surveys are likely to meet strong resistance, not just in the SAP, but in the higher echelons of the Ministry of Law and Order. They are costly in personnel hours, and because of the need for repeated surveys to indicate any fluctuations in local perceived crime priorities, are unlikely to be sustained in any one force area, over time. The alternative, as conducted by the British Home Office, of biannual national surveys, does not meet the particular local requirements of heterogeneous South African society. However, as in the UK, there is no reason why certain communities could not be targeted experimentally through the survey approach in order to provide a sampling of more universal perceptions of policing priorities over time.

A fourth example of external rule-tightening within the orthodox reform programme relates to the handling of complaints against the police. As we saw in Chapter Two, in South Africa, the complaints system has been of derisory value. It has been completely unable to deal with police abuses that may be perceived to derive from the influence of the police culture. But the changes recommended from the orthodox approach – in particular, for the expansion of the 'independent' investigating and reporting agency – fails to satisfy. That recommendation, like most of the proposals detailed above, seeks to 'blame the culture' (and the individual police officers immersed in it). An independent complaint agency is portrayed as a relatively effective device for constraining such rule-breaking.

In practice, two types of complaint systems have emerged in English-speaking liberal democracies. What differentiates them is whether the entity responsible for the complaint process has the authority to impose a decision in response to complaints on the police or not. Where the answer is 'no', they tend to operate as a source of recommendations to legislatures and councils who can, within the limits of the doctrine of police independence, put pressure on government and through them the police. In both these systems, the police, more often than not, retain at least an initial right to investigate complaints and take action in response to them. As this account suggests, a critical feature of such complaint systems is that they tend, like the criminal justice system they mimic, to operate reactively in response to complaints by individuals and to solve problems by blaming and punishing individuals. In a society in which organizations shape and control subjectivity and the actions that flow from it, it is the 'management of organizational life' (Rose 1989: 2) that clearly should be the principal focus of accountability not individuals seen as getting their instructions directly from 'the law'. This conception that individuals rather than organizations are a central focus of concern, is clearly inadequate as is the conception of the modern state as 'an entity which was developed above individuals'(Foucault, cited in Rose 1989: 1).

In response to this individualistic and reified conception there have been repeated calls in liberal-democratic countries for a more remedial response to complaints against the police that will direct attention to the police organization rather than simply to autonomous individuals within it (Goldsmith 1991; Shearing 1990a). This development has gone some way to respond to the obvious inadequacy of a 'just deserts' approach to accountability but it is fundamentally flawed by its location within the framework we have outlined.

A final approach to tightening the external rules over the police culture lies in the variety of monitoring schemes which have scrutinized police practice both in the West and in South Africa, over recent years. Monitoring schemes are intended to restrain police culture and the conduct it promotes, by placing the police under the scrutiny of persons drawn from the communities they serve. These schemes seek to identify and report on the extent to which police deviate from the norms of democratic policing. Some of them may operate like the Lay Visiting scheme (see above) which can exercise a degree of internal scrutiny. The Monitoring strategies recognize the problems of access experienced by incorporative strategies.

The general function of these initiatives is to rectify the restricted access citizens have to police activity. They may operate outside of the police stations at city-wide level (Ericson 1982) or at community level (Jefferson, McLaughlin and Robertson 1988). In the United Kingdom and North America such schemes generally seek to ensure that police deviance is kept within check and, second, that positive action with regard to crime does not unduly benefit middle-class communities to the detriment of services to other groups. In South Africa, monitoring schemes – which have become an important feature of the political scene – have moved beyond monitoring in the narrow sense of observation to include an interventionist peace-making, lay policing role (Marais 1992b).

This interventionist mode, which has been described as 'deep monitoring', depends on the establishment of 'intensive personal relationships between individuals and organisations within and around' communities (UMAC 1992). What links these 'deep' schemes to more conventional monitoring schemes is their shared concern with 'stopping the violence'.[24] Schemes that embrace deep monitoring operate as a form of governance rather than simply as a device for restraining the agents of government (see Chapters six and seven) as their monitors act to maintain order and bring about peace. An example of a deep monitoring group that emphasizes peace-making is the Transvaal-based Community Dispute Resolution Committee (CDRC) whose mission is to serve 'the broader community of South Africa by assisting with the development and enhancement of appropriate dispute resolution capabilities within communities' (Mission Statement March 1991). These groups, which have worked largely outside of the structures of formal governance, have developed as part of the struggle against apartheid.

One of the earliest and perhaps the best known of South Africa's monitoring groups is the Black Sash, a women's organization that became prominent in the 1950s, when women wearing black sashes stood in silent protest in public against the brutality and injustice of apartheid. This role developed into one of monitoring the South African state as women from the Sash became unauthorized lay visitors in situations like courts and demonstrations, as witnesses whose presence would constrain government officials. From this beginning, monitoring has expanded enormously within South Africa with scores of local groups and numerous international groups participating. While international groups, like Amnesty International and the International Commission of Jurists operate exclusively as monitors in a narrow sense, many of the local groups combine a witness with an interventionist function in their monitoring. A recent example of this was the involvement of monitoring groups as a Joint Forum on Policing as both witnesses and mediators in Cape Town's recent 'taxi war' (Collins 1992).

The twin functions of providing accounts of what took place and intervening as peace-makers were formalized in 1991 with the signing of the multi-party National Peace Accord which sets in place formal structures for monitoring the actions of the security forces and the major political parties. These structures blur the lines between observation and intervention at a formal level in ways that directly parallel what has happened at a more informal level. At present both these formal and informal structures are operating simultaneously.

At the observational level, monitoring schemes provide an audit function (Marais 1992) that responds to the critique of the 'individual' focus of police complaint systems we noted earlier (Shearing 1990a) by uncoupling the scrutiny of government officials from complaints. In such schemes, it is the monitoring agency that decides on the focus of attention, not a complainant, though of course this may be influenced by complaints. In adopting this principle, these groups operate as informal ombuds-bodies to provide a 'supervisory shadow' to oversee the operation of government on behalf of communities. This notion is illustrated by Gelhorn (1966: 226–7) in relation to the Swedish ombudsman system, where prosecutors, judges and prison governors make decisions fully conscious of the potential intervention power of the ombudsman.

In the context of state policing, the monitoring ideal is for police malpractice to be forestalled rather than sanctioned, by a realization of community observation. However, local monitoring groups work under difficult constraints. They are frequently the subject of police harassment, they may become 'captured' by officials through exposure to them and they are dependent on the press to publicize their findings. Furthermore, as monitoring groups are frequently established at moments of crisis and staffed by volunteers, simply maintaining themselves is often a constant problem. These problems and similar problems in South Africa have led for calls for a more permanent national monitoring scheme. The National Peace Accord signed by the major political parties in 1991 is a significant move in this direction. More recent calls for monitoring structures in South Africa that include an 'international presence' seek to respond to the National Peace Accord's reliance on 'illegitimate' government structures by involving an outside body, such as the United Nations, in monitoring (Shearing 1991).[25]

The limitations of culturalist and rule-tightening strategies

The difficulties with the general body of proposals that stem mainly from the orthodox approach to reform are considerable. Underlying them is the thesis that the state police – and especially the rank-and-file – are the problem. Policing as an arena of debate is left unquestioned. It avoids the larger political questions of the democratic mandate of policing. It focuses in practice on police culture. It reduces the problem of transforming the SAP to essentially one of removing aberrational, historical defects. Modify the practices on the ground by infiltrating and constraining police culture and a solution is possible.

This argument critically ignores our discussion in Chapter Three. Police culture does not operate independently of the larger state exigencies. The analysis of discourses of state policing in South Africa demonstrates a clear link between rank-and-file cultural practices and the imprimaturs of the apartheid state. The major difficulty lies with the move from an acceptance that South Africa requires 'democratic policing' to the premise that this should be accomplished by cloning the policing arrangements from a country with a liberal-democratic political tradition. Our reason for questioning this premise is not that South Africa presents unique problems that require unique solutions, nor is it that South Africa has nothing to learn from the experience of liberal-democratic countries. We reject both these arguments.

First, South Africa's policing problems are not unique, and the claim that they are is frequently little more than a disingenuous attempt to resist reform. Second, as the considerable success of Namibian police reform indicates, the cloning of existing Western police practices would go a very long way to improving South African policing. Much democratic policing, as the multinational Goldstone Panel on Mass Demonstrations (Panel 1992) has argued, is considerably better than what has happened in South Africa and even the worst would probably be an improvement. Our argument is that South Africa can and should do better than existing Western policing and in doing so it can and should contribute to the development of the problems of democratic policing. South Africans should not simply be entering the global arena to which they now have access as beggars ready to take and implement a received wisdom. It can and should approach what the democratic world has to offer critically, as active participants in an ongoing process of police reform.

Policing in Western democracies has moved a considerable distance towards the realization of the principles that guide it. The best of liberal-democratic policing, however, is policing that is critical of its accomplishments and is striving through an 'institutional reflexivity' (Giddens 1991: 2) to move beyond them. It is this reflexivity that South Africans should be emulating. What is required in South Africa is not cloning but a reflexive monitoring of policing both in South Africa and elsewhere so that it can take its place as a full participant in the debate over policing that is evident everywhere.

This is not to argue that South Africa cannot and should not learn from the lessons of others. This, however, is very different from simply 'buying' their 'models.' As Friedmann phrases it:

> There are temptations in a comparative effort to examine the possibilities of importing some aspects of successful policing from one country to another . . . a policing tactic should not be imposed when it does not fit.
>
> (Friedmann 1992)

Consideration of the specificities of the context are crucial to decisions over such transplants (1992: 203–4). Learning from others requires the adoption of a critical stance towards their institutions. The task is not one of locating a 'package' to adopt but of contributing to a conversation about how to realize democracy policing in the face of the wide variety of impediments that mitigate against this.

Put in more theoretical terms, there is no pre-existing 'truth' about policing, or for that matter anything else, to be located and adopted by South Africa. The task is to engage in an ongoing search for the 'better' where what is 'better' will be discovered progressively through ongoing reflexive debate. We seek to 'disturb and incite' rather than to 'comfort and tranquillize' (Connelly 1987: 125) so as to encourage South Africans to engage in a critical debate about what democratic policing can mean.

In developing our thesis, we maintain that the difficulty with the conventional cloning approach to police reform is that it defines reform as a technical problem requiring a technical solution rather than as a conceptual problem requiring a conceptual solution. In challenging this technological stance, here and in the remaining chapters, we argue that it is precisely the conceptual framework within which this technical debate over policing has been located that is the problem at issue. As South Africans search for a new mode of policing, it is the established frame that guides conventional reform that they must question if they are to develop an approach to policing that does not trap them within an outmoded conception.

ACCOUNTABILITY – SALVAGING ELEMENTS OF THE ORTHODOX PROPOSALS

As our review of the problems associated with South African policing, the support the police culture receives from wider discourses and our review in this chapter of reform strategies makes clear, we recognize that transforming the SAP is going to be enormously complex and difficult. South Africans, however, will have no choice but to tackle this task if the dream of a new South Africa is to be realized. If South African policing is not transformed, South Africa cannot be transformed. As recently as 26 July 1992, Dr Jonathan Gluckman, the pathologist who gave evidence for the Biko family at the inquest into Steve Biko's death, decided to 'go public' in a desperate call to the De Klerk government to 'stop the killing' of people in custody because he 'can't stand it any longer.'

> I get speechless. I get sick at heart about the whole affair. It goes on and on and on. I don't know how to stop it. I don't know how to stop it. I don't think the government knows how to stop it. . . . These [his files] are the fruit, or detritus, of a lifetime. Ninety per cent of the people in these files, I am convinced were killed by the police. I have constant evidence of police handling people in a vicious manner. My impression is that they are totally out of control. They do what they like.
>
> (*Sunday Times* 26 July 1992)

Transforming this police force is going to have to begin with a government with the will, determination and strength to insist upon change. In this we are heartened by the research one of us recently undertook in Namibia on the experience of transformation by a determined government with a police force that was until that country's independence part of the SAP. As one of the officers interviewed there phrased it, the police in Namibia began to change when everyone realized that the government was serious about change.

Within liberal democracies the issue of accountability (understood both as being both answerable to and controlled by some authority) has been a concern around which debate about policing has developed. Central to this debate has been a deep-seated suspicion of the trustworthiness of governments. This suspicion has its source in the very nature of representative democracies. A government, within such a democracy, is formed by a political party that promotes policies that reflect the interests of its constituency. This constituency very rarely includes a majority of citizens. This is so for at least two reasons. First, the citizens who elect a government seldom constitute a substantive, or even a simple, majority of the electorate. Second, government decision-making is very often influenced by well-resourced lobby groups who, for the most part, work behind closed doors to persuade governments to promote the interests of their clients.

To place the state police directly under the control of such governments would be to put in the hands of a partisan set of politicians an extraordinary powerful resource that they can use to promote partisan interests. Under such a system the police, it is feared, will become a partisan tool of a political constituency. This concern has given rise to the widespread acceptance, both in Britain and in countries whose law has developed under British influence, of a conceptual mechanism designed to distance the police from government. This mechanism is based on a distinction between administrative and operational issues and the associated notion that with respect to operational matters police officers exercise an original rather than a delegated authority (Marshall 1965). The argument used to develop these concepts into a distancing mechanism are as follows.

While it is reasonable for governments to provide direct guidance to the police with respect to administrative questions, this is not the case in operational matters. In these matters, that include those activities associated with law enforcement and keeping the peace, the police should take their direction from the law rather than from government because law represents a more general public will. The law, so the argument goes, may not perfectly reflect the 'public interest' but it comes closer to doing so than do the inevitably partisan directions of particular governments. In this conception, 'the law' is accorded a reified, autonomous character that separates it from government at the same time that it is accorded a 'voice' that speaks to the police on behalf of 'the people'.

Perhaps the most famous expression of this doctrine of police independence is the statement by Lord Denning, who argued that a chief of police:

> is not the servant of anyone, save of the law itself. No Minister of the Crown can tell him that he must, or must not, keep observation on this place or that; or that he must, or must not, prosecute this man or that one. Nor can the police authority tell him so. The responsibility for law enforcement lies on him. He is answerable to the law and to the law alone.
>
> (1968, 1 All ER 763, at 769)

While the validity of this reasoning has been challenged (Lustgarten 1986; Stenning 1981), it continues to dominate considerations of police accountability in many English-speaking liberal democracies. This distancing mechanism has embedded in it a problem that becomes apparent as soon as it is put into practice. The problem is that 'the voice' of 'the law' is seldom, if ever, unambiguous. Law requires interpretation and this requires discretion. Given this the critical question becomes the regulation of discretion in ways that are consistent with the doctrine of police independence.

The review we have undertaken in this chapter makes clear that simple once-and-for-all answers are not available. Establishing police democratic policing is going to require ongoing debate and dialogue and the incremental development of structures and processes that operate simultaneously at a variety of levels. This is the lesson of the experience we have reviewed here. None the less, the struggle over community-responsive policing that has taken place both within South Africa and elsewhere does provide guidance. Our reading of this experience suggests five essential lessons that South Africans should heed as they move to transform their police. First, the hope that impartial policing can be achieved through the doctrine of police independence is a chimera that should be rejected. If the doctrine of police independence has not promoted impartial policing in countries like Britain and Canada with a long democratic history, it is unlikely do so in South Africa, where the police traditionally have been employed to deny the majority of South Africans the most basic human freedoms. All that this strategy would do in South Africa would be to embed the practices and values of the old regime within the new state. While this might be favoured by those who will resist the transformation of South Africa into a democratic state, it is not one that the democratic movement can countenance. Police independence is simply not an option anyone seriously interested in transforming the South African state should contemplate as a device for establishing an impartial police that respects human rights. The police in a new South Africa should be directly and unambiguously accountable to political authority. The essence of democracy is that governments must bear responsibility for the action of their officials. This responsibility is not incompatible with the requirement that officials should act within the limits of law.

To conclude that the doctrine of police independence should not be imported to South Africa is not to deny the problems of partisan government that it was meant to avoid. These problems, however, should be faced directly rather than avoided. It is here that the South African experience with monitoring is most instructive.

This brings us to our second conclusion. The way to deal with the temptations governments will inevitably face to use the police for their own partisan ends is to make the activities of the police and the decisions of the government with respect to them as transparent as possible to as many people as possible. In that sense, many of the reform strategies described as 'orthodox' in the discussion above, remain viable in a more radical account. State policing and the decisions that governments make in controlling it should be a public matter and so far as possible visible to all. This should be done by institutionalizing monitoring of the police, government control of policing, as an essential feature of a new South Africa both at the level of the state and civil society. What the international and the South African experience suggests is that this should be done at the political level through the creation of an ombuds-type body (Shearing 1991) as a constant shadow over police and government to review police actions and governmental control over the police. Only the presence of such an independent body with unrestrained access to state policing and the structures that produce it at all levels will ensure political accountability.

To ensure political accountability, such a body should not have the power to intervene directly in any way. Its task should be purely one of observation and reporting. It is the task of the government to govern effectively and to do so in a manner that upholds the new South African constitution. The task of an ombuds-body is to make this process of governance transparent so that it can be assessed by the people to whom government and the police are ultimately responsible. To permit the supervising body to intervene directly in the process of governing is to create a further institution that must itself be monitored. The essential function to be performed by an ombuds-body is to ensure that the police and government are compelled to answer for their actions so that they can be controlled. It is this compulsion not professional independence, that will protect the people of South Africa from governmental exploitation of the police for partisan ends.

Our third conclusion is that monitoring should not be restricted to the political level. Lay monitoring, despite its problems, not only provides a basis for holding the police directly accountable to communities but it is a device for building community confidence in the police. In South Africa, where the police have for a very long time been seen as an enemy of the people, and where suspicion of government is particularly deeply rooted, monitoring that has its roots in civil rather than political society is likely to be especially important. The South African experience of civil monitoring under apartheid is testimony to how effective such groups can be in restraining both the police and government and in placing alternative proposals on to the policy agenda. While these monitoring groups have filled a gap created by the absence of legitimate monitoring mechanisms at the political level, they can and should play a role once such structures are developed. The cynicism about government and politicians internationally, and the impetus it has provided to civil monitoring initiatives, should caution against any suggestion that the mechanisms that have developed within South Africa should be allowed to wither once a legitimate democratic government has been installed.

Our fourth proposal is that monitoring schemes at both the level of political and civil society should be based primarily on an audit principle that should include but not be limited to complaints. Exclusively complaint-based mechanisms not only provide a very partial system of supervision but tend to shift attention away from the critical issue of remedy to considerations of justice, which, while obviously important in themselves, must not be permitted to replace remedy (Shearing 1990a). It is only through an emphasis on remedy that the source of problems that require reform can be identified and rectified (Shearing

1990a). For a monitoring system to operate as a supervisory shadow that restrains policing, it is essential, especially in South Africa where a large portion of the population has been intimidated by the police, that monitoring be audit rather than complaint-based.

The principal of universal audit-based monitoring was the principle behind the United Nations supervision of the police during the Namibian transition period. While this worked to enable a successful election to be held, it was very, very costly. Universal monitoring can at best only be sustained for short periods and may not be a possibility at all in South Africa given the size of the task. In South Africa during the transitional period and beyond, effective audit-based monitoring should take place both in response to crises and through the targeting of specific arenas where systemic problems can be identified (Marais 1992). It is here that complaint systems can be articulated with audit-based systems as a source of data on the instititutional location of systemic problems.

Fifth, it is essential if South African state policing is to be held accountable, that what police do is visible to monitors at both a political and civil level. To provide for this it will be necessary that transparency be accepted as a principle of South African policing at an organizational level.

There are, as we have noted, many problems with the steps that are being taken to increase the transparency of police action. The lesson, however, is clear. The creation of 'trails' of police action that permit the retrospective reconstruction of what has taken place are essential to effective monitoring. This is a matter that will be contentious within South Africa, as it has been elsewhere. The state police will vigorously resist attempts to make them more accountable. The tendency internationally, however, is for police to accept a greater and greater degree of scrutiny and the transparency that this requires. The South African police must required to submit to at least similar levels of scrutiny.

In these proposals, we have limited ourselves to a consideration of monitoring as scrutiny of the governance rather than as a form of governance itself. This is not because we do not believe that the interventionist tendencies, which involve 'monitors' in doing policing rather than simply observing it, are unimportant. On the contrary, we consider them to be of vital importance to the future of South African policing. The issue of intervention is, however, wider than the question of restraint that has been our focus here. In the final two chapters we turn our attention to community involvement in the business of policing itself.

Chapter 6

Processes of ordering in the townships

> The support these committees enjoy is a great source of concern
> to the Police. Africa has a long history of merciless dictators, and
> there's no telling what the teenage street committees will develop
> into if they are allowed to grow without any standards set by the
> community.
>
> (*Servamus* February 1991 'Policing in Soweto')

POLICING AS ORDER-CENTRED NOT OFFENDER-CENTRED

In this chapter, we explore the local, popular policing initiatives that
have emerged in the black townships of South Africa both in response to the failure of state policing to protect black communities,
and as part of black struggle against apartheid that has shaped so
much township life. We map out the emergence of the beginnings of the
alternative ordering processes in South Africa, which challenge conventional Western conceptions of policing. It is an account that
contests the inevitabilities of the primrose path, and the Western
impedimenta, of the evolutionary development of policework. In
Chapter Seven, we explore the possibility of developing a policing
system in South Africa which recognizes key elements of this experience of alternative ordering. The central proposition of the previous
chapter was that the SAP could be transformed towards orthodox
Western policing. This, as we will reiterate in our final chapter, is
something that should be done. It is not, however, all that should be
done. To think of policing reform as exclusively the reform of the
SAP is to embrace three problematic assumptions. It presumes a
crude unilinear evolutionary model of policing, moving towards
more and better state policing. It embodies an imperative of progress,

a path along which all ex-colonial police forces must travel. At the end of the day, all 'underdeveloped' police institutions will converge on the Western police bandit-catching Utopias. Further, it assumes that policing in South Africa, both historically and in the present day, means state policing. By sleight-of-hand definition, other institutions that might serve to – among other things – deal with crime, are denied the rubric 'police'.

Implicit in this thesis is a further questionable assumption. Policing, it is presumed, is above all else concerned with crime and the application of force in its control. Crime-fighting is typically understood to mean catching criminals and taking them before the courts. Within this perspective 'community' is simply regarded as a resource that the police should tap to improve their 'bandit-catching' capacity. Thus, a commitment to crime-fighting and community in the contemporary discourse of 'community-policing' refers to programmes to improve police performance as 'bandit catchers'[1] by making better use of community resources and in particular its intelligence capacity.

An example is the 'Crime Stoppers' programmes that have become so ubiquitous (see, for example, Carriere and Ericson 1989). Such schemes encourage people to become more actively involved in assisting the police in solving crimes by cooperating with them more fully as police informers. These, and similar initiatives, celebrate and affirm a vision of police as determined 'bandit catchers' by appealing to citizens to help the police to become better at it.

Within this vision the famous Peelian adage that the police are the public and the public are the police, is read to mean that the police and the public should see themselves as partners in a fight against crime and criminals. Crime-fighting is conceived as a 'war' in which the police and criminals fight with each other for supremacy.[2] In this war a 'win' for the police is a successful prosecution.[3] This metaphoric imagery celebrates the police as modern gladiators whose knowledge and weapons set them apart as technical specialists who 'own' policing. Policing is conceived as a professional not a lay enterprise. Ordinary people should assist the police but, as lay persons they are seen as in no position to do policing themselves. Good policing requires good, well-trained police and tough courts, who are not soft on criminals, who will bring to a satisfactory conclusion the work of the police.

In South Africa, where the police have for decades paid virtually no attention to the protection of black communities, the prospect of a crime-fighting police is, not surprisingly, very appealing. What could be better than to have the police turn their attention away from brutalizing black South Africans to protecting them by fighting crime? And what better way to do this than to take a feather out of Namibia's cap and ask one or more of the countries whose police have been doing this for years, and who have been honing their professional skills to assist in the transformation of the South African Police into an efficient crime-fighting organization? This course of action, as we have and will continue to argue, has merit only if it is framed within a wider context of reform.

This state police-focused vision of reform, which encourages South Africans to import established models from elsewhere, assumes that people in these other countries are satisfied with policing as bandit catching. While people in these countries do undoubtedly celebrate this conception of policing in media dramatizations of a struggle between good and evil, and while they may hold the police in high esteem as protagonists in this battle, they have been increasingly troubled by the failure of bandit catching to secure their persons and property. Put bluntly, Western policing has been strikingly unsuccessful in 'controlling crime' despite the multitude of innovative schemes (Cumberbatch 1984; Trojanowicz and Bucqueroux 1990).[4]

In response to this failure, communities (in particular, middle- and upper-class communities, with the resources to take control of their policing) have actively employed alternative methods of providing for their protection. These initiatives have been quietly transforming policing in ways that profoundly challenge the traditional bandit-catching conception of crime fighting. In South Africa, this challenge extends beyond the emergence of private security to grass-roots initiatives that have emerged in response to apartheid. In this chapter, we review these developments in black communities. We will argue that in responding to the failure of the state to protect them, they have promoted practices of civil policing that, while highly problematic for a whole host of reasons, should be recognized and drawn upon in developing a reform agenda for South African policing.

Although community-ordering institutions in South Africa have varied enormously, several features that cut across much of this diversity can be identified.

The first is a focus on the reduction of risk of harm to persons and to their property. To police, means to regulate life in ways that will promote safe and secure environments. This focuses attention on the states of affairs, or outcomes, to be promoted rather than on the identification and punishment of offenders.

A second feature is the extent to which this activity is related to and integrated with other activities that regulate community life. This is seen most clearly in the activities of 'Civics' (Civic Associations) that have developed as popular alternatives to the municipal governments installed by the South African state. Thus, for instance, street committees formed within the context of these Civic Associations have taken responsibility for a variety of ordering activities that included thefts, assaults, domestic disputes, evictions, dangerous areas, the regulation of shebeens, sewerage disposal, garbage disposal and the like. Policing ceases to be a specialized, separated function to be located in a separate institution and is integrated with other duties.

Third is the manner in which a whole range of resources in addition to coercion are deployed in response to the risk. Policing ceases to be a matter of solving problems on the basis of the resources to which the police have access, especially physical force, and instead draws upon a wide range of resources available to communities.

Fourth, and closely related to the third feature, policing is not understood as a function monopolized by a specialized body of persons but rather as everybody's business. Policing is understood as a people's or popular enterprise to which everyone can and should contribute. This shares responsibility and promotes the use of a wide range of skills and knowledge.

Fifth, local arrangements for regulating community life are related to wider structures. Control over the police is seen as having a variety of loci depending on what level of community organization is at issue, from the street, to the neighbourhood, and so on up to more encompassing structures. This is not merely a matter of top–down restraint but of exchanges that provide for the voicing of the various interests, conflicts and tensions that make up communities at different levels. There is no idealization of community founded on some mythical consensus in this process. Rather, communities are understood as networks of people, sometimes identified in spacial terms, but often identified on the basis of shared interests and shared 'circuits of communication' (Foucault 1977: 217), who differ in their views of order and the means to be used to promote it. Processes of debate are established which encourage the open airing of these differences. While these processes are frequently hierarchically structured so that more general levels of dialogue (for example, at neigbourhood level) are seen as binding on more local ones (for instance, at street level), it would be a mistake to think of this simply as top–down control. The agendas and dialogue at wider and spatially more inclusive levels are structured by what has already taken place at more local levels. In social processes, the principles of democratic control, are given expression in the context of an emphasis on dialogue and wide participation.

Finally, most community-ordering processes focus on the reintegration of the person into the community rather than their stigmatization and exclusion. What is encouraged in such cases is a community-centred focus on healing both the community and the relationship between the community and the offender. The process is one that Braithwaite (1989) has termed 'integrative shaming' in which healing takes place both through an acceptance of responsibility for harm to the community and a commitment to take steps through concrete action to repair the damage.

In making these features our focus, we are not being myopic to the ugly spectacles of violence that have come to be associated with 'people's justice', both in South Africa and elsewhere. The brutal and widely reported attack in Los Angeles on a white motorist who happened to drive into a group of male black Americans protesting against a white jury's acquittal of brutal white police officers who had participated in an equally ruthless attack on a black motorist,[5] or the 'necklacing' of a suspected informer, plucked from a crowd and set alight by a petroleum-filled tyre hung over his shoulders, in a South African township, hardly present an appealing picture of civil policing or 'non-state ordering'. Popular justice within South Africa, and elsewhere (Johnston 1992), often has this cathartic and brutal quality. Similarly, a critique of state ordering does not guarantee that the legal history of the alternative on which township ordering draws, is rosier. One myth about former British colonies in Africa is that British rule bequeathed a legacy of justice. An equally stubborn counter-myth presents a 'pre-colonial Merrie England' (Chanock 1987: 6). Some European anthropologists, like some African scholars, portray traditional African societies as containing remarkably equable harmonious legal processes. African customary law is portrayed in dramatic contrast to the colonial legal inheritance:

> the African method would tend to adjust disturbances of the social equilibrium to restore peace and goodwill, and to bind or rebind the two disputing groups together in a give-and-take reciprocity. The European method would tend to widen the gulf between the

two groups by granting all rights to one of them to the exclusion of the other, because it would in general concern itself with the facts and legal principles and take no cognisance of social implications.

(quoted in McNally 1988)

The truth is somewhere in between. The story we want to tell draws on events that have been of little interest to the world's media. It is an account of more mundane events in which many black South Africans have sought quietly, with little fanfare and spectacle, to take charge of the ordering of their communities and to do it in ways that promote an approach to policing that contrasts with the dominant approaches elsewhere being offered for export to South Africans. It represents the gentler, more humane face of people's justice, that exists side-by-side with the more brutal.

Traditional forms of criminal justice – a bastardized inheritance

Traditional African society (acknowledging all the disparate systems under that general rubric) had its own central structures of dispute processing and of policing. According to Sanders, the traditional unit of African society was group-centred. Customary African government was frequently based on principles that sought consensus through dialogue. Legal proceedings were community affairs in which a central aim was to reconcile the disputing parties and to restore harmonious relations within the community:

> the purpose of the court is not to discover and apply a rigid law. Its function is to try to provide a compromise which will as far as possible be acceptable to the parties and will be regarded by the community generally as the right decision. The aim is restore an equilibrium which has been disturbed or to provide compensation for a wrong which has been committed.
>
> (Suttner 1968: 437)

Precedents were not required, although the application of law in previous situations might, in difficult cases, act as a guideline. There were few rules guarding the admissibility and relevance of evidence. Character testimony and previous convictions were commonly used in the decision-making process and there were no hard and fast rules regarding the burden of proof. The accused was typically not asked to plead and all persons were regarded as competent to give evidence although the mental state of the witness could be taken into account and would determine the weight given to evidence. The court would take into account decisions of bodies such as informal family councils. Legal process aimed at restoring the community equilibrium, through restitution, reconciliation and compensation:

> in the eyes of the African, there is no justice where the equivalent of loss is never obtained.
>
> (Mwansa 1986

A central feature of African legal systems was a concern to shame the offender and then to reincorporate him or her, once that initial expression of community repugnancy had been demonstrated. Unlike Western courts, where, as Braithwaite has argued (1989), the aim is to stigmatize and reject the offender, traditional African courts tended to avoid as far as possible the segregation of the offender with the possible marginalization of him or her into a sub-community of similar social rejects.

Legal anthropologists have also documented limited evidence of policing in non-industrial societies, features often overlooked by studies that have focused directly on the process of dispute resolution (Bouman 1987). These practices had two items in common – they were often tightly interlinked with the local judicial process, and, like the traditional courts, their central function was to restore the community equilibrium or social order. The legal classic by Llewellyn and Hoebel (1941) details police-like activities among the North American First Peoples. Among many such examples the French Metis of Western Canada adapted the democratic system of policing of the buffalo hunt to their new townships on the Saskatchewan (Brogden 1991a). In African society, there are several illustrations of indigenous policing systems. These could exist as institutions in their own right or, more commonly, as part of wider justice processes.

Bouman has described a complex example of the first type in Botswana (1987). In the traditional society of the Tswana people, four systems of policing were apparent. Mutual social control was central:

> every man in the community should consider himself a policeman. That is why everybody held himself responsible if anything wrong happened where he was.
>
> (Chief Tshekedi quoted in Bouman 1987)

Second, mephato or age-cohorts of young men could be called on to arrest offenders and to execute sanctions. Ward headmen could use force to police their local territories. Finally, the chief could directly appoint his own policemen (Bouman 1987). Often, however, traditional African policing was submerged within the overall criminal justice process. Abrahams gives such an example from Tanzania:

> Every man . . . had to be equipped with bow and arrows and with a gourd stem whistle which was blown in emergencies. If a theft was committed, a hue and cry was raised and the thieves were to be followed by the young men of the village. The whistles would alert the young men of neighbouring villages who would in turn forewarn others in the same way.
>
> (Abrahams 1987: 181–2)[6]

The white South African state gave some recognition to traditional African ordering practices in establishing – in the early days of the Union – a dual system of criminal justice. What this meant was that black people would experience elements of a different process from that of whites. Legal dualism (or pluralism [Santos 1977]), the co-existence of legal models and institutions somewhat independent of and distinct from the official dominant legality, has been a feature of most societies with a colonial past. In South Africa, the separate systems of white courts and of Bantu Commissioners Courts, established in 1927, gave superficial recognition to black African history. The Commissioners Courts institutionalized a separate structure of law and authority in specific cases.[7]

These courts were similar to colonial courts elsewhere, like, for example, the local courts established by the British in Tanganyika, which were as Moore notes:

> to be run by Africans and would apply African 'customary law' but in a manner consistent with basic British legal principles and the objectives of the colonial administration.
>
> (Moore 1992: 12)

The Minister could confer the authority of chief as a judicial authority on any named black person he considered suitable to deal with a range of minor criminal and civil offences by black people.[8] Indigenous law was to be applied in so far as it was not repugnant to the principles of 'natural justice' (as determined by the white state) and public policy. The stated object was to provide an inexpensive, simple and familiar legal procedure for black people – one free from

Western technicalities and within easy reach of the communities it
was to serve (Van Niekerk 1986) and one that appeared to draw – at
least superficially – on certain traditional African practices. In particular, it dispensed with many of the safeguards of common law.
Again Moore (in a comment on a pamphlet prepared for British
administrators in Tanganyika) is instructive. The tone and message of
the pamphlet, she argues, is a 'double-think' of simultaneous
endorsement and rejection:

> The sermon that Africans and African institutions must be respec-
> ted is stated again and again. But the disapproval of African prac-
> tices is also clear.

(Moore 1992: 17)

A generous appraisal of the Black Administration Act was that the
government hoped to create a simple and inexpensive apparatus –
'located on the boundary between state law and indigenous or local law'
(Merry 1991: 163) – for settling disputes between black people, with
their cases tried by experts in indigenous law and customs (Hund and
Kotu-Rammopo 1983). The later development of Makgotla (traditional
courts in the township setting, about which we will have more to say
below) was a less overt replacement for such structures.

This form of legal dualism, however, differs dramatically from the
contemporary medley of policing and judicial practices that are documented in this chapter. Fundamentally, the Commissioners Courts
created 'poor law for poor people'. Not merely did they act as a primary
strategy by which the white state could maintain legal control of black
people, but their very procedures were grotesquely weighted against the
accused. Guilt was commonly assumed, a plea bargain forced on the
suspect. In minor cases, the 'suspect' might be locked away for a few
days as a salutary 'punishment' before a withdrawal of the charge,
followed by internal deportation:

> in the Commissioners Courts, the formal law model of adjudica-
> tion gives way to a process of justice moulded to the requirements
> of bureaucratic efficiency.

(Hund and Kotu-Rammopo 1983)

Immense policing and judicial discretion ensured that the black
courts were not so much a parallel structure of justice but very much
(like the apartheid system itself) the second tier of a two-tier system
in which due process rights were the prerogative of those in the

higher reaches. An African person was in effect subject to three legal processes – the customary law of the Bantu courts, South African law proper, and later the apartheid legislation. The development of the black courts simply added to the legal discriminatory burden:

> these courts came to be seen by much of the black community as an instrument in the hands of the apartheid regime.
>
> (Van Niekerk 1986)

Legal dualism, as Dugard has forcibly argued, has simply served to reinforce apartheid (Dugard 1978). State-imposed legal dualism in South Africa also accommodated a two-tiered policing system.

> Throughout this century, South Africa has always had two policing strategies, one for the white population, another for the blacks. In the case of the 'apolitical' whites, the British model of the police as friends and protectors of their interests is the dominant one. The level of police penetration into white 'ordinary' communities and suburbs is minimal; whites face a low degree of harassment at roadblocks, and generally in their presence, the police seem to be acting within their legal powers.
>
> (S.A. Outlook 1987: 5)

Legal dualism implies the coexistence of different forms of legal process. In the South African case, this has meant one system for whites and another for the black majority. Such a dualistic form has been roundly condemned by critical commentators as 'uneconomical, inefficient, and sometimes unjust' (Suttner 1968: 451; Dugard 1978). Such critiques assume that dualism as a principle (as opposed to that state practice) must necessarily provide second-class justice for supposedly second-class people. Thus, in his early work, Suttner presumed a tiered system of judicial process with traditional systems composing the bottom, residual, layer. Certainly, Southern African history has several examples of hierarchical dual systems, with the traditional practices occupying the lowest rung.

In neighbouring Mozambique, during Portuguese rule, the colonialists incorporated certain traditional laws with tribal courts headed by authoritarian chiefs, paid agents of Portuguese government (Isaacman and Isaacman 1982). Merry identifies this as a general tendency and source of criticism.

> In both core and peripheral countries, popular justice ideologies portray a transformed social world yet enact one which replicates

the power relations of the political system and the system of state law which created them in the first place.

(Merry 1991: 173)

Fitzpatrick notes this symbiotic relationship as follows:

where alternative justice works specifically in conjunction with state power, it does so on the basis that such power is limited and that alternative justice makes good this deficiency. Alternative justice does what the state cannot.

(Fitzpatrick 1992: 200)

However, hierarchical ordering systems are not the same as horizontal ones where the indigenous processes are not qualitatively inferior to those of the state (Fitzpatrick 1992: 212). It is possible – as the township experience demonstrates – for the processes to remain separate (Spence 1982)[9] but not hierarchical. Despite their abysmal record, the Commissioners Courts did have one merit. They recognized the relative legitimacy of an African system of justice that was notionally independent of the colonial experience. However, the Commissioners Courts were a gross and illegitimate distortion of an authentic inheritance. They were a bastardization of traditional African criminal justice, failing to acknowledge the core ethos of the African tradition on which they drew, namely that it was community-centred rather than offender-centred.

In two other critical ways, the structures devised by successive South African governments for black people differed markedly from the later township developments. The former were an attempt to impose a uniform process across South Africa for black people. It was a centralized system with the final judicial determination remaining in the hands of a white judicial structure. The township structures that emerged out of the process of struggle have sought to encompass decentralized forums of power where policing and justice have been reconstructed as a direct challenge to the centralized criminal justice processes of the state.

The dual system of the South African government relied on an atavistic view of black people and black traditions, who required a familiar system relevant to the needs of 'primitive peoples', under white tutelage. But quite apart from those racist assumptions, there was a failure to recognize the problem of periodization. Like comparable European legal systems before the onset of industrialization, traditional practices have a limited time-span. Ironically, colonial practice (self- interestedly) recognized certain limitations on tradition. Under British rule, Africans were allowed [to maintain] customary law but subject to constraints and under the overriding imprimatur of colonial rule. As colonial rule was institutionalised, indigenous legal process was gradually subordinated to European law and often restricted to contracts over marriage, land tenure, and succession.

(Bapela 1987)

Within the colonizing perspective, subject people were slowly weaned, step-by-step, away from historically inappropriate, degrading, legal structures.

However, the ideals symbolized by such traditions have a currency independent of the limits of practices. Legitimacy of present township ordering processes derives in part from those historical values of community-centredness. But that legitimacy also derives from two other phenomena – the development of the community-ordering processes in the course of the struggle against white hegemony. It also stems from the maturation of structures relevant to the period and location in the course of struggle – that is in not taking the crumbs of the dominant formation's view of an appropriate trajectory from a bastardized past to a synthetic future, but in constructing original practices relevant to the present.

Contemporary township ordering processes have drawn on traditional sources in the same way that contemporary Anglo-Saxon policing draws on the image of the Saxon tythingman.[10] The legal dualism of township ordering processes is as similar to tribal courts, as the community 'bobby' is to the tythingman.

The construction of township dispute resolution and policing

The advantages of retaining alternatives to the state system of policing and judicial processing have been acknowledged in several works. Dugal (1981), for example, in reflections on the Namibian experience, has proposed a system of local and community courts, possessing civil and criminal jurisdiction, to dispose of the more petty disputes, supplemented by a network of informal forums or tribunals, each serving a small section of the community. The role of these would be limited to arbitration and conciliation. Attendance would be voluntary and decisions not legally binding but persuasive. These informal courts, he argued, could be the backbone of a new, more democratic, more proximate, and more immediate legal system. An examination of the community-ordering processes constructed in the townships in the last decade makes plausible the thesis that such structures could coexist with the formal alternatives and not be regarded as inferior to them.

The central thread that runs through these alternative township structures is the concern by those immediately present, to construct some new form of order out of problematic situations. The disputes may range from the polarities of homicide and forcible rape to those of organizing rubbish collection. But each has in common the necessary search for a communal resolution that affects those affected by intimate, order-disturbing, problems.

Township ordering is self-generated and self-regulating. As the life-world of the townships changes, so do the rules and processes of ordering practice. Customary African ordering through law has shown a remarkable capacity to adapt to different levels of struggle and different pressures (Prinsloo 1987). In the townships, these ordering systems, the combination of judicial and policing functions, vary in character, in form, in longevity, in substance and in composition. In spite of this variety, they capture in important ways the strength of an indigent tradition that has remained intact despite, or perhaps because of, the imposition of the restrictions of the apartheid system. Their legitimacy has been shaped as much by the process of struggle against apartheid as from tradition.

Six often overlapping township ordering processes can be observed. First, there are the relatively informal street patrols and People's Courts which have become increasingly merged into the Civic Association structures. Second, there are the Makgotla, the attempt to maintain or reconstruct the traditional *Gemeinschaft* tribal courts in the *Gesellschaft* of the townships. Then, in descending order, there are the several cultural movements which have assumed certain responsibilities for peace-keeping and dispute resolution in certain townships – such as the Vukani Vulimehlo People's Party in Mamelodi (Moses 1990). There are small semi-private organizations forged for specific purposes – such as the protection of the territory of a shebeen. There are also the multiplicity of gangs which have historically become an endemic part of South African township life.[11] Ordering has also been carried out by assemblies or crowds, gathered to mete out punishment to people labelled as 'enemies' for reasons such as their participation in oppression as informers. Finally, there are informal networks of neighbours consolidated in occasional bands to deal with matters such as garbage collection and the protection of persons and property.

Traditional justice in the townships – the Makgotlas as criminal justice surrogates

Our principal concern in this study are the first two ordering processes, namely the Makgotla and the People's Courts. The Makgotla represented an attempt to revive customary African judicial tradition within the townships (Sanders 1985). Like the kitskonstabels, Municipal Police and vigilantes, they provided a surrogate system, a buffer between the township and the white government. Thus, they sought to reinforce the view that black people, being socially inferior, would be most suited to an apparently more tribal system of justice.

Makgotla operated mainly in the Transvaal townships around Johannesburg, Pretoria and Vereeniging. They cohered around a tribal base and often had relatively conservative court presidents, whose primary ties were not to the township itself but to rural areas and their traditions. This agrarian power base was reinforced through to the surrogate black town councils. Their notorious reputation in the townships appears to have two principle sources. First, they invariably found against the accused and second, they were used by tribal elders as a vehicle for dealing with those who erred from traditional, rural norms. For example, they were used to punish 'errant' children in support of conservative familial social norms. In short, they were used as instruments of an authoritarian tribal culture.[12]

The Makgotlas were, in effect, a surrogate criminal justice process that reflected the view that a more primitive kind of tribal justice was appropriate for 'unsophisticated' people. Although commentators sympathetic to black resistance vehemently criticized the Makgotlas, many people participated in them because there was little else available.

> There can be no doubt that the law of Makgotla is the law of the jungle . . . a significant proportion of law-abiding people in Soweto support the Makgotlas . . . out of desperation because the civilised law, order, and justice system which the whites brought to South Africa has failed to protect township dwellers from rampant crime and from criminals who operate with something close to immunity.
>
> (Quelane *Star* 7 July 1991)

The Makgotlas collapsed during the State of Emergency, following the flight of their township Council mentors. Their more organic replacements were the alternative ordering systems, encompassed by the umbrella term, 'People's Courts'.

Township ordering systems and the development of a competing criminal justice process

While the major features of the intentions and practices of People's Courts can be traced back to traditional African concepts, they were, unlike the Makgotlas, clearly linked to the struggle against apartheid and were viewed as alternatives to its structures. This constituted a major break as these courts were conceived of as a 'peoples' challenge to apartheid not as an imposed surrogate structure. They could not easily be incorporated. Equally importantly, while they embraced certain traditional practices, they also confronted traditional notions of authority. In some cases, this challenge assumed a generational form, as young people assumed a dominant role in ordering processes that took action against their elders. Most importantly, these ordering processes legitimated themselves on the basis of a claimed 'popular' rather than a traditional mandate. Authority was claimed on the basis of local acceptability as a source of pragmatic resolutions to practical problems as well as on the basis of their struggle against the state.

Suttner (1986), in a revision of his early critique of legal dualism, welcomed the development of the People's Courts in the mid-1980s. Noting a Leninist tradition in their formation, he argued that local township structures which developed to furnish local crime control and dispute resolution, had a latent political function. By organizing opposition to state structures, they advanced the struggle against the state. In addition, as crime and local disputes exacerbated intra-class schisms which divided black people among themselves, indigenous structures that worked to resolve such divisions were to be welcomed.

While such heroic analyses ennoble what were hesitant beginnings of oppositional new township ordering, they nevertheless point to several important features of these processes. First, they were local in terms of personnel, of problems, of authority, in procedures and in accountability. Second, they also demonstrated a very clear commitment to mediation, reparation and restoration of the communal equilibrium. Although coercion is clearly a key resource in communal problem-resolving, it is not an end in itself. Third, they celebrate diversity. Different 'histories of struggle' are viewed as promoting and justifying different ordering processes. Divergences in ethnic traditions, in the composition of township communities – sometimes riven by the factors of traditional culture, of property, of gender and especially of age – ensured no direct replication of ordering processes. Finally, and perhaps most crucially, there is no neat division between the policing of the streets and the decision-making in the People's Courts. Nor in the judicial context is a distinction drawn between civil and criminal matters. There is a high degree of vertical and lateral integration. Anglo-Saxon conceptions of the divisions of functions have not the same clarity – or of relevance – within township ordering.

Self-policing in the townships

To document such self-policing as a significant mode of ordering in the townships is not to make a novel contribution to police history. Self-policing has always been a common practice both in South Africa and elsewhere. For example, there is now historical evidence that in the Anglo-American context, the New Police of the nineteenth century coexisted with measures of self-policing in working-class areas. Part of the apparent 'success' of the state police in Victorian England was, it appears, due to the fact that local working-class communities continued with their own ordering systems independently of the rise of the new domestic missionaries (Johnston 1992). Relative community harmony was maintained despite – rather than because of – a state police institution. Do-it-yourself policing was not invented on the streets of the Rand townships but has an historical pedigree elsewhere. In South Africa, as elsewhere, voluntary self-policing has historical legitimacy.

Given the unique character of the racial and class repression in South Africa, and the solidaristic bindings that have emerged from the struggle, there are few similar examples of self-policing elsewhere arising in opposition to – as opposed to tacit cooperation with – the state police. However, one important study of communities under legal and political threat has demonstrated a practice of communal self-policing similar in functions and organizational structure to that of the townships. In Chile, the emergence of the Left Revolutionary Movement during the right-wing Frei government, resulted in squatter camps (where the Movement had its base) developing what were initially self-defence units against the state police. They came to

> perform internal police functions. . . . They broke up fights and caught petty thieves whose activities not only caused personal loss but also threatened general morale and increased suspicion. In some cases, they simply 'beat-up' the thief, in others they tried to fine or expel him. The militia served as police, judge, and jury.
>
> (Spence 1982: 231)

A primary concern of those institutions and their successor (the Vigilance Front, under the Allende government) was to avoid the development of a separate specialized police force wielding excessive or arbitrary force (ibid: 235).

South African township history is filled with examples of self-policing practices, formed in the vacuum left by state policing, and often in opposition to that institution. In the black townships, rises in local crime have regularly been countered by the development of volunteer street patrols. Goodhew (1990), for instance, has detailed the ebb and flow of a variety of agencies under the rubric of 'Civic Guards',[13] in the black areas of Johannesburg between the 1930s and 1950s. These bodies, he argues, were a response to two related pressures – alienation from the state police (white and black), and rising crime. A major source of alienation, as we have already argued, was the arbitrary criminalization under the Pass and Liquor laws. Clearly, such policing enjoyed no local legitimacy, especially as the SAP in its township forays demonstrated minimal concern for community ordering problems. In Sophiatown, in Newclare, in Western Native Township (WNT), in Alexandra, in Benoni, in Orlando and in Pimville, the combination of a brutal and corrupt SAP and a rising crime rate, gave rise to a self-help policing system in the form of voluntary street patrols (Goodhew 1990).

The source of black estrangement from state policing went beyond the race-regulated regulation of township street life:[14]

> The ignorant, young, brutal Afrikaner policeman has become something of a cliche amongst blacks . . . unable to speak any local black language, barely literate, and the product of the extreme racial codes of the Afrikaner rural hinterland.
>
> (Goodhew 1990: 6)

Black officers of the SAP were similarly despised, possessing even lower qualifications for the job than their white 'colleagues'. Hostility to those educated black people who appeared to 'play white' was a particular feature of state policing style on the Rand throughout the history of the South African state police:

> the semi-educated types who are inclined to be very insolent . . . when asked for his pass . . . he will smoke a cigarette, and adopt a surly attitude, practically inviting a man to assault him.
>
> (quoted in Goodhew 1990)

What was also apparent in parts of the Rand between the 1930s and the 1950s, was the pragmatic relative tolerance by local white administrators of what amounted to a dual system of policing. In WNT, for example, the township Superintendent in the early 1930s was content to supplement state policing with voluntary patrols of residents who would bring suspects to the Location Office where he would decide whether or not to hand them over to the SAP. Later, during the Emergency period, other local administrators (and especially white shopkeepers, subject to consumer boycotts) also acquiesced unofficially to local ordering processes (Price 1991). This acceptance of voluntary private policing by local administrators contrasted with the vehement opposition from senior SAP officers and eventually by the Government, which finally prohibited any endorsement of such organized self-policing (Goodhew 1991).

Over the years, self-policing has developed sporadically across the townships in response to specific crises and to the failures of the SAP. For example, in the Western Cape, Scharf notes the existence of Amavoluntiya in the townships in the 1960s and 1970s. They instituted patrols to deter 'robbers and petty thieves from molesting residents' (1988). Similarly,

> in Manenberg, the people formed themselves into groups that responded to concerns that the Police were slow to respond to. This happened in the late 70s. It was more of a crime prevention function. They had a network system and a hooter would go off and then the men would go out.
>
> (respondent quoted in Shearing and Mzamane 1992: 26)

Ten years later, in the Pretoria township of Mamelodi, voluntary crime prevention merged with a more political role, where a campaign to 'root out crime' converged with attempts to deal with 'hooliganism' in which local gangs masquerading as 'comrades' used a boycott campaign as a cover for extortion.

> We decided to launch an operation clean-up to weed-out criminals and hooligans using the political struggle for their own ends.
>
> (*Weekly Mail* 9 May 1986)

This link between crime and politics is a relatively common feature of such voluntary policing initiatives' development. Thus in Gugelutu, near Cape Town, the Youth Brigade of the ANC organized street patrols to control crime in the state policing vacuum of the

Emergency period. Similarly, informal 'self-defence units' mush-roomed during this period in Alexandra and in the Uitenhage town-ships to protect the locals against persons suspected of being supported or encouraged by the state:

> We have been the victim of non-stop hooliganism and brutal killings by men in balaclavas travelling in combis. They damage property and have forced people to flee from their houses.
>
> (*Weekly Mail* 10 October 1987)

Similar self-policing structures appeared at Diepkloof in Soweto:

> We can no longer stand idly by while our wives, children, and property are being attacked. We have no option but to defend ourselves.
>
> (*Weekly Mail* 6 May 1986)

Such units mobilized patrols from adult men and youths, often with explicit political allegiances to the ANC to keep the peace, with the primary purpose of checking on people carrying unauthorized weapons and, in the tradition of eighteenth century English polic-ing[15] 'to get rid of all unwanted elements' (*Weekly Mail* 6 May 1986). In the Western Cape townships, the politicization of youth groups and the new experience of militancy involved the recruitment of youth for informal policing on streets (unlike elsewhere maintaining a separate identity from the black political organizations [Scharf 1990]). Both as a source of protection against state policing and other non-state elements, these structures operated to protect 'people and property from 'outside' forces' (Harrington 1992: 180). According to Sapire – discussing self-policing in squatter settlements, 'one of the motives of social policing was to protect the community from the intrusion of the municipal police' (1992: 684).

The street committees constituted the link between self-policing and more encompassing local ordering processes. Thus it was not uncommon for those accused of offences to be brought before a group of residents in a trial presided over by the street committee chairperson (Price 1991). These links between self-policing and community justice processes could also be 'tolerated' by the white administrators. Goodhew notes a pre-war structure in Pimville, in which the local Advisory Board institutionalized an informal court to deal with suspects apprehended by the Civic Guard (1991). In the more settled ordering processes, self-policing and the street com-mittees formed the foundation of a larger socio-political pyramid.

The People's Courts – informality, unity of functions, and heterogeneity within a pyramid structure

By 1987, major alternative ordering structures were evident in many black townships in South Africa, some 400 People's Courts being noted by one observer (Seekings 1989). These Courts, which developed during the most recent period of struggle with the state, have been characterized by the organizational features we have already noted. Three are, however, worth reiterating. First, most of them were informal, relatively non-institutionalized. Second, the distinction between a policing function and a judicial function was often blurred. Third, while a general pyramid model of organization of the ordering process was typically present, specific structures varied with local exigencies.

The first two features are captured in Moses's account of a Mossel Bay People's Court:

> Most of the cases concerning the youth were dealt with on the spot where the offender was found, or the nearest place from there. If for example, you were found and it was discovered that you had stolen half a loaf of bread, then you would get fifteen lashes on the spot over the buttock, or if it was said that the price of the bread was 25 cents, then you would receive 25 lashes. There was for example a guy who had stabbed a dog and he could not explain why he did it. So he was found guilty and was given five lashes there on the spot.
>
> (respondent quoted in Moses 1990)

This vertical integration of the criminal justice process was accompanied by a process of lateral integration. 'Crime-work' rarely existed as an entity in its own right. Dealing with crime was immersed in a realm of related street problems. Policework in the townships, as in traditional African society involved a range of duties in which the only common element was that they constituted 'trouble' for the local residents – from rubbish collection to intoxication to dealing with 'disorderly youth'. This vertical and lateral integration constitutes a significant feature of much community 'justice'.

Despite the disparate origins of the township ordering processes, the integration between the different components generally followed the same pattern while remaining, in specifics, a product of the locality. Street policing was one element of that larger pyramid. Structures evolved as streets and areas groped their way towards more integrated networks and in response to Civics' pressure in seeking to bring some 'discipline' to spontaneous groupings. The nature of these structures varied within the larger social context. Thus voluntary policing varied from apolitical constructions to democratically motivated initiatives that were part of larger political formations. The journal *Frontline* held that the more radical version – the street committees

> grow out of the need of the people to defend themselves against State repression . . . and in response [to] the ANC calls to make the country ungovernable and apartheid unworkable . . . the main idea is to forge them into 'contingents' that will be part of the process towards a total people's war.
>
> (*Frontline* Christmas 1986)[16]

While this statement appears to have reflected more hope than any observable reality, the street committees did increasingly become preoccupied with a variety of basic functions of governance – problems of crime, of garbage and night-soil disposal, of breakdowns in water supply, of determining opening hours for shebeens, settling domestic disputes, of turning empty lots into parks, and of reinstating tenants evicted by the state (Price 1991). Scharf noted 'dozens' of such street committees in the Cape Town township of Langa.

Where formal structures emerged, they tended to be simple and logical although the rubric under which they operated varied. Thus, in townships near Witbank in the Transvaal, each ward was divided into street committees with a 'street captain' as the leader who solved most small disputes.

> If he or she failed, these were passed to sub-committees. Senior crimes were dealt with by disciplinary committees. Street policing, and the courts were part of wider more complex problem-solving structures.
>
> (*Weekly Mail* 28 September 1987)

In Mamelodi, if a resident was dissatisfied with decisions of street committee, it was referred to the block committee. The matter could potentially be taken to the highest level of the Civic (if the decision was eventually likely to affect the whole of the township) where, if necessary, it was determined by vote. At the lower rungs of the pyramid, there were separate committees for adults and youths 'because of the peculiarities of their experiences and needs'. But the generations were merged at the level of the Civic in order to eliminate possibilities of conflict (*Weekly Mail* 9 May 1986). Generally, the more serious the problem, the higher the level. Petty crime and domestic disputes were dealt with in street committee meetings. Punishment for more serious offences like murder was meted out by the supreme agency (which also resolved matters such as night curfews for shebeens [Swilling 1988]). A schoolteacher from Kagiso, who sat on an appeal court of elders, describes the practices at the apex of the pyramid:

> we hear the cases again (in an appeal court of elders) and weigh the evidence a little more carefully. Usually, we confirm the community's judgement but reduce the sentences.
>
> (quoted in Price 1991: 210)

In that case, the appeal committee drafted codes of conduct which stressed the need for due process, the right to a defence and the right of appeal. These structures were developed most intensively in the Eastern Cape but the best-documented examples are those of Mamelodi and of Alexandra.

As we have indicated, these pyramids have been shaped by several sources. An Atteridgeville case (*Weekly Mail* 30 April 1987) suggests two alternatives sources. An adult and four minors were charged with furthering the aims of the ANC by constituting a People's Court and intimidating people to participate in it. They were also charged with kidnapping the 'accused' to bring them to trial, and with extortion in requiring the latter to compensate a complainant for broken spectacles, and of assault with intent to do grievous bodily harm by threatening to sjambok the 'accused' before the Court.

> A police witness claimed that the Court was part of communist-inspired Mandela plan imported from the Soviet Union. He handed a sketch to the judge of the 'M-Plan' to show how it worked. However, counsel for the accused argued that court was not communist-inspired but based on African tradition whose chief exponent was the 'father' of African nationalism, Anton Muziwakhe Lembede, and that Mandela merely translated tradition into practice in the form of M-plan. This was in keeping with ANC ideology in borrowing ideas from other ideologies in the development of indigenous structures of government. These structures were adapted to needs of urban government.
>
> (*Weekly Mail* 1988)

The incorporation of People's Courts within a pyramid structure is, of course, not peculiar to South Africa. Exiled ANC cadres had experienced them in Zimbabwe and Mozambique, where they were established to 'counter official structures regarded as illegitimate because they were established against the will of the people'. In the Chilean squatter camps, similar pyramid structures had emerged (Spence 1982). By the mid-1980s, there was considerable experience of ordering systems in neighbouring countries on which the UDF could draw (Makamure 1985). Not that that experience was all positive. An account from Zimbabwe suggested that rather than representing, in the post-colonial state, a parallel pyramid to that of the 'official' ordering process, they had become in the new political context a second tier to that official structure, providing an inferior service for poor people, and simply consolidating an outdated and semi-feudal tribal law within the new structure.

Price suggests a more prosaic source for the township processes than that suggested in the comparative studies. Within the tumult of the early Emergency period, groups of young comrades had already divided up the turf within which they would seek to control crime, to administer discipline, and to re-make the urban landscape with clean-up campaigns. The UDF, responding to some of the apparent excesses of radical zeal, and seeking to bring some organizational discipline to them, built the pyramid on top of the street committees. Political theory then entered, with an attempt to merge these local structures into a potential country-wide structure, as an alternative to that of apartheid (Price 1991). In some communities, these abuses were a major stimulus to setting up formal street committees by the UDF which, in naming more mature court members, aimed to achieve greater discipline from above and more accountability from below. Thus 'kangaroo courts' in many townships were transformed into a rudimentary criminal justice system (Price 1991). While the detail varied from townships to township, the democratic pyramid structure was the typical form of eventual organization.

As the following example of an ordering process in Alexandra illustrates, their origins, while located in systemic problems, could be quite fortuitous. As a consequence of the 1986 killing of a youth in a police shoot-out, several youths gathered at the house of his mother. Two women came to complain to them that the SAP would not record complaints about their husbands who had assaulted them (they had been told, sardonically, to report the violence to the 'comrades' or to the 'Archbishop,' that is, to Archbishop Tutu). Consequently, the youths began to deal with complaints brought by adults, started an anti-crime campaign and confiscated weapons from unauthorized people. Similarly, in Nyanga, in Cape Town, the first recorded People's Court was set up to deal with the problems of the local art centre where young people had stolen the copper telephone wires. The art centre members convened a court in response (Scharf 1990).

Inattention by the police to complaints about crime was a central cause for the development of people's policing/courts. If there was an accessible alternative agency to the state police, ordering processes were unlikely to evolve. In Graafwater, in the Western Cape, the establishment of a para-legal and social work advice office resulted in further deterioration in relations between police and the 'coloured' community (the latter community preferring the advice office to the police station to settle disputes). Further, the advice office could facilitate conflict resolution without the usual

> drawn-out and intimidating bureaucratic procedures in the begin-
> ning, the local police did not take kindly to this loss of faith in
> their service and avenged this by insisting that heavy fines be
> imposed on people convicted on charges for public drunkenness.
> (Fernandez 1991: 47)

Consequently, the office assumed central ordering functions. In Mamelodi, in a similar situation, the youth organization (MYO) stepped into the vacuum resulting from the collapse of the town council (such as the breakdown of garbage collection) and the withdrawal of the SAP from even notional crime functions (*Weekly Mail* 9 May 1986). Consequently, MYO launched a policing campaign, 'Operation Clean-up', to deal with the general problems of detritus, vegetable and human, and hooliganism in the name of the 'struggle'. In Mamelodi, as in many other townships, 'normal' policing had ceased both because the SAP was preoccupied with the political events and because they had little interest in community protection. Events such as the consumer boycott of 1985 had led to entrepreneurial thieves robbing shoppers in the guise of policing the boycott. In Langa, the police violence and the aftermath of 1985 led to the emergence of a similar alternative structure. The disappearance of the police from crime work created a breeding ground for a 'young marginal acquisitive population' (Scharf 1990) to which voluntary policing was a natural communal response.

In sum, with the incorporation of the *ad hoc* street committees and People's Courts within the larger Civic structures, more formal procedures were adopted in the politically conscious townships to standardize ordering practices, and to achieve a measure of account-ability. Irrespective of the variation in the quality and durability of the alternative ordering processes, from township to township, certain principles and practices were nearly universally evident.

The procedures of ordering

Popular ordering practices combined several elements, modified by the exigencies of apartheid, the demands of township life, and the socio-political commitment of their propagators. They reflected limited traditional African practices. Dispute resolution, problem-solving, was to be immediate and communally responsive. Lay justice was a defining feature – trial by one's peers reflected a traditional commitment (and a major diversion from recent white South African criminal process). As we have noted, they generally differed from the Makgotlas, in denying inequality in process (especially between the elders and the youth), presuming equal status and rights of those who participated, whether as officials or as accused (in Mamelodi, for example, incorporating female adjudicators and sometimes very young people as part of the participating court assembly).

But they also retained traditional features (Hund and Koto-Rammopo 1983). In the judicial process, findings rested not only on the facts of the case but also on the reputation and character of the accused. A central aim was to prevent the breaking of relationships and to achieve a measure of reconciliation between the disputants, it required an analysis of the total history of relations between parties and not just the substantive issue.[17] Punishments for infractions were group-directed rather than individual-directed. A Mamelodi example demonstrates this point, representing an attempt to formalize existing *ad hoc* practice.

> It was then that we hit upon the idea of setting up street committees to deal with problems affecting a particular street . . . met about once a week dealing with domestic problems such as a husband deserting his family and moving in with a girl-friend. Usually the man is fetched and brought to the court to say what led to the walk-out. Several marriages have been saved this way. (At times, a young man spends all his money at the shebeen without supporting his parents). He appears before the court and after being shown the folly of his ways, he is usually given five lashes with a cane.
>
> (Hund and Kotu-Rammopo 1983)

Sanctions were intended to serve several purposes. Custody (apart from on rare occasions) was simply not feasible, and in any case, alien to custom. Punishment therefore had to exclude the dominant, graduated, Western practice. Its primary function was to serve the collectivity by repudiating acts seen as harmful to the community – not to deal with the particular needs of the offender. Paul Mashatile of the Alexandra Young Congress claimed:

> Although we have taken over some law and order functions, our aim is not to mete out punishment, but to educate and restore the right values within the community.
>
> (quoted in Carter 1991: 116)

It must symbolically repugn an act which threatened the unity of a community that required solidarity in the face of the apartheid machine. The findings of the Nyanga court, for example, were based on 'discipline, organisational accountability, recognition of the true enemy (the apartheid state and its institutions) and an understanding that intra-black crimes were divisive and counter-productive to struggle' (Scharf 1990).

In sentencing, a distinction was frequently made between shaming and stigmatization (Braithwaite 1989), with the latter being avoided as it was likely to drive the offender away – possibly into an oppositional camp with consequences for communal solidarity. Shaming was typically preferred as it was a temporary state which, while manifesting the community anger at the offence, also allowed reintegration once that disgust had been expressed. Such reintegration was sometimes sought through the re-education of the offender. At other times, it was promoted through sanctions aimed at restoring or improving the moral and physical fabric of the community. One such 'community service' option in Nyanga required offenders to repaint the houses of elderly community members. Similarly, in Mamelodi, a youth court encouraged 'community service orders' that required offenders to build parks and rockeries in the open spaces of the township and ensure that they were kept watered (*Weekly Mail* 9 May 1986). An attempt at reintegration would follow – thus in Nyanga, community service would be followed by a requirement for an appropriate offender to join the Youth Brigade of the ANC in order that he or she could be re-socialized and subject to communal discipline. Once disciplined and 're-educated' the ex-offenders became members of the court in turn in order to continue that socialization process (Scharf 1990). A key judicial aim was to show offenders that they had not been abandoned by the community.

More serious offences – such as forcible rape – might be dealt with by public whipping or sjambokking. Whipping had the particular benefits of immediacy, of calculated, measured punishment, and afforded a public shaming experience of temporary duration. Members of the Youth Brigade took turns to administer the whipping in order to emphasize the collective nature of the punishment (Scharf 1990). Where fines were imposed, the sums collected could be used productively for expenses ranging from the purchase of chemical toilets to the payment of lawyers' fees (for local people accused in the state courts) (Sapire 1992). Democratic accountability was both a necessity (decisions made locally could have wider repercussions) and a central principle of an ordering process which sought higher standards than that of the authoritarian South African state. The pyramid structure enabled street committees to affirm the decisions across the community:

> (for example) a street committee decided that shebeens had to operate until 10pm. This decision affected a particular street [but] other committees had to discuss it with their own residents together with the shebeen owner (each person in the street are members of the street committee apart from collaborationists). If the member is dissatisfied with decisions of the street committee then it is referred to the block committee. The matter can be taken to the highest level of the Civic where if necessary a vote can be taken. A decision likely to affect the whole of Mamelodi is passed upwards.
>
> (*Weekly Mail* 9 May 1986)

Justice was essentially 'popular' (Sachs 1987) in the radical and practical meaning of that term. The language was open and accessible. In many cases, the legitimacy of this informal process was increased to the extent to which it disavowed formal practices:

> Here [in Mamelodi] we do not concern ourselves with legal technicalities – like in the Magistrates Court where, if you have a good lawyer, you get off.
>
> (*Weekly Mail* 9 May 1986)

However, the more institutionalized People's Courts adopted several European features. They were, for example, courts of record, in that previous decisions were regarded as binding. There were, however, important modifications. Horizontal integration was maintained, civil and criminal cases being dealt with together (although the former, as in the case of a domestic dispute, only came to People's

Courts as a last resort if they could not be dealt with at street level). Cross-examination practices were different from the formal courts, aimed not at finding loopholes in the defence but rather in highlighting that the accused's conduct was not acceptable to the community. At the same time, it attempted to show him or her their mistakes, and how the accused should remedy them – not trying to entrap the offender. Cross-examination was meant to be educative. At the end of the day's hearings, the members of the Court might – as in the Nyanga case – hold a post mortem and education meeting on 'people's justice'.

The reaction by the State

Several phases can be identified in the State's reaction to the emergence of alternative ordering processes. With the Makgotla institutions that were evident prior to the Emergency, there was relative tolerance. They were functional in neutralizing potential township violence and in instilling a relative respect for the State's 'law and order'. Indigenous structures were allowed to exercise their own forms of social control as long as they did not threaten apartheid. They relieved the state courts of township cases. They minimized the work-load of the SAP. Being under the influence of local surrogates, such as the Community Councillors, gave them some legitimacy with the State, especially after the Soweto uprising of 1976. When faults appeared in such processes, the State could wash its hands of the affair by invoking the rhetoric of formal justice, while affirming the 'primitiveness' and 'barbarism' of informal process (Moses 1990).

Initially during the Emergency the State's response to the People's Courts was simply criminalization. Punishments by People's Courts were deemed simple acts of criminality. Persons participating in the People's Courts were charged with public order offences such as 'assault'. Later, there was a different, more considered, reaction. The development of alternative structures in the townships, independent of those of the State, were subversive, a deliberate challenge to white rule and threatened the surrogate township structures. As the State came to appreciate this political challenge, charges were more likely to relate to political sedition than to common crime (Scharf 1988).

Academic discourse framed that repression:

> The South African Police, looking after complex national interests, is confronted by [a] complex society. It is quite evident that radicalism will rear its ugly head. Increasingly more the police

will have to police the so called alternative structures perpetrated (not created) by the radicals.

(Smit 1988: 22)

The State and the white Press represented the community ordering processes as instruments of barbaric intimidation and repression, used by township agitators to enforce the compliance of 'moderate' residents in unpopular activities such as boycotts and strikes (Seekings 1989).

At the local level, state policing reacted with the predisposition of criminality. Actions of self-defence by township residents were simply forms of crime irrespective of the factors which had led up to the 'trial'. A typical example is the Atteridgeville incident referred to above.

The following account of the incidents surrounding one such police incursion into the alternative realm in the Western Cape township of Khayelitsha vividly illustrates the State's reaction, and the way the event was interpreted by the police within the wider complex of relations between state police and township residents.

On 8th August, Macassar residents captured a man who was raping a local woman in the bushes nearby. An agreement was made with the rapist's family that a fine would be paid to the rape victim and the residents kept the rapist in 'custody'. At about 1pm on 9th August, the rapist's sister arrived with a police van, BHJ742B, to come and fetch the man. Residents explained the situation to the police and the police left. At about 6pm, another van, BFW519B, arrived with the sister and two black and one coloured policeman. The policemen assaulted Mandla Shuku and when Jantjies tried to intervene, threatened him. Jantjies ran away and the police fired shots at him. A number of women were also beaten by the police and a scuffle broke out. The police fired tear gas and left with the rapist. At about midnight, the same policeman and two others returned in plain clothes and on foot. They went to Jantjies' house and knocked on the door. Jantjies was out and a visitor opened the door. The police fired two shots and the visitor fell down. The police then set the house alight. Jantjies' wife who was inside the house managed to escape but could not remove the visitor's body as the fire spread too rapidly. The police then went to the house of another activist in the area, Mnyani, fired shots at the door and then set it alight. The house next door also caught fire.

On 12 August, Jantjies went to the Site B police station and spoke to Major Heunis and a white captain. He pointed out the three police-men involved in the incident. Shuku has been charged with attempting to necklace the rapist. Residents deny that there was any inten- tion to kill the rapist as they were waiting for the family to return with the fine. They claim that the charge is an attempt to cover up the police assaults, shooting and burning of the houses.

(ANC Women's League, West Cape, Memorandum on Khayelitsha Crisis 8–9 August 1991, Abraham Jantjies, Macassar)

This incident demonstrates a number of points – that the practice of self-policing, of ordering at the street end of the private–public continuum, could occur with the maximum of informality. Self-policing was directly integrated in the judicial and dispositional functions. Second, the residents were faced with an immediate problem of what to do with a violent offender when there was no formal process available – techniques of capture, of interrogation, of trial, of reparative sentence and of custody until the penalty has been paid – were instantly improvized. The state police reaction was conditioned by a wider alienation from the community, and permitted an exemplary exhibition of the power of the state police over those who dare to question its mandate and the rights of the individuals who compose the local state police.

An experience in Graafwater similarly underlines the local character of police reaction to the development of alternative structures:

in the beginning, the local police did not take kindly to this loss of faith in their services and avenged this by insisting that heavy fines be imposed on people convicted on charges for public drunkenness.

(Fernandez 1991: 47)

Harassment of local voluntary policing was common:

They hamper the communities efforts to control ordinary crime. Once the community comes out and patrols then the Police come out and they start searching the people doing the controlling. They look for small knives etc. But they do nothing to disarm the gangsters who are causing the trouble.

(respondent quoted in Shearing and Mzamane 1992: 7)

But central state directives reflected a political rather than a 'criminal' concern. During the Emergency period, the street committees and their structures of self-policing and judicial process came to symbolize not just an alternative criminal justice process but also an embryo form of community government which offered a political threat to the State:

many of these alternative structures were the first targets of the State crackdown on June 12, 1986. . . . the police detained all of 200 leading activists (in Mamelodi) who ran the courts and street committees.

(Boraine 1988: 2)

These arrests reflected a state policing ideology that combined a perception of the threat to white rule posed by the development of black ordering structures together with an underlying racism. An SAP comment on the Soweto community ordering processes is instructive:

understaffed and overworked, these [police] stations never were the most popular spot in town. Intimidation of the public by the Soweto Civic Association's Street Committees add further complications to this problem. The street committees, or 'People's Courts' enjoy growing support from the community – albeit in some instances forced. They undermine by taking the justice into their own hands. Predictably, no mercy is shown when the *ad hoc* administrators of justice mete out punishment. They stridently accuse the S.A. Police of inefficiency, the courts of procrastinating, and the sentences as laughable. The alternative they offer is to find, judge, and sentence perpetrators themselves in far less time than the system takes. All of which sounds reasonable in a crime riddled society, but meanwhile back at the ranch, policemen are regularly ambushed, street names and numbers of houses obliterated and people are intimidated not to lay charges. Not exactly the conduct one expects from a society demanding a better police force.

(*Servamus* February 1991)

At command level, the SAP viewed the emergence of such processes not as a direct response to community needs and to its own failures, but rather as a deliberate challenge to the State.

At the same time, the so-called 'People's Courts' emerged and attempted to take over the legal and judicial functions of the Police and courts of law.

(*Annual Report* 1985)

Formal proscription followed with political criminalization replacing social criminalization. Information on the township ordering process was limited, preventing publication of any material or comment on any structures:

in which members of the public are incited or encouraged or which is calculated to have the effect of inciting members of the public . . . to prosecute, to try, or to punish persons by way of unlawful structures, procedures, or methods purporting to be judicial structures, procedures or methods, or to subject themselves to the authority of such structures, procedures or methods.

(Proclamation 97 (1987) in terms of the Public Safety Act 1953)

By the late 1980s, the vast majority of the more institutionalized People's Courts had been destroyed by punitive state police action (Scharf 1988). In the Eastern Cape, half of all detainees arrested during the Emergency were imprisoned because of their involvement in People's Courts (*Weekly Mail* 20 November: 1986). This widespread repression ensured that by the early 1990s, attempts to network the township ordering systems had largely failed and the informal justice processes had retreated back to an underground, *ad hoc*, existence.

Problems of township ordering processes

There were, of course, many imperfections in the local structures, arising from a combination of repression and from lack of wider knowledge. Some committed commentators had painted an initial rosy picture. For example, a year after the imposition of the Emergency, in Mamelodi:

> Within this relatively short period, much was achieved. Order and peace reigned in the township, children were made to respect their parents and the crime rate was reduced considerably. . . . The comrades strived to combat any kind of misconduct by members of the community. They succeeded in guaranteeing the safety of the people in the township to a considerably larger extent than the police force.
>
> (*Frontline* Christmas 1986)

But in the longer term, the ordering processes being borne out of unremitting pressure, inevitably manifested those strains. The failures of the state police to provide for local requirements, inevitably, in some contexts, led to a rough-and-ready alternative. The tension of formal illegality; the constant threat of arrest and harassment by the SAP; the attempt to maintain a notional fairness and accountability in vicissitudes of township life; and the existence of major schisms in many townships – between young and old, between men and women, and between different ethnic groups – ensured that practice was rarely Utopian.

Informal ordering processes in other countries have been criti- cized on several counts. Offenders often treat the processes cynically – appreciating that if any punishment is imposed, the formal state apparatus might deny the legitimacy of the process, reinstate the offender and punish the community agents. The development of such systems, even in a revolutionary situation, may be an attempt to reinvent the wheel (Santos 1979) – a return to past ordering traditions is impossible, given the development of a complex differentiated society. Abel (1982) has argued that such informal practices may simply widen the net – bringing misdemeanours into a more formal process, matters that could well have been left to families or neighbours to sort out more effectively and with no stigmatizing consequences. It might provide second-hand justice for second-hand people – at least, in the state system, there is some notional regard to the rules and procedures of law. Informal processes might be 'captured' by sectional interests. Powerful figures in the community who might hesitate to use the formal system or wish to avoid its expense, could use the cheap local alternative to maintain oppression.[18] Many similar studies of comparative ordering processes have noted the lack of communal participation, after an initial period of high involvement (Turk 1987). Local voluntary policing may degenerate into a system of vigilantes exercising private power (Dahrendorf 1985: 74). Other criticisms of informal ordering processes are less relevant in South Africa – that it would, for example, lead to more rather than less state control by permitting intervention into the privacies of everyday lives.

Such Western critics have generally assumed a peaceful co-existence between the tiered formal and the informal, with the lower, informal sector acting as a feeding source for the second, pushing miscreants up the ladder. Conversely, in that ordering hierarchy, the lower tier may become a poaching ground for professionals from the formal sector seeking further profit – lawyers out to extend their practices by advertising the value of 'professional' representation in the second sector and consequently devaluing the 'informal' character of the proceedings.

However, the horizontal nature of the two systems of criminal justice in South Africa, where the existence of the township ordering processes is a *de facto* denial of the legitimacy of the state system, precludes the substance of these latter criticisms. There were few cross-over points. Criticisms of the informal ordering processes often assume a positive interactive relation with the formal sector.

Commentators sympathetic to black resistance have given weight to the former condemnations, denouncing the undemocratic nature of many such structures as bands of youths set up so-called 'kangaroo courts' and give out punishments, under the control of no-one with a democratic mandate, this is not people's power.

(speech by Zwelakhe Sisulu quoted in Price 1991)

Certainly, the processes could be used pragmatically and relatively cynically. Private 'prosecution' processes have always been open to abuse.[19] Personal vendettas were pursued through some township courts. In Mamelodi, for example:

people would come to us claiming that their neighbours or whoever had insulted them or assaulted their child. In some cases, the courts would try the person in absentia without caring to listen to the other side of the story. Some people took advantage of this type of undemocratic procedure and would fabricate charges against people they had a dislike for. . . . in some cases, a person would go to a committee in a different street to report an incident that allegedly happened in the street in which he lived. The offending party would then be fetched and punished. This led to people reporting incidents that had occurred several months or even years ago.

(*Star* 7 July 1991)

In the KTC squatter camp, a Court was operated by 'extortionists' posturing as comrades.[20] In Nyanga, a Court staffed by 'non-affiliated youth' rarely acquitted, and the informal machinery appeared to be used on occasion for personal vengeance. Qwelane has argued, that whereas tribal courts and Makgotlas tried cases between recognizable parties, the People's Courts 'usually base their evidence on faceless accusers and the accused is almost always guilty before the hearing' (Qwelane in the *Star* 7 July 1991). A court operating under the banner of the UDF prosecuted political activists without any apparent authority from the parent body (Scharf 1988). Despite the legitimacy given to the informal process in many townships, local realities and needs led sometimes to personal rather than to communal advantage.

Many of these problems occurred where the various disparate street committees and local courts had not been incorporated into the pyramid of the area committee or Civic Association: 'without a broader order around them, they can easily descend to kangaroo courts' (*Frontline* Christmas 1986). Where different and occasionally competing ordering processes existed in the same township, a potential litigant could 'shop around' until he or she could find one that might offer them personal advantage. The secretary of the Mamelodi Youth Organization made the point forcibly, that while the Courts were created mainly to deal with petty crime 'this led to other elements using the courts to settle personal feuds'.

Where the Court attempted to try servants of the white state, such as local councillors, other problems appeared. Scharf (1988) notes the collapse of the Nyanga Court after it had punished a councillor's family by lashings. The councillor refused to accept the jurisdiction of the court. The result was the arrest of most of the members of the Court. Those who did not accept the legitimacy of community justice and ordering process – informers and local councillors – had an alternative resource, the state criminal justice process. Township ordering processes could only work effectively as long as they were regarded as legitimate by all those who appeared before them – or dared not resort to the state system.

There were further criticisms of the standards of justice meted out by the People's Courts. Lacking any universal procedures and tariff of punishment, sanctions could be excessive, leading to community dis-avowal as the punishment tariff was increasingly raised at the demand of militant members (Scharf 1988). Contradictory pressures often led to dissatisfaction. Community approval exerted pressure towards leniency, whereas the inability to incarcerate and the seriousness of many offences exerted a pressure towards summary justice (Allison 1990). While there is little evidence to suggest that established People's Courts have resorted to the ultimate barbarity of the 'necklace' (Scharf 1988), local exigencies have often meant arbitrary procedures and violent outcomes (Price 1991). The common criticism of the township ordering processes is that they have commonly flouted traditional African norms by allow-ing members of the younger generation to try their elders. In the more institutionalized structures, separate courts for young and old were eventually created. But given that many of the local informal processes were created in the heat of the struggle by young comrades seeking immediate solutions to pressing problems, there are several incidents of courts being delegitimated in this way. Scharf notes such incidents bringing the Gugelutu court into disrepute (Scharf 1990). Complaints about similar practices were raised with the Alexandra Action Committee:

> youths who controlled them were very aggressive and would accept no criticism. Alexandra residents generally favoured the idea of the Courts but opposed the excessive use of lashings.
>
> (*Weekly Mail* June 1986)

Conversely, there are examples of the People's Courts (in a practice inherited from the Makgotlas) being used as weapons by the elders of the community, as instruments of general disciplining for young people, largely irrespective of evidence of criminality (Seekings 1989). Scharf documents a further criticism from the Western Cape. In that case, the post-punishment reintegration process – requiring that ex-offenders be re-socialized by joining the Youth League that formed the Court – resulted, at the end of the day, in those ex-offenders becoming a majority in the Court. One consequence was an escalation in the tariff of sjambok strokes for relatively minor offenders, with few accused being found not guilty (Scharf 1988).

Conclusion – township ordering in the transitional period

Township ordering processes in South Africa have, given the obvious constraints, been subject to little objective analysis and evaluation.[21] Given their formation within the confines of the apartheid system, they have been subject to considerable criticism both from the organizations of the white state and also from within the leadership of black 'struggle' organizations. More generally, such processes elsewhere in the context of revolutionary struggle have, as we have noted, encountered sustained and almost overwhelming academic critiques. Developing township ordering processes as an alternative to those of the apartheid state faces major obstacles.

In the succeeding chapter we consider the broad outlines of a proposal for a dual system of policing, that draws upon the energy that has given such life to popular ordering while responding to the criticisms we have just outlined. The challenge, we believe, is to take advantage of the 'immense community involvement' in ordering 'in a way that neither crushes its spontaneity on the one hand nor permits manifest injustice on the other' (Sachs 1992: 226). In responding to this challenge, we argue that despite its many problems, the seeds of a more equable ordering system can be found within the township experience and that this should be related to developments elsewhere, to provide new directions for South African policing. The key to constructing a new satisfactory dual system of civil and state policing is, we maintain, the establishment of forums of dialogue that provide for ongoing conversations between civil and state structures, that will identify and coordinate policing resources in the maintenance of local orders that endorse broader standards.

Chapter 7

Towards a dual system of policing

Policing is something worth fighting for and the struggle shapes both the forms and functions of policing.

(Marenin 1992: 28)

In our review of non-state developments within South Africa, we identified challenges to the oppression of apartheid that sought to promote policing practices that protected rather than disrupted black communities. In particular, we noted an emerging conception of policing that was community-controlled and that was concerned with problem-solving, security and community integration. These practices, we argued, were part of a widespread endeavour on the part of black people in South Africa to refuse to participate in the institutions of apartheid. They represent an attempt by communities to take direct responsibility for policing in ways that do not contribute to their continued exploitation. These challenges resembled developments that have been taking place elsewhere in response to a growing critique of the 'catch 'em and exclude 'em' approach to policing (that we have termed 'bandit-catching') that has come to dominate police practice in liberal–democracies.[1]

In this chapter, we turn our attention to these other developments as experiences that South Africans should consider as they construct the institutional arrangements that will shape a new South Africa. In this discussion, we recognize the critical issue of avoiding the problems that have accompanied so many of the attempts (as reviewed in the last chapter) to develop forms of policing that are directly controlled by, and responsible to, people at a local level. We consider first the changes that have taken place elsewhere with respect to the policing function. We then turn to a consideration of their implications for South Africa in relation to indigenous developments.

POLICING AS PROBLEM-SOLVING

The central development in contemporary policing reform has been a move away from the 'bandit-catching' function that has dominated state policing to a 'problem-solving' approach. This move has been presented in the context of two different understandings of the recent history of policing. As these understandings promote distinctive visions of the role of the State and civil society in policing, they have different implications for the future of South African ordering.

We will present these understandings as different narratives about the development of modern policing. The first narrative is a state-centred one that expresses what Johnston (1992: 184) has recently termed 'an obsessive preoccupation with the study of public [state] police personnel' that insists on identifying modern policing with 'the police'. As this story, and the model it advocates, is being vigorously promoted by police reformers, its vision is one that South Africans will be urged by many progressive 'police experts' to embrace.

The second story is a revisionist account that challenges the first story's 'obsessive preoccupation' with the State on the grounds that it fails to acknowledge an enormously consequential change in the structure of ordering that has resulted in policing becoming both despecialized and decentralized. In contrast to the first story, this pluralist narrative provides conceptual space for the communitarian tendencies (Braithwaite 1989; Gardbaum 1992) we have identified in the grassroots manifestations we reviewed in the previous chapter. Unlike the first narrative, it is a story that South Africans are unlikely to hear from police experts. None the less, as it embraces a vision that resonates with the developments of indigenous civil policing, in which 'law is ordinary and everyone has law' (Fitzpatrick 1992: 212), that have been so important to the history of ordering in this country, it is a story whose lessons South Africans should carefully consider.

Narrative of the state police as problem-solvers

Our first story provides an account of the emergence of a new state police, at the turn of the nineteenth century, in response to the inadequacy of earlier private policing initiatives to cope with 'the irresistible force of industrialization and its control problems' (Reiner 1985; Brogden et al. 1987). It traces the way in which this new specialized police has struggled to become an effective keeper of the peace.[2]

In outlining these developments, Sherman (1992) identifies the American police scholar Herman Goldstein as the source of a recent consequential move from bandit-catching to problem-solving in which police attention has shifted from legal to community definitions of wrong-doing.[3] Goldstein advocated abandoning the criminal law as the organizing framework for defining policing problems, replacing it with substantive patterns of behaviour.

'Taking the problem apart' was the most important step Goldstein advocated, to be followed by a diagnosis of the problem's causes and some hypotheses about the problem's possible solutions. It is this emphasis on clear definition of highly specific problems as targets for police attack which gives the problem-orientated policing strategy its name.[4] In this shift to problem-solving, two things in particular have happened to revolutionize the police and their approach to policing.

First, and most importantly, the police have recognized that it is disorder rather than crime that should be their concern (Wilson and Kelling 1982, 1989; Skogan 1990). Eck and Spelman (1987) make the point (in the course of a critique of bandit-catching and the crime-control mentality on which it depends) that most citizen concerns are not directly related to crime. Rubbish on the streets, noise, abandoned and ill-maintained buildings, barking dogs and the like, form the bulk of calls for police service. In many areas, residents judge these problems to be more serious than street crime. But still, police are orientated to crime control.

> Given the attention police have paid to crime over the years, one would expect that they would have learned to control it. In fact the opposite is true.
>
> (Spelman 1987: 34)

Second, the shift of focus from crime to disorder has served to de-emphasize the importance of physical force, which becomes less critical as a resource. While bandit-catching with its focus on detention might require physical force as its essential resource this is not true when disorder is the central concern.

Eck and Spelman illustrate the implications of these two crucial changes in the police role conception with the following anecdote.

> Charles Bedford couldn't sleep. Most nights, his residential Newport News street was quiet, marred only by the low rumble of an occasional truck on Jefferson Avenue two blocks away. But lately,

Friday and Saturday nights had been different: groups of a dozen or more rowdy teenagers kept him awake, with their loud music and their horseplay. There had been no violence. But there had been some vandalism, and the kids seemed unpredictable. More disturbing, the kids came from another section of town, miles away. One sleepless Friday night it became too much. Charlie Bedford called the cops. . . . Sergeant Hogan was on duty when Mr Bedford called. He assigned the problem to Officer Paul Summerfield. Summerfield suspected that the source of the problem might be a roller skating rink. The rink had been trying to increase business by offering reduced rates and transportation on Friday and Saturday nights. At two in the morning, as he drove north along Jefferson Avenue to the rink, Summerfield saw several large groups of youths walking south. Other kids were hanging around at the rink. Summerfield talked to several of them and found that they were waiting for a bus. The other kids, he was told, had become impatient and begun the three-mile walk home. Summerfield talked to the rink owner. The owner had leased the bus to pick up and drop off kinds who lived far from the rink. But there were always more kids needing rides at the end of the night than the bus had picked up earlier.

Officer Summerfield returned to the skating rink early the next evening. He saw fifty or so youngsters get out of the bus rented by the skating rink. But he saw others get out of public transit buses that stopped running at midnight. And he saw parents in pyjamas drop their kids off, then turn around and go home. Clearly the rink's bus would be unable to take home all the kids who would be stranded at closing time. Summerfield left, perplexed.

Officer Summerfield consulted Sergeant Hogan. They agreed that the skating rink owner should be asked to bus the kids home. Summerfield returned to the rink and spoke with the owner. The owner agreed to lease more buses. By the next weekend, the buses were in use and Summerfield and Hogan saw no kids disturbing Mr Bedford's neighbourhood.

Sergeant Hogan summed it up: 'Look, we can have the best of both worlds. People here can get their sleep and the kids can still have fun. But we can't do it by tying up officers and chasing kids every Friday and Saturday night. There has to be a way of getting rid of the problem once and for all.'

(Eck and Spelman 1987: 31–2, 36–7, 49)

In this story, the police still 'own' policing though they are now willing to enlist the help of others. What has changed is the way in which they think about it. This message dominates contemporary police and scholarly understandings of policing. Indeed, it is so hegemonic that the second story, which we will outline in a moment, about the growth of civil – and in particular corporate – policing is not even acknowledged. For these reformers, the second story simply does not exist. There is only one narrative and it is a police-focused story in which the police and their advisers are presented as the heroes of a reform process initiated by them.

The policy implications of this story are straightforward. Now that the bankruptcy of bandit-catching policing with its strategies of 'panda cars', 'unit beat policing' and the like has been recognized and innovative thinking within the police community has realized a new vision, what is required is, first to refine this new way of thinking, and second, to spread this conceptual revolution throughout the police community.

The policy implications for South Africa are equally obvious and can be summarized as follows:

Yes, Los Angeles was burnt as black horror over the acquittal of the police who mercilessly beat Rodney King turned into anger that was unleashed in a pandemonium of violence against anything 'white'. But that all has to do with the old policing and an old era. It is simply evidence of the bankruptcy of this force-based, reactive, bandit-catching approach to policing. But, fortunately, a new era of community attentive policing has dawned. So what South Africa needs to do is take advantage of all the 'Research and Development' that has taken place in the global police community.

The people of a new liberal-democratic South Africa need a problem-solving state police, sensitive and responsive to community definitions of disorder, and made up of police officers who are willing and able to provide communities with solutions to their problems. What a new South Africa needs is a police who, like the new generation of police, think about policing differently. South Africa requires a new problem-solving 'community-orientated' police.

This vision of a new police will strike a responsive chord with all those South Africans who have lived for so long under the heel of a police who have systematically ignored their concerns. In response to this story many people are likely to acknowledge that when they have pleaded for more effective crime-fighting (see Shearing and Mzamane 1992) what they really had in mind was problem-solving state policing.

We believe that this favourable response is likely to change, however, once South Africans reflect on the consequences of promoting a new all-purpose problem-solving state police who will, like the police of apartheid, continue to be part of every aspect of their lives as paternalist problem-solvers. While South Africans will want to embrace a problem-solving, disorder-based approach to peace-keeping they will not, we suspect, want to embrace a strategy that is premised on the continuance, indeed the further development of, an expansive state police who consult them but who ultimately 'own' policing.

This brings us to the crux of the first narrative, namely the way in which it sets up the problem so that it appears that the only way in which disorder can be adequately responded to is by accepting direct police, and hence state, involvement in people's lives as problem-solvers. In reflecting on the future of policing within South Africa, it is important for South Africans to recognize that that conclusion does not logically follow. Promoting problem-solving is not the same thing as promoting the police as all-purpose problem-solvers. The development of policing as problem-solving is something that can be done, and what is more has been done, without radically broadening the role of the state police from crime to disorder. Furthermore, it is important for South Africans to recognize that if the recommendations of the first story are accepted, the empowerment of the police that this will promote will affect the poor far more than it will the more affluent, as the latter, as we have already suggested, have already taken steps to ensure that they are not dependent on the state for their routine policing.

Narrative of the state police as one community resource in problem-solving

This brings us to our second narrative which is about how problem-solving has developed as a central feature of policing without requiring an expansion of the state police role. This is an account that the first story systematically, and very deliberately, silences. It is a story about how the middle and upper classes, through the corporate entities which organize so much of their lives, have moved their policing from bandit-catching to problem-solving in ways that have limited rather than expanded the state police intervention in their lives. This narrative challenges the first story on four fundamental grounds. It argues that:

1 policing is not something that the police 'own';
2 the move from bandit-catching to problem-solving is something that has already taken place on a massive scale without a change in the police role;
3 the impact of this change has to date been limited primarily to the policing of middle- and upper-class communities;
4 the move to problem-solving has not been driven by the vision of 'police' reformers but has emerged as a result of global changes that have 'redesigned the role of the State as facilitator of trans-national capital requirements' so that the 'regulatory functions of the nation-state have become derivative, a kind of political fran-chising or subcontracting' (Santos 1992: 135).

What differentiates this narrative is that it is a story about 'polic-ing' rather than 'the police' (Johnston 1992; Shearing 1992d) in which it is increasingly difficult to establish 'where state regulation ends and where non-state regulation begins' (Santos 1992: 132). It is an account of a 'quiet revolution' (Stenning and Shearing 1980), that finds visible expression in a 'rebirth of private [civil] policing' (Johnston 1992), that has enabled ordering to become the respon-sibility of corporate entities and the communities associated with them.[5] This story recognizes the conceptual changes that have shifted the focus of policing from bandit-catching to problem-solving that the first story identifies. It argues, however, that these changes have taken place within the context of, and because of, structural changes, 'a transnationalization of the legal field' (Santos 1992: 135), to do with the expansion of corporate entities and their role as sites of social life that has resulted in policing becoming increasingly the responsibility of corporate communities (Shearing and Stenning 1983). These communities may be fairly stable over space and time, as is the case with a residential community, or may be as temporary as the communities created by visitors to recreational sites such as Disney World, or they may be 'deterritorialized' (Santos 1992: 136) interest-based or functional communities.

These changes have fundamentally reshaped modern policing from something that is 'owned' by one institution, the state police, to something that is located in a whole variety of institutional contexts. Policing has been 'pluralized' within a 'world system' (Santos 1992) so that it is now something that is 'owned' by, and done by, a variety of entities (Macauley 1986). Commercial banks, for instance, – which may or may not be transnational – respond to disorder, including the disorder of crime, on behalf of their staff and customers in ways that seldom involve the state police. In doing so, they govern a corporate community.

It is these structural changes, it is argued, that have prompted the change in the way policing has come to be conceived. This is so because, from the perspective of corporate communities, it is not the criminal law that is the most relevant source of definitions of disorder but rather the values and objectives that define the 'community', be it 'imagined or symbolic, real or hyper-real' (Santos 1992: 136). In these communities, disorder comes to mean such things as loss of profit, threats to the security of staff and customers, and so on (Shearing and Stenning 1984). In this story, the state police are seen as one player among many in the business of policing – and as the player who is very often the least important.

It is structural change signalled by the emergence of, among other things, 'mass private property' (Shearing and Stenning 1983) that has driven and facilitated a shift in focus from bandit-catching to problem-solving. This shift has as its basis both a focus on disorder as well as on the availability of an interest-based will to participate in policing and capacities that have made it possible to solve problems in new and novel ways. This argument is nicely illustrated by an anecdote (circa 1980) one of us overheard about the way in which policing in a Canadian company was challenging the bandit-catching approach that was, and still is, associated with state policing. Employees of this company had been stealing portable power tools such as drills, saws and the like. This had resulted in significant losses to the company. In response, the company's director of security – an ex-state police officer – was asked to come up with a solution. His proposal was that he should arrange for undercover agents to gather evidence on who was removing the tools. He would then arrange for these people to be stopped and searched as they left the plant in a swoop on a particular day. Those found to be in possession of tools would be dismissed and prosecuted. When this proposal was presented to the vice-president to whom he reported, instead of finding approval for his bandit-catching solution he was chastised for not understanding the nature of the objectives and values of the corporation. It was explained to him that the criteria by which his solution was to be judged was its utility in contributing to company profits and the morale of the staff. The solution he proposed, it was pointed out, did not measure up on either count. Its implementation would mean that time and energy would have to be spent on catching the culprits and prosecuting them, well-trained people would be fired, new employees would have to be hired who would be just as likely to take tools home with them, these new recruits would have to be trained, morale would be damaged, and so on. In short, far from solving the problem he had been asked to address, his solution would contribute to it. The director of security was instructed to come up with a problem-solving rather than a problem-creating solution. His new solution was to establish a tool library, from which tools could be borrowed.

In the context of our second story, the 'discovery' of problem-solving policing by state police, is seen, at best, as a belated recognition of what non-state civil policing has been doing for decades. Problem-solving, in this account, has emerged as a strategy because policing has become increasingly community-controlled and organized. It is the structural changes of global privatization[6] that have driven the shift to a problem-solving policing. Problem-solving does not require police intervention.

In this account, the loci of control and assistance are reversed. Instead of the police using communities as a resource to tackle problems, it is 'communities' – be they territorially based or deterritorialized – who, on occasion, use the police to assist them to supplement their civil policing (Shearing et al. 1990). From this perspective, what is valuable about 'the police' is their licence and capacity to use force (Shearing 1992d). Critically, in this narrative the more traditional role of the police as a source of coercion is seen not as an error, or a failure, but as a resource that forms part of an institutional network that encompasses both the State and the civil society (Ericson 1992). The police are seen as valuable, not because they are all-purpose problems-solvers, but because they are equipped in terms of legal authority, capacity and knowledge to be bandit-catchers, and because bandit-catching is sometimes what is needed. This story is critical of the expansion of the police role promoted by the first narrative because to expand the police role as general problem-solvers is not only to involve them in arenas for which they are not well suited but, more disturbingly, it is to undermine the value and autonomy of civil society.

What is essential about this policing network, it is argued, is that its 'victims' are responsible for the coordination of security resources. Thus, to take a well-known example, in Disney Worlds it is the Disney Corporation that manages the problem-solving to do with the 'vandalism, rowdy behaviour, drug use, drunkenness, noise', not the state police. From the perspective of this account, the policy proposals of the first story are viewed as advocating a dangerous expansion of the State at the expense of civil society. In contrast, the second story advocates a 'reversal of power' over policing (Marenin 1992). It is a story about the manner in which governance is not, and should not be, a monopoly of government (Macauley 1986). It is a narrative that describes and advocates the growth and development of a vibrant civil society (understood as the space between individuals/families and the State (Braithwaite 1989)) in which corporate entities and the communities they make possible become the sites of governance. It is a story that recognizes that 'people – "ordinary", non-professional people – have competently operated locally-based but extensive legal orders' (Fitzpatrick 1992: 212).

What is significant about this story for South Africans is that it recognizes that the development of policing as an inter-institutional phenomenon has not enhanced local, civil control over policing in an even-handed way. On the contrary, control over policing has followed the contours of wealth and power. Poorer people, who do not have much influence over corporate entities and the institutions they manage, have not been empowered. They, in contrast to the more affluent, remain consumers rather than the producers of both civil and state policing.

POLICING FOR A NEW SOUTH AFRICA

If the lessons of the second story are to be heeded by South Africans, policing reform in their country should be based on the following principles.

1 First, the focus of reform should be policing not the police.
2 Second, policing should be understood as a product of a network of interrelated institutions operating at different levels and with different knowledges and resources.
3 Third, policing should be located primarily in the institutions of civil society.
4 Fourth, civil society should be understood as fractured and as made up of cross-cutting territorially-based as well as 'deterritorialized' communities.
5 Fifth, the state police should be defined as specific, not as all-purpose problem solvers.
6 Sixth, their problem-solving role should be organized around their capacity as bearers of force.

7 Seventh, force should be recognized as but one resource among many in peace-keeping.[7]
8 Eighth, the use of force should be strictly licensed and its use should lie primarily with the state police.
9 Ninth, constitutional restraints should apply to all features of peace-keeping.

REFORM OF THE STATE POLICE

The implications of these principles are that the reform of policing in South Africa should proceed on two levels. The first level of reform should focus on the state police and their role in policing. Reform at this level should be conservative. The aim of reform would be to establish the police as a body of people who can be recruited to use force in responding to disorder, provided these requests are consistent with the criteria laid down by the law and the vision of dominion that would inform it. Reform at this level would recognize the SAP as playing a part, but only a part, in the provision of security. The principal emphasis in these reforms would be on making the police responsive to communities, and ensuring that they are held politically accountable for the way in which they exercise their role.[8]

There is much to be done at this level. The continued evidence of SAP failure as crime-fighters and bearers of force makes clear that this task of reform will be difficult. The most recent indictment of the SAP as a competent traditional police force is to be found in the findings of a British team of two police officers, an academic and an ex-police officer who led the team. The team examined the police response to the Boipatong massacre (in which not only did hostel dwellers murder township residents in a night raid, but the police, immediately after F.W. de Klerk had visited the township, fired on a fleeing crowd), at the behest of the Goldstone Commission established under the National Peace Accord to investigate violence and intimidation (Waddington 1992b). In his Report, Waddington concluded that the deficiencies that they uncovered 'amount to a basic failure' on the part of the SAP, 'to serve the people of Boipatong' (1992b: 46). This failure, the Report argued, was not a matter of direct 'complicity'. 'Omissions arose not from deliberation, but from incompetence' (1992b: 46). The SAP, Waddington wrote, 'suffers from serious organisational [problems]' that include 'inadequate command and control', 'ineffective intelligence and contingency planning', 'unobstructed investigation', and 'insufficient awareness of community relations'.

The good news, the Report notes, is that these problems can be remedied in a relatively straightforward manner because, if there is one arena in which the SAP can learn relatively directly from other countries, it is as crime-fighters.[9]

> Fundamental as these criticisms are, they are equally remediable, since they involve not the replacement of individuals, but the establishment of structures and methods of policing that are familiar elsewhere in the world. If these defects are to be addressed it will require thorough reappraisal of the entire organisation, backed by political will to ensure sufficient funding.
>
> (Waddington 1992b: 46)

The Report's conclusion that the replacement of individuals is not required arises both because of the impression the team had of the 'dedication' and 'commitment' of SAP members 'in junior commissioned and non-commissioned ranks' (Waddington 1992b: 1), and because of the woeful inadequacy of the systems they found in place. While this does not negate the difficulties that the police culture, and the discourses that surround it, will pose to reform, it does suggest that these problems will not be insurmountable.

If the Waddington Report is correct about the commitment of junior police, and if a legitimate new government dedicates itself to reform, the major impediment to change at this technical level will be managerial resolution and it is here that individuals will present a problem. This obstacle has been noted by Allister Sparks[10] in an editorial commenting on a letter he received from the General in charge of the SAP's Internal Stability Unit, defending its tactics at Boipatong:

> what really concerns me is the outlook which [the General's] letter reveals; here is a member of the police general staff presented with an eye-witness report of an incident in which men for whom he is responsible opened fire at point-blank range, without warning and without orders, on an unarmed crowd and keep up their fire for nearly half a minute while the crowd flees in panic until two are dead and 29 wounded, and he shows no interests in the content of that report. [The General's] letter reveals not the slightest concern with the facts of what happened that day. He knows from the report which he read that I witnessed the whole

thing from start to finish, yet he does not ask me whether I can furnish him with further details, whether I can make myself available to the general staff to give them a fuller account and perhaps answer some questions. No, his interest is confined to making an exculpatory public relations response with a bunch of clippings that have nothing to do with the incident in question. That is the heart of the problem. Week after week, evidence comes out of police incompetence and malpractice, yet the response of the authorities is to deny and obfuscate in an attempt to safeguard the image rather than to probe and rectify in order to build a new image.

(*Cape Times* 29 July 1992)

As we have emphasized throughout the first part of this text, the problems associated with the SAP's role as oppressors are the consequence of a deep-rooted 'institutional complicity' or 'organisational deviance' (Shearing 1981b) in which the SAP's capacity as a police organization have been shaped by myriad decisions at a whole variety of levels that have made it a competent oppressor but not a competent protector of black communities. SAP members have in the past had neither the will nor the capacity to police black communities in a protective, cooperative manner. Their training, deployment and equipment have motivated and enabled them to control blacks and protect whites. They are not organized or prepared to protect black communities. As this inability is deliberate, it points to what can perhaps be described as a 'deliberate incompetence'. While this may not be 'direct complicity', it reflects an institutional complicity.

Reshaping the SAP so that it becomes a competent source of community protection will be a mammoth task. The central issue involved in this task will not, however, as Waddington suggests be a problem of vision, but rather a matter of the will of the State to reshape the management and rank-and-file culture of South African policing (Weitzer 1990) by putting in place internal and external mechanisms of control that are backed with the sanctions required to give them effect (Shearing 1991b). The 'interests and capacities of the post-settler regime' constitute, as Weitzer (1990: 18) has argued, 'the master variable' in determining the transformation of security policy and practice. Critical to the establishment of a police dedicated to community protection will be a state with the will and capacity to require the SAP to 'cut free from the past' (Weitzer 1990) through demilitarization and abandonment of its 'security policing' functions. Whether such a governmental will is forthcoming will depend on the outcome of the political contest that is taking place over the control of the South African state.

If the political will to establish the SAP as a crime-fighting force dedicated to the protection of communities is established, there is enough understanding of the processes of transformation, and what is required of state police in their role as bearers of force in the service of community protection, to ensure that a new SAP can be created despite the difficulties. In this respect, the changes taking place in countries like Namibia, and similar dramatic changes that have taken place in police forces in a variety of places, where there is demonstrated political determinism, provides grounds for considerable optimism.

Whether there will be the political will and capacity to bring about the organizational changes that this first level of reform requires, depends on a variety of factors – including the extent to which the police and other security establishments are subject to 'systemic liberalization' (Weitzer 1990: 10). This is required both during the transition period as 'lasting, substantive democratization requires liberation of the security system' (Weitzer 1990: 12), and thereafter (Mathews 1986: 290). Systemic change at this level is crucial to what has become almost a mantra of transition in South Africa, namely 'creating a climate for reform'.

A key factor in the transformation of the security forces – both as a result of direct influence on these forces and the creation of the will and capacity on the part of the State to change – is the impact of civil society. Weitzer cites Stepan (1988) as follows in drawing attention to the importance of an active civil society for transformation: 'lasting democratization requires social forces to "revalorize democracy" and commit themselves to holding security agencies accountable' (Weitzer 1990: 22). Thus, in contrast to the situation in 'settler' states where the security establishment 'actively seeks to maximize their autonomy from civil society' (Weitzer 1990: 6), what is required is systemic change which will enhance the influence of a broadly based civil society over security forces that will counter the 'differential access' to influence over the 'security core' (Weitzer 1990: 9; 1991) that characterizes 'sectarian' societies and, of course, many other more liberal societies where partisan influence so often dominates (Morgan 1987). An active civil society will also directly influence the will and capacity of a new state to bring about change in the security forces (Weitzer 1990: 22–3).

Finally, at this level, there is the issue of the social values underpinning the new state police of South Africa. Standards are required to act as the totemic device by which the community will guide the practices of the state police in the implantation of commitment to the conception of social justice that we have termed dominion. State policing has always operated with partisanship as guided in practice by the signposts of the police culture and by the imperatives of the institutional order. Finite resources have been translated into selectivity in order maintenance and in law enforcement. Traditionally, and inevitably, in societies structured to maintain social imbalance, that partisanship has always been borne most negatively by the lower social strata and by disadvantaged groups. To paraphrase a famous quote from Anatole France, the application of an equal measure to manifest unequals simply increases inequality. As the jurist, Pashukanis, once argued succinctly, conferring legal equality upon social unequals serves to reaffirm their inequality. Inequality of condition in the townships, and among different social groups, as compared with the white suburbs, makes their inhabitants more susceptible to unequal sanctioning. Simply put, the problem of the battered wife is not to be solved by reconciling her as a subordinate with the no-longer-battering husband. What the new South Africa requires is a system of ordering for social unequals that treats them as unequals, but in a positive fashion, in order to compensate for that social inequality. Legitimacy of a new policing system rests in part on the structured commitment of state police officers to recognize that social inequality, and to seek to compensate for it by positive rather than negative actions. It is this that is the vision of dominion. As Jefferson and Grimshaw (1984) have argued in their perceptive approach to police accountability in the UK, public or social justice is critical to developing policing positively. Police responsiveness to the community should be assessed not in terms of whether or not it fits within the broad remit of a notional democratic mandate but in terms of its commitment to act within the criteria of social justice. Democratic control of state policing means the ability to judge and sanction police members who do not reflect, in their discretionary practice, their commitment to a code of social justice that seeks to realize dominion.

POLICING THROUGH CIVIL SOCIETY

This brings us to the second level of reform which will be our principal concern in the remainder of this chapter. What is required at this level is a new vision of policing rather than the implementation of an existing one. The question to be addressed here is what role civil society should play in the promotion of dominion and how this is to be accomplished. The principles we have outlined provide general guidance. They argue that reform at this level should seek to place responsibility for policing on local structures that would be required to direct, support, foster and coordinate peace-keeping as a central feature of civil society.

This proposal is very different from what is normally meant by community policing or schemes that seek to enhance community police liaison (Weitzer 1992). These schemes focus attention on the police and involve endeavours to provide greater citizen support for the police, greater input into what the police do, as well as more ongoing supervision of the police by the community. What we have in mind would certainly contribute to these objectives but these effects are secondary. At the heart of our proposal is a scheme which will promote self-policing that operates within an environment that permits it to be coordinated with state policing. Our concern here is the promotion or 'resurrection of civil society' (O'Donnell and Schmitter 1986, cited in Weitzer 1990) in ways that will ensure it plays a central role, not only in monitoring and contributing to what the police do, but in taking direct responsibility for policing as part of a radical process of democratization.

In middle- and upper-class communities, this would mean on the one hand encouraging and facilitating existing networks of private policing and, on the other, monitoring these systems to ensure that those who provide these policing services comply with constitutional guarantees of dominion. In this arena, the issue of restraint will be the principal policy concern as there is a long history of abuse involving private policing within South Africa (Grant 1989). In poorer communities, the focus of reform would be on creating networks of civil policing by developing those features of 'popular policing' that are consistent with the democratic and constitutional principles that dominion requires. Daniel Nina provides an account of recent developments in Alexandra that illustrate this policing of civil society according to popular justice standards:

> the interaction with the [state] police or state institutions, does not mean that they have become what is popularly known as a 'sell-out'. In fact, the police are still not trusted by most of the people in the community, but the interaction with them [police]

is determined by the community itself. When and for what reason to call the police is a community decision.

Serious matters such as rape and murder, will require the [state] police – a decision taken since 1990. But other crime-related matters such as theft or burglary, will be sorted out, most of the time, between the community structures. In other words, the community has learnt to operate, developing its own culture and practices of popular justice so that when necessary it interacts with the state legality.

(Nina 1992: 21)

It is at this second level of civil policing that reform is going to be the most difficult because it is here that novel structures need to be developed.

Towards a new civil policing

We begin our discussion of reform at this second level with the report of a 'multi-national panel' (of which one of us was a member) that has recently reported to the Goldstone Commission on the 'lawful control of demonstrations' (Panel 1992). What is significant about this report, for our purposes, is that it implicitly accepts the conception of liberty as dominion and applies the reform approach we have outlined to an area of policing that, as the label 'riot policing' makes clear, has traditionally been regarded as a 'hard' rather than a 'soft' policing arena.

The Panel developed its approach by doing what we have argued must be done, namely looking to 'experiments' at the cutting edge of policing rather than to established models. These practices were then used to develop principles from which they derived their recommendations. The nub of their report is their proposal that the effective policing of demonstrations requires the participation of both the state and civil policing institutions. This civil–state co-ordination is spelt out in the Executive summary to the Panel's Report as follows:

A democratic public can properly insist upon demonstrations and protests being carried out peacefully without violence. The responsibility corresponding to that right is agreed in the first instance by three parties:

– those organizing demonstrations
– the local police or state authorities, and
– the police

The Chief of the Rotterdam police terms this tripartite allocation of responsibility, the 'safety triangle'. Properly managing a demonstration requires combining and coordinating tangible resources of these three parties to assure that the demonstration will be peaceful as well as effective. The relevant resources for managing the demonstration thus go far beyond those in the hands of the state police. They include provision of necessary facilities (e.g. first aid stations or toilets), of speaker systems and platforms, and of help in dealing with vehicular or pedestrian traffic. Both by careful pre-event planning and by coordination during the demonstration itself, the three partners can draw upon these as well as the authority of the organizers and of police in managing the demonstration (Panel 1992: i–ii).

The Panel's proposals for this tripartite conception (Ayers and Braithwaite 1992) of policing responsibility arose out of a review of 'riot policing' in several Western democracies that revealed not only a growing recognition that policing should be orientated towards problem-solving but that it should involve civil society and the State as policing with both the determination and the capacity to engage in order maintenance. In each of these countries, the development of public order policing had been guided by a recognition that the coercive capacities available to the State provide only one of the means, and often the least important, required in the maintenance of public order. The Panel was also cognizant of the extent to which the use of civil resources, in the form of marshals, had become an effective feature of crowd control in South Africa and in Namibia where the demonstrations and the rallies associated with their first elections had been policed almost entirely by marshals.

It was this combination of domestic and international experience that persuaded the Panel to propose the adoption of a strategy of community policing, in the literal sense of self-policing, in partnership with state policing as the basis for the maintenance of public order within South Africa. What it sought to achieve through its proposal for the establishment of 'safety triangles' to plan for and police demonstrations was a system that would provide both for local definitions of order that were consistent with more 'general standards', and the routine coordination of civil and state resources to maintain this order. Significantly, the SAP, along with the ANC and the Inkatha Freedom Party, have endorsed this proposal.[11]

These proposals for a policing strategy that is grounded in and respects both interest-based and territorial community concerns (Santos 1992; Giddens 1991) may well prove, in retrospect, to be the turning point in the emergence of a 'post-Boipatong Era' in which South African policing leaves behind its back-to-front, upside-down, looking-glass character. South Africa's tragedy is also its opportunity. The transitional period is a conjunctural one – the crisis at so many levels of the State and civil society creates a seedbed for dramatic change. This is the time for creating an imaginative vision of a partnership of state and do-it-yourself policing. Setting out the terms of this partnership requires both vision and imagination for it is out of dreams, not merely the ashes of the past, that a new, and hopefully better, tomorrow will be born.

Dreams, however, if they are to shape practices, must recognize the realities of the present and the past. In South Africa, these realities include the enormous hostility of many black people to the SAP. This hostility extends to the very idea that is central to this text, namely, that policing can be liberating; that it can, and should, promote dominion. We recognize this not as a prohibition to reform but as a challenge which must be confronted. Our recommendation for a dual civil-state policing system that arises from our acceptance of the lessons of the second narrative, also requires, as we noted in Chapter Six, that we address the legacy of suspicion that surrounds dual policing systems in both colonial and more recent contexts. Criticisms of dual policing systems are especially telling in countries like South Africa where there has been a history of 'the recruitment of indigenous people to enforce the laws of the colonial power' (Havemann 1988: 72; Brogden 1987a and 1987b). In such circumstances, policing, including policing that involves people from oppressed communities, is, more often than not, no more than

> the terror necessary to keep an exploited population in check. If that policing is done by the locals themselves, so much the better. It is cheaper and hides the power and interests of the exploited classes behind the facade of service and accommodation.
>
> (Marenin 1992: 21)

Dual policing in South Africa is associated with poor justice for poor people. It has been used as a tool of apartheid to widen the net of social control. 'Bantu courts' have operated as a second tier of a dual system in which black people were not only patronized but were subordinated to a body of 'traditional' law that was used to serve the ends of the oppressors. In South Africa, duality of policing has mirrored the duality of apartheid and enforced its provisions. It has promoted one law and one order for whites and another for blacks. As the Hoexter Commission argued:

> that inhabitants of the same country should purely on the grounds of race be criminally prosecuted in separate courts . . . is by any civilised standard unnecessary, humiliating, and repugnant.
>
> (quoted in Corder 1983)

We are aware of these criticisms, and more besides. However, we believe duality in policing can, should and indeed must be rescued from its colonial past and its contemporary abuses. In arguing for this we are especially mindful of the fact that a system of dual policing already exists in middle-class and corporate arenas in South Africa and elsewhere. In these areas, what is provided is not 'inferior', 'colonial' policing but enhanced protection for the communities involved. Most middle- and upper-class Westerners, for instance, are in the course of a normal day, exposed to both state and civil policing structures in coordinated networks that both enhance their security and give them greater control over what security will mean.

Ericson points to this multi-layered feature of contemporary policing in commenting upon a story about a Canadian police officer who completed sixteen separate reports and forms in the course of investigating a single traffic accident. The 'knowledge' generated by these forums was channelled to a variety of institutional locations both inside and outside the police. What this anecdote indicates is that public policework is entwined with a number of other institutions involved in the provision of security, and that these institutions 'have . . . needs and interests that the police respond to routinely. . . . Policing involves myriad public and private institutions, including the public police, that act as guarantors of security with respect to particular matters over which they have jurisdiction. The public police constitute, and are constituted by, a wide range of public and private arrangements in society' (1992: 5–6). Such multi-layered systems of policing and regulation are common in the Western world (Johnston 1992; Macauley 1986; Santos 1992).

Civil policing structures that have not been colonized by the State already exist within black townships in South Africa. Their acceptability to communities, however, depends on their isolation from the SAP. This opposition to the State and state policing operates both as a source of legitimacy and a difficulty, for this opposition promotes a vacuum of constitutional restraint. This lack of deterrent has led both to the exploitation of popular civil policing initiatives by an oppressive government, by gangsters, by warlords and by unruly youths. What is required, and what the Goldstone Panel has sought to do, is to rekindle a positive vision of civil policing that works within and respects constitutional guarantees that promote dominion. It is this dream that provides the motivation for so many of the popular policing initiatives that have sprung up in black communities all over South Africa.

TOWARDS A PARALLEL SYSTEM

The place to start in developing a vision of new forms of policing that gives expression to the principles we have outlined is with a 'bottom-heavy' system that has as its foundation a network of civil institutions. Policing, it must be recognized, is a problem-solving process in which the resources available to the state police – in particular, coercion and the authority of the State – are best deployed in combination with other resources located within the institutions of civil society. If civil peace is to be guaranteed then a wide range of resources and knowledges should be employed. The challenge is to find ways of doing this on a routine basis in ways that will ensure that civil institutions will have a say in the definitions of local orders (be this how a march is to be organized, what is acceptable in a local park, what sports fans should be permitted to do in demonstrating their pleasure and displeasure, what noise levels should be permitted on a street, etc.) the decisions to be made about their preservation and the resources to be deployed.

This challenge, as we have suggested, has been responded to with enormous success in corporate contexts where civil authorities have, for a variety of reasons, accepted responsibility for policing to such an extent that private or civil policing is now a significant feature of most Western countries (Johnston 1992). These are onerous responsibilities but they also are empowering ones that permit those who are directly affected by an order to take primary responsibility for its definition and promotion. The acceptance of an obligation for peace-keeping has provided the middle and upper classes, and the corporate entities that promote their interests, with control over decisions as to how order will be maintained. Under this arrangement, middle and upper class policing has became a fractured rather than a unified system in which policing is undertaken by a host of different civil authorities who coordinate resources with those of the State in the maintenance of order. These arrangements are 'untidy' in the sense that what happens differs from one location to another. What one hotelier, for instance, does to provide for order for their guests and staff may be very different from what another one does. These differences are, however, limited by national and regional requirements – property law, contract law, criminal law, labour law and so on.

It was just such a scheme of local, plural autonomy operating within broadly defined limits that the Goldstone Panel has argued should be institutionalized with respect to the policing of demonstrations. In the system they envisage, the police and the organizers of demonstrations should each be responsible for the problem-solving that the policing of demonstrations requires, with the organizers having the initial and primary responsibility. Thus, for example, it is the organizers who, after having agreed to conditions that will govern a march, are expected to enforce the order established by these conditions through the mobilization of trained marshals.

The Panel recognized that any system that sought to exploit a civil capacity for policing must recognize the very real potential for harm that accompanies the use of resources. This potential, they argued however, was not a cause for making the policing the exclusive responsibility of the public police. Rather it requires the establishment of procedures to limit this harm in the same way that the use of the state police requires the institution of protections in the face of the enormous potential for harm posed by these police. In developing these limits the Panel insisted first, that the use of physical force as a policing resource should, with strictly limited exceptions, be monopolized by the state police and second, that national criteria be established to regulate the contours of the relationship of the civil–state arrangements and the limits of local definitions of order. Third, they responded to the parallel danger of civil policing simply becoming a tool of the central state by insisting that the primary responsibility for policing rest with civil institutions and by making the local authority the locus of political accountability with a judicial appeal mechanism for challenging specific decisions of this authority.

These proposals for a decentralized system of civil–state policing provide a model, not simply for the policing of demonstrations, but for policing more generally. While their concern is with demonstrations, there is nothing in the model they outline that limits it to such events. On the contrary, their recognition that a wide variety of institutions and communities associated with them, whose interests range from the cultural to the political, have both the will and capacity to engage in policing, point to the more general application of their proposals.

A dual policing system built on these principles not only responds to the problems associated with 'popular policing' we reviewed in the previous chapter but impinges directly on the problems associated with private security in South Africa where 'armed response' is a common feature and where formal coordination with the state police and the local authority within a regulatory scheme that deliberately seeks to integrate resources and protect dominion is not required (Grant 1989). Acceptance of the Panel's model as a basis for a dual civil–state system of police would thus respond to the potential for abuse of both private security and popular policing – including the concern over private armies.

The challenge in applying the Panel's recommendations as the basis for a dual policing system more generally is to develop forums for negotiating the deployment of a network of inter-institutional policing resources to promote locally negotiated orders. What is required is for every interest-based and every corporate and residential community to be part of a network of triangles of safety in which the definition of order and the requirements of policing are the subject of an ongoing dialogue.[12] The Panel's conception of policing as orchestrated through such a network provides the basis for generalizing their recommendations.

Within this conception, what the transformation of South African policing requires, is the development of an infrastructure at the local government level that can accommodate and coordinate a multiplicity of 'triangles of safety'. A start has been made in developing such a structure in the National Peace Accord in its proposals for the establishment of dispute resolution committees at both the regional and the local level. What is required is a mechanism that local groups and the state police can use to develop 'contracts' with respect to the role each should be playing in keeping the peace. We propose, following the Goldstone Panel, that such mechanisms form part of the bureaucracy of local government. What we envisage is a system whereby the state police are required to contact local communities (both territorial and functional) and that these communities in turn should be required to contact the state police, and that these interactions should take place under the auspices of the local authorities. What is required is a flexible negotiative structure in which the order that is to be achieved is a consequence of a dynamic process of interaction between local and state agencies.

That such a network can be quickly and effectively established is evident in the extraordinary speed with which negotiations over demonstrations have been established following the release of the Panel's report, and the extraordinary changes this has wrought in the policing of public demonstrations within South Africa. The successful policing of the ANC/COSATU-initiated 'mass action' of August 1992, in which hundreds of thousands of people took to the streets and occupied buildings and parts of cities, is eloquent testimony to the practicality and success of the Panel's proposals. So too is the terrible tragedy of the march into the Ciskei in September 1992, when twenty-eight people were shot dead when the Ciskei security forces did not abide by the Goldstone Panel's proposals.

At the core of the Goldstone Panel's proposals and our recommendation that their scheme be generalized, is a claim that there is a determination as well as a capacity on the part of civil institutions to become directly involved in policing. This claim will be questioned by some in the light of the historical argument that the 'new' state police owe their existence in large part to a lack of will on the part of communities to undertake their own policing (Critchley 1979). However, it is precisely changes in this willingness, motivated by changes in the organization of social life, that account for the emergence of private security (Johnston 1992; South 1988). Furthermore, as we have argued in Chapter Six, there is widespread evidence of commitment to direct civil involvement in policing in popular ordering initiatives. Similarly the Goldstone Panel noted the extensive voluntary use of civil policing in the arena of demonstrations both here and elsewhere. In each of these cases the will to participate in self-policing is related to the direct control it provides over orders that directly effect peoples' lives.

In recognizing the commitment on the part of communities to participate directly in policing, the Goldstone Panel, however, also argued for the importance of seeking to maintain and foster this will by providing legal incentives. The argument they developed was that the right to protest carried with it an associated obligation to ensure that the protest was peaceful. This responsibility placed on the organizers of demonstrations a duty to ensure that protest was peaceful. This 'due care' responsibility is well recognized in law and it provides a legal incentive for much self-regulation including the self-policing provided by private security. Thus, to use the example of a hotelier again, there is an obligation on someone who offers space for hire to take due care in providing for the safety of those who will occupy that space. It is this due care responsibility that provides the basis for generalizing the legal incentives that the Panel proposed. What is required is to develop the implications of this obligation in the variety of circumstances that include such things as the requirement to maintain a peaceful neighbourhood. The commitment to self-policing will be secured if the institutional incentives are re-inforced with legal incentives. In taking this position, we are drawing on the ancient tradition of 'frankpledge' that was so essential to early Anglo-Saxon and Norman policing arrangements (Critchley 1979) and arguing for its rebirth and revitalization.

Policing reform in the new South Africa should both seek to empower people at a very local level to determine the order in which they will live their lives and to police it themselves. What is required to set out the specifics of such a system is the establishment of a National Task Force, under the auspices of a legitimate authority to develop detailed proposals on 'self-policing' with respect to a legislative framework and model procedures for the establishment of networks of 'safety triangles'. This task force's mandate should include a requirement that it examine the existing legal framework for, and practices of, private security with a view to making specific recommendations as to the control of the private security industry within South Africa in ways that will ensure that it operates within the context of 'safety triangles' and national standards of public justice that will ensure that broader community interests are not trampled on.

CONCLUSION

In our recommendations for a dual system of policing, we have recognized the existence of networks of cross-cutting, interest-based communities, the necessity of recognizing broad as well as sectarian concerns in any attempt to order the affairs of people who share a territory, the critical importance of central control over the distribution of physical force and the wide distribution of knowledge and resources relevant to policing within civil society.

Specifically in arguing that much of the burden of policing should rest with civil institutions, we have sought to recognize that governance is a civil as well as a state responsibility and that an acceptance of this should guide policing policy. This has led us to propose that the traditional conception of policing as an activity that the State provides for passive 'clients' should be replaced with one that recognizes these 'clients' as active co-producers of the security policing seeks to guarantee. In taking this position, we have argued that South Africans should eschew those reform initiatives which argue that the state police should become general-purpose problem-solvers and instead map out for themselves a process of reform that emphasizes self-policing as the front line of peace-keeping and that insists that the state police play a limited, albeit vital, role in a problem-solving network.

In making these proposals we have argued for a reform process that recognizes community differences and encourages community participation and control over ordering. At the same time, we have insisted upon national limits on the deployment of coercive force and on local definitions of order. These proposals seek to respond to the substantive inequalities that have accorded middle- and upper-class communities considerable autonomy over their own policing by making similar possibilities available to those who have been excluded from these advantages.

Liberty, understood as dominion, will be enhanced in South Africa to the extent to which the determination and capacity for order definition and order maintenance is located, both in the institutions of civil society and the State. Bringing South Africans out through the mirror of their looking-glass world requires a recognition that the conventional top-down, state-centred, conception of policing must be (to mix metaphors) turned on its proverbial head. If South Africans are successful in doing this, they will not only go a long way towards realizing their dream of a new society which will empower those whom apartheid has deprived, but they will be contributing to the emergence of more democratic and responsive policing everywhere.

Notes

METHODOLOGICAL NOTE

There is a methodological impasse, broken with difficulty. It is no fault of critical South African academics that research on policing in South Africa is notable for its relative barrenness (Frankel 1980). One commentator on South African policing (Brewer 1990) who has conducted careful research in a not dissimilar Emergency context, that of a Northern Ireland police station, would have received no such access in pre-Peace Accord South Africa. Research on policing is always difficult. In Western societies, the tradition that everything about policing is defined as secret until proven otherwise has been paramount. In South Africa, that problem has been compounded by law. There is little of the research that has deluged Western criminology – from police culture to problems of police accountability. The 'closed' nature of the political system together with the military nature of the SAP means that most state police practices have been defined as beyond legitimate public concern. Parliamentary debates have indicated that the line between criticizing the police and subverting the 'national interest' has been a very thin one. State paranoia over police secrecy has evinced a variety of legislation. For example, the Police Act 1958 prevented publication of 'untrue material' relating to police misconduct with the onus of proving the veracity of the material on the publisher. Act 64 of 1979 placed an onus on the person to prove his/her allegations against the police with a penal sanction of R10,000 or five years' imprisonment for failure (as used most recently against the *Weekly Mail* [*Cape Times* 4 April 1991]. In that case, as the *Cape Times* said, it was 'rightly perceived as a means of covering up police transgression'.) The Police Amendment Acts 1958 and 1980 prevented the publication of information relating to the constitution, conditions, methods of deployment, or movement of any force concerned with the prevention of 'terrorism'. Since 1989, the system has become technically more open in the anodyne Annual SAP Report.

A principal tactic of the SAP, and more generally the South African government, in responding to allegations of police brutality, has been to discredit affidavits by victims and newspaper reports as 'politically motivated', 'subjective' and 'unscientific', (most recently in the case of Dr Gluckman's revelations over 'deaths in custody') while at the same time making it exceedingly difficult to gather more reliable evidence. There is no doubt that such affidavits and news reports are sometimes partisan or false and the failure of the *Weekly Mail* (although we pay due homage to some of the courageous investigative journalism that has sought to expose the crimes of apartheid) adequately to document charges it had made before the Goldstone Commission into violence and intimidation, is a case in point. In relying on newspaper reports as a major source of illustrative material, we acknowledge that we have in those instances used material whose reliability can be questioned. However, our use of such material is, we believe, defensible in view of the remarkable consistency between such 'subjective' reports and findings that have been exhaustively substantiated. While there may be specific cases of victims' reports being exaggerated, or simply false, the sheer volume and consistency of those reports requires that they be taken seriously at the same time as the difficulties they present are acknowledged. To refuse to make any use of victim-based reports, because it is so difficult to gather validated evidence within South Africa, would not only fail to recognize an important source of information but would unnecessarily discredit the testimony of hundreds of thousands of victims whose only motivation has been to tell the story of their experiences.

1   Through the looking-glass

1 Adriaan Vlok, the Minister of Law and Order who lost his post in the context of the 'Inkathagate' scandal.
2 It is this distinction that underlies the differences between those South Africans who believe that the protections of a new constitution should be limited to traditional first generation rights (political) – that guarantee formal equality, and those who believe that a new constitution should include second (socio-economic) and third (peace, security, identity, dignity, environment) generation rights – that seek to guarantee sub-

stantive as well as formal equality (Sachs 1990: 8–9). The idea of dominion is fundamental to the African National Congress proposals for Bill of Rights that argues for an acceptance of all three generations of rights in a constitution that 'acknowledge[s] the importance of securing minimum conditions of decent and dignified living for all South Africans' (ANC 301: 15).

3 See the original collection of essays on colonial policing by Anderson and Killingray (1991) and also Brogden (1988 *et al.*).

4 Davis (1990), in his account of the private and state policing of Los Angeles, provides a vivid account of the experiences of the urban lower classes, in a lucid study that predates the Los Angeles riots of May 1992.

5 We use the term 'privatization' in this text to refer to the return of what are at present state-controlled assets to individuals, communities and social classes in civil society. That usage differs markedly from the practice of privatization in certain Western societies, which involves the transfer of state assets to corporate profit-making companies

6 For examples of the early critical literature on definitions of policing, see Cain (1979), Marenin (1992) and Klockars (1985). Conventional definitions of the state police as *internal* ordering institutions are flummoxed by South African state practices. The SAP has frequently engaged in external actions – the ill-fated 'Police Battalion' spent most of the Second World War in captivity after surrendering at Tobruk. During the Rhodesian/Zimbabwean struggle, some 3,000 SAP members were used in support of the state 'security' force. SAP members participated in the invasion of the sovereign state of Angola. Conversely, the South African Defence Force (SADF) has acted internally – suppressing industrial risings and Afrikaner rebellion during the period of Union status and has been frequently called upon to act in the townships in more recent years. The traditional divisions between the military and the police task have largely disappeared in South Africa (Cawthra 1992: 10).

7 On the government side there has been much said about matters such as prioritizing crime detection rather that state security with the subsequent merger of the Security Police and the detective branch into a new Crime Combatting and Investigating Department. The White Paper that recommended this was notable only for the absence of any comment on the question of democratic control and accountability. There has been a haphazard implementation of a few reforms – for example, setting up local police community forums; negotiating codes of conduct between police and local communities; integrating training facilities (see Rauch 1992b). Wonderland has produced more idiosyncratic developments – a consultant in 'creative thinking' has been hired to teach the SAP how to avoid being racist, Casspir police vehicles are to lose their camouflage and be repainted blue as an aid to a bobby-on-the-beat image, and the Riot Squad has been renamed. Most recently, and most encouragingly, the Minister of Law and Order has announced new complaint provisions and the retirement of approximately a third of the General Staff as the start of a process of restructuring.

Detailed police reform has not figured high on the ANC's agenda. Transitional demands have included calls for less aggressive crowd control methods; some local accountability; the dismissal of brutal police officers; the integration of ANC personnel into the force; establishing a 'public policing committee' to govern training, recruitment and management; an independent complaints agency; the enactment of a code of conduct for all police personnel; the limiting of police armaments to only those necessary for 'normal' law enforcement and the detection of crime; and an affirmative action programme to promote black officers. The ANC also planned ground-level monitoring devices – a Police Ombudsman working with Reporting Officers (envisaged as independent lawyers), and the establishment of 'Certified Community Monitors' with independent powers – such as unfettered access to police stations. Disciplinary hearings would be publicly open and include civilian representation (see ANC proposals to CODESA 1992). Academics have laid out a tentative agenda. For instance, Weitzer (1990) has proposed a number of pre-conditions – the scrapping of the discriminatory legislation; the reorganization and retraining of police riot squads in less lethal weaponry; tighter selection controls to screen out Rambo-style and racist recruits, and more politically neutral forms of training. Precedents derived from the transformation of the Namibian Police have included instituting forums of police–community contact (Police Public Relations Committees) and the importance of demilitarization (Nathan 1990). Baynham (1990) has listed several priorities – increases in pay and better conditions of work; a doubling of force size; crime control rather than security prioritization; a separate riot squad and consequent removal of heavy weapons from largely untrained officers; affirmative action over black recruitment and promotion; and a measure of decentralization. Independently of specific problems with all these proposals, they suffer from the myopic conceptual problem that the reform of South African policing means little more than changing the state police.

In noting these recent proposals for SAP reform, we should recognize that there is little new about such orthodox attempts to grapple with the essence of SAP structure and practices. For example, as early as the mid-1930s, there were clear arguments articulated for a reconstruction of the SAP:

> there is no doubt that the bullying methods of certain members of the police force may be ascribed, in part at least, to a predominantly military training. Though an amount of military organisation and control is essential, more emphasis should be laid on the civil duties of the police and less on their military duties, more emphasis on providing for the security of law-abiding citizens and less on the necessity for securing a large number of convictions.
>
> (Franklin 1935: 169)

See also Simons (1934).

8 The emerging literature on 'problem-solving' state policing is referred to in Chapter Seven. A detailed problem-solving and Community Policing reform programme for the SAP is contained in Brogden (1993) Memorandum to the Minister of Law and Order's Report to the Committee on Police Standards and Codes of Conduct, Pretoria.

2 Policing apartheid – violence within the rules

1 As reported in the House of Assembly Debates, 5 February 1982 col. 230.

2 Although there has been much talk during the current round of South African reforms about the death of apartheid, it has yet to be abolished. The eradication of the more visible features of apartheid such as 'whites only' areas and the pass laws has reshaped the surface features of apartheid but has not touched its political or economic dimensions.

3 Of shootings in the Western Cape in 1985, the UCT Medical Research Project found that more than 50 per cent of the people wounded were shot in the back (ninety-three of them being killed – *Weekly Mail* 9 May 1988). For similar examples of double-size birdshot being used without provocation by police officers, see the *Sunday Tribune* 14 December 1986 and the *Argus* 21 August 1987.

4 A similar incident is recorded in Maokeng township near Kroonstadt where two boys were killed after stoning a Protea Furnishers truck: 'The police then threw off a tarpaulin and started shooting at the unsuspecting youths' (*Star* 17 May 1990). An important analysis of policing killings (in the Western Cape) is Hansson (1989).

5 Similarly, a confessed Sobantu robber alleged a variety of assaults and torture, as he was processed through arrest to interrogation. He claimed to have been kicked all over the body, including his testicles. While naked, he had been handcuffed, and suspended on a stick between two tables – the bag over his head being drenched with water so that he could not breathe. Eventually, the stick broke and he felt a 'hot' pain in his wrists (the suggestion of electric shocks). Both arms were broken. The police claimed his injuries had been caused when he escaped and fell into a donga in the dark (*Natal Mercury* 10 September 1986).

6 There is of course now much evidence of selective assassinations by SAP officers. The former SAP Captain Dirk Coetzee's unpublished autobiography provides graphic detail of assassinations. Poison, as well as gunshots and parcel bombs were apparently common devices in dealing with ANC activists and others by the Security Police. The bungling of several such attempts does not detract from the view – if Coetzee's account is correct – that much SAP violence was organizationally-directed, if outside the criminal law.

7 A chilling display of these official explanations is to be found in the long list that scrolls by at the end of the film on Steve Biko's murder, *Cry Freedom*. See also the revelations of a state pathologist, in the *Independent* 26 July 1992 about the number of deaths in custody and the blanket refusal of the State President to recognize the reality of daily life in South African police stations. Hochschild (1991) quotes the black poet, Chris van Wyk, on such police explanations of deaths in custody:

> He fell from the ninth floor
> He hanged himself
> He slipped on a piece of soap while washing
> He hanged himself
> He slipped on a piece of soap while washing

He fell from the ninth floor
He hanged himself while washing
He slipped from the ninth floor
He hung from the ninth floor
He slipped on the ninth floor while washing
He fell from a piece of soap while slipping
He hung from the ninth floor
He washed from the ninth floor while slipping
He hung from a piece of soap while washing

Brutality in obtaining confessions has a long history. Duncan (1964) quotes one boastful police detective, explaining how an investigating officer made local black people confess to cattle theft:

> There are three ways. The first is that we hit them. The second is electric shocks. And the third is the gasmask. The shock usually works as they are terrified of electricity. But the gasmask always works. That way you put the gasmask over his head. Then you tell him that if he won't talk, you'll stop the air going in so he can't breathe. Then you stop the air. When he faints you let the air go in again and bring him round. Then you tell him that this time you were merciful. You brought him back from the other side. The next time, if he doesn't talk, you're going to let him stay there. When this happens, they always talk.

Although Duncan's detailed accounts of torture by the SAP is now thirty years' old, the most recent evidence (Fernandez 1991) suggests that while some things may change in the SAP, brutality to exhort confessions does not.

Understanding police brutality in obtaining confessions in South Africa has been too focused on the perceived pathology of individual police officers. While police brutality in that context clearly owes something to the aberrational characteristics of individual police officers, effective controls over it must pay more attention to systemic factors. In practice, most evidence given in court in South Africa appears to derive from confessions. Detective work is limited to post facto collation of material. Limited resources and historical tradition has resulted in the confession becoming the 'normal' way of obtaining a result. One clear way of lessening police violence is to disallow confessional evidence (unless accompanied by severe safeguards). While that situation might make policework more difficult in achieving convictions, it would vastly improve the experience of the many thousands of South Africans subject to the police brutalizing experience – on this see M. Brogden (1993) 'The Social Organisation of Police Torture', paper given at the British Criminological Conference, University of Cardiff, July.

8 See the original discussion of these concepts in McConville and Baldwin (1981) and their use in the South African context by Steytler (1987).

9 Similarly, Minister Le Grange: 'and the public could not be jeopardised by the actions of individual policemen' (*E.P. Herald* 2 October 1985). See among many similar aberrational accounts, the Cillie Commission 1980 on the police and SADF killings in Soweto in the mid-1970s:

the police themselves used force but only as much as was needed to maintain order or restore the peace and order to protect lives and property. Rioters were not treated roughly, but firmly. It was possible that there may have been exceptional cases where a policeman went too far because of his own mental makeup.

(Commission of Inquiry into the Riots at Soweto and elsewhere
from 16 June 1976 to 28 February 1977)

10 A more extreme version of this complicity is the extent to which the police have encouraged and cooperated with vigilante groups – see Chapter Four and Cawthra (1992: 12–13) and Haysom (1989).

11 There is little external access to records of police deviance other than that which appears in the Court records. The SAP Annual Reports never record offences committed by police officers. One alternative source, the Commission for Administration's Annual Reports, analyses criminal offences committed by other public functionaries, but members of the police are not within its scope. SAP Standing Orders governing disciplinary matters are not readily available as public documents. Evidence on the degree of police deviance and on the reaction by the State to it, therefore, is patchy.

12 In part, this permissive quality of law with regard to policing relates to the general powers of the SAP. Despite the Roman-Dutch tradition, complexly, criminal law draws largely on Anglo-Saxon common law. This second source has a particular implication for the totality of the power of the SAP – the latter's possession of twin powers of arrest and prosecution. The power to arrest, to lay and specify charges, and to conduct prosecutions (although rarely practised), is at the bedrock of police legal authority. The police in South Africa consequently exercise considerably more authority over suspects as compared with most civil law countries (where police authority has traditionally been limited to the arrest function) and common law countries (such as Canada with a developed separate prosecutorial office) and even England and Wales, which belatedly recognized the enormity of the combined power (Royal Commission on Criminal Justice, 1981). In its inheritance of English criminal law, the South African criminal justice process and state police institution has not been exposed to the critique of that duality which has occurred elsewhere. By this criterion alone, the legal status of the SAP is anomalous. On proposals for change with regard to certain of these matters, see the discussion in Chapter Five.

13 The legal accountability of the South African police officer is confused. In practice, the law appears to allow the State to disavow any action by a police officer that embarrasses it in front of an international audience. It enables the South African state in certain circumstances to escape liability for the wrongful acts of police which can be explained away as aberrational. This discretion originates in the English legal doctrine that the police officer is an independent professional citizen free from control of state – but this is anomalous in South Africa where the police officer is prima facie a servant of the State. There appears to be a conflict between common law and statute in determining the legal status of police officers – for a detailed discussion see Milton (1967) and Dendy (1989).

14 As in the extraordinary case of the private security officer Louis van Schoor (*Independent on Sunday* 5 April 1992). Over a four-year period, Van Schoor shot at least 101 people, killing 39 of them. In at least 25 of the fatalities, he was cleared of any illegal action, under section 49 (2) of the Criminal Procedure Act (also Chapter Four, note 23).

15 Police killings under this clause rely in part on the ancient notion of the police officer as a citizen-in-uniform. Police officers assume the citizen's right to defend his or her property. This is a dubious proposition legally in South Africa and perhaps more importantly, ignores the fact that, unlike citizens, the police have alternative resources to that of physical force. A citizen has only him or herself. Conversely, the police are more disposed to kill because they have firearms readily available, unlike most private citizens, and are by training and attitude predisposed to use them.

16 The euphemism of 'assisting police with their enquiries' (already abolished in England and Wales, from which legal system it derives, because of its misuse by the police) is of major assistance in avoiding legal control. The suspect's position is only formally voluntary because he or she will be arrested if they do not agree to accompany the police. In that case, the police are not required to inform suspects of their rights not to go to station or to answer any question. The 'helping with enquiries' euphemism was abolished in England and Wales by the Police and Criminal Evidence Act 1984 (PACE) because of the way it allowed the state police to avoid formal restraints. It remains largely unchallenged in South Africa (see Chapter Five). Similarly, the abolition in Britain of the Judges Rules by PACE because of their lack of sanctioning authority has not been paralleled in South Africa.

17 The requirement of section 13 of the ISA on the police to provide humane treatment is simply an internal administrative direction to the police and not subject to judicial interpretation. It is left to the police to give content to the terms 'humane manner' and 'rule of decency'.

18 There are also specific legal problems in checking on the police. There are substantial discretionary powers vested in them by the criminal laws – for example, in the powers affecting the holding of drug suspects. A person who appears to be withholding information may be arrested and detained indefinitely for interrogation and only released when the magistrate is satisfied that she has answered the questions put by the police. In the case of suspected offences, the suspect can be kept in detention for long periods, depending on the discretion of the Attorney-General – neither the accused nor her representative has any access to that decision-making process. In the case of a person held in custody by the police, and who is believed to have been injured by them, the police can certify him or her to be too ill to come to court to make such a case – the Court will then direct the suspect or accused to be held in a specific place until well. He or she does not have access to an independent private doctor:

> in most cases the investigation of [such an] assault. . . . of a suspect is entrusted to the very same police who were implicated in the matter.
> (Fernandez 1991: 64)

19 There is limited evidence of magistrates apparently colluding directly with the SAP. In a Natal case, during the State of Emergency, the Security Police were discovered to be giving secret briefings to magistrates (*Weekly Mail* 17 January 1986). In that case the judiciary formally forbade those magistrates from undertaking any related court cases.

20 Attempts to monitor internal rules potentially rely on varied record-keeping devices (which outside the Emergency context could potentially be produced in Court as evidence) – the pocket-book diary, the personal file (one section of which deals with all complaints against the officer), the Unit Information Incident Book, the Information (communications) Book, the Section Commander reports, the Attendance Register and a Sick Book. Other reporting systems under Police Regulations include Section and Platoon Reports, radio reports and Divisional HQ Reports. Video records are also commonly available of township incidents – most divisions now have video units. There are several problems with such records – where they in fact are accurately kept. During the Emergency, the SAP relied heavily on section 66 of the Internal Security Act which allows the Minister to prohibit the use of such documents. Second, inclusion of such material (which may in any case, have been 'imaginatively constructed') in a court case, provides an apparently 'factual' account of events, thereby delegitimating other, verbal, accounts. For an important UK criticism of such recording practices see McConville *et al.* (1991) and Chapter Four (passim).

21 An academic on UNISA's Police Science degree and a former senior officer in the SAP.

22 See the overview of this argument in Weitzer and Repetti (n.d.).

23 As in many other countries, the South African Attorney General expects a higher standard of proof against the police before starting a prosecution.

24 A legal clause of 1955 stated that identity numbers need not be worn. Several months after the Peace Accord, which attempted to tighten up the requirement for police identity numbers, senior officers in several districts had still not made that requirement mandatory.

25 For other state institutions, the limit is three years.

3 Police culture and the discourse of supremacy

1 The Patrys Speurklub was sponsored by the Afrikaner National Party. Its journal (*Patrys*) urged these child police to go on raids against blacks in police vehicles 'I have again helped to arrest two Bantu, and I very much enjoyed going on these raids' boasted one child in a letter in the February 1966 issue. These child police were often rewarded for arresting blacks and encouraged to look on them with contempt, calling them such names as 'porridge lips' (October 1967 issue).

The Patrys Speurklub has been documented in several publications (see, for example, the *Manchester Guardian* 'Mr Vorter's Bedtime Stories') although accounts of it have been ruthlessly suppressed in South Africa. The most detailed account of the Patrys Speurklub is contained in John Clarke's article for the Sydney University publication *Honi Soit* (1 July

1971). A South African *Sunday Express* (31 January 1966) provides a graphic illustration:

> South Africa has about 10,000 'junior detectives' between the ages of 12 and 18 who actively help the police with their work. Four of these boys who live in Johannesburg have in the past few months arrested 15 Africans a day. . . . Armed with blank-firing pistols, whistles and handcuffs, the four youths – all aged 16 – spent their school holidays arresting an average of 15 Africans a day. All of these boys belong to a country-wide Junior Detective Club organised by the Afrikaans boys' magazine *Patrys*. . . . 'They are recognised by the SAP and our unofficial leader is Brig. Gideon Joubert, the South African C.I.D. chief. . . . Many of these boys join the police after leaving school . . . (they) have orders to make contact with the nearest police station as soon as they join the club.' The four Johannesburg boys arrested only Africans, mainly for pass and tax offences. They handed them over to the police pick-up vans or took them to the nearest police stations. They had their own equipment and were planning to equip them-selves with walkie-talkies.

We are grateful to John Clarke for this material.

2 In orthodox writings, police culture has been construed as an impedi-ment to the implementation of organizational goals (see a review of this literature in Shearing 1981a and Goldsmith 1990). As more recent research has argued, in practice, such conflict between cultural practices and the legal rules has been grossly overstated (McBarnet 1981; McConville *et al.* 1991).

3 See the BBC documentary 'Children of God' on the Cape Riot Police, April 1991.

4 See the discussion on the Groenwold as the source of legal ideology in Afrikaner nationalism in Turk (1981).

4 Township policing – experiencing the SAP

1 For example, the Boputhatswana police killed eleven people in one incident in March 1986. There is an exceptional account of the activities of the KwaZulu Police (which some observers have depicted as the private police force of the Inkatha Freedom party) in *Obstacles to Peace: the Role of the KwaZulu Police in the Natal Conflict*, Legal Resources Centre (Durban) and Human Rights Commission (Durban), June 1922. A scath-ing account of the political bias, brutality and maladministration of the KwaNdebele Police is contained in the lengthy Report of the Parsons Commission (1992).

2 See Cain (1979) for a conceptual account of defining the police in terms of its key practices.

3 See, for example, Carlin *Independent* 16 May 1992, and Beresford *Guardian* March 1992.

4 Labelled as crime and public disorder prevention – criminalizing the programmes of the extra-parliamentary opposition and 'presenting resist-

ance as senseless violence perpetuated by people who have no commitment to civilized standards' [Davis 1990: 307] in a state discourse which
has its own history. See Turk (1981) for a criminological discussion of
this issue.
5 Noted in Sachs (1975) – see other evidence in Prior (1989).
6 As in other parts of the British Empire (Brogden 1988).
7 Even the Boers themselves underwent a short period of criminalization
   by Pass under the 1901–2 British police administration.
8 See also Wells (1982) for detail of the way male state officers used the pass
   legislation as a device for 'interfering' with women. For early accounts of
   the permissive use of the Pass Laws see Burger (1943) and Simons (1956).
   Both emphasize the importance of the ubiquitous 'pick-up van':

> A cruising police motor van picks up any natives without the proper
> passes and takes them straight to the charge office. Many Johannes-
> burg Natives state that the police tear up their passes after arrest so as
> to be sure of a conviction. . . . The treatment of arrested natives is far
> from gentle: they are shoved and pulled instead of being allowed to
> walk naturally, and attempted explanations are frequently treated as
> insolence. If a man is wrongfully arrested on a Saturday night, he may
> spend the week-end in gaol and receive no compensation when the
> case is dismissed on Monday morning.
>
> (Burger: 164–50)

Simons illustrates the experience from a local folk-song

> Nantso i-pick up van.
> Manje sikwenze nto ni, Pick-up van?
> Ngapha nangapha yipick-up van.
> Manje sikwenze nto ni, Pick-up Van?
> (There is the pick-up van.
> Now, what have we done to you, Pick-up Van?
> All around us are pick-up vans.
> Now, what have we done to you, Pick-up Van?).

9 As in the raid on a Stellensbosch hostel in 1988 and the convictions of
   some 500 residents under the trespass laws.
10 The Reservations of Separate Amenities Act, 1953; Admission of Persons
   to the Republic Act, 1972, and the Prevention of Illegal Squatting Act,
   24 of 1952.
11 For example, by the Hoexter Commission on the grounds that the
   process of administrative criminalization produced contempt for the law.
12 Extraordinarily, the outside world has often had a more detailed experience of policing in the townships than have South Africans themselves.
   The South African Broadcasting Corporation has been remarkably
   restricted in its production of television news on township experiences,
   even since the lifting of the Emergency legislation. Posel (1989) gives a
   clear indication of the way such material is presented inside South Africa:

> The SADF and the SAP have been consistently presented on tele-
> vision in ways which evoked a sense of order, control and strength.

Police and soldiers were rarely seen shouting or running. If they did run – when charging a crowd of township youth or university students, for example – the action seemed organised and strategic. When collections of police or soldiers were seen standing together, lines of command and an authority structure were usually clear. Likewise when Casspirs were seen on the move, the image was one of slow, deliberate action, proceeding in a military formation . . . presented as a different sort of collectivity from that of the township residents not simply as a seething homogeneous mass in which individuality was obliterated, but rather an orderly, purposeful and controlled grouping . . . violence by the police or army was described as defensive, protective, action.

(Posel 1989: 269)

13 Superficially, there appears to be a shortfall. In 1986, there were roughly 1.4 police per 1,000 population (roughly half that of Western countries). This figure was projected to rise to 3.4 per 1,000 by 1990. A uniformed establishment of 96,000 and some 14,000 civilian employees was planned for mid-1991. Some measure of comparison is available by recognizing that the UK, with a population of 55 million, has 129,000 uniformed officers and some 55,000 civilian employees. By 1992, the SAP was planning to train some 10,000 recruits a year, having just purchased the SADF base at Oudtshoorn for that purpose. For details of SAP training, see *Human Resource Management: Training and Development of Skills*, Pretoria, 1992.

14 This is not the place to deal with an exposition on the rise in crime in South Africa but briefly the explanations that have dominated conservative South African criminology have sought to apply 'universal' explanations such as those to do with individual and/or cultural pathological approaches. For example:

It is particularly worthy of note that crimes against the person and crimes relating to indecency and immorality have a very much higher relative incidence among the Natives and Coloured than among the European.

(Freed 1963: 48)

More common in recent, years have been versions of modernization theory which have explained township criminality as an inevitable consequence of the urbanization process in the course of 'development' – see for example Ndabandaba (1987) and the review by Shearing (1990b).

What such approaches remarkably ignore is the effect of apartheid itself in creating the conditions in which intra-class crime has become one strategy for survival and produced a general brutalization of the black under-class – on this, see for example, Turk (1981), Sloth-Nielsen (1987), and Van Zyl Smit (1990).

15 Information provided by SAP generals at the meeting at SAP Headquarters with international participants at IDASA Conference on 'Policing the 1990s', Vanderjylpark, 5–8 October 1992.

16 For an early and apparently unique study of the criminal statistics see Van Zyl Smit (1977).

17 See, among many others, Carr-Hill and Stern (1979).

18 Whose contribution however is more token than real (Rauch 1991b).

19 Implemented, 1989, although to date fewer than 100,000 private security guards have registered. They have citizen powers, not police powers. Under the Act, Security Officers must be registered, observe a code of conduct, and pay a Fidelity Bond (one expensive factor that has deterred many from registering). For details, see Grant (1989).

20 Super Cops, for example, claimed an (improbable) 3–4 minute response from cars that are constantly on patrol. There are nearly 300 burglary alarm companies serving mainly the white suburbs of Cape Town alone.

21 For example, the 1983 Waterpan Mine incident:

> the Police acted only when the security division of the mine and the mine authorities called in their help because they could no longer control the situation.
>
> *(Annual Report* 1984: 9)

22 As one recent *Annual Report* describes it 'Policewomen also receive finishing-off lectures in make-up, deportment, and social etiquette'. See Rauch (1992b).

23 Carter provides a graphic game picture of the hostility to one black SAP officer who had lived in Alexandra township (by 1986, the only black SAP officer still living there) for 25 years. It was claimed that Sergeant Mothibe had killed six people in the township on different occasions and had allegedly deliberately provoked attacks in order to justify those killings. Carter also documents a mass revenge attack on Alexandra township by some three hundred black police officers from the local Kaserne Barracks on local activists in Alexandra in March 1986, after the shooting of a black officer. In that incident, some 14 people were killed by the police. No disciplinary actions or legal proceedings against those officers are recorded. See C. Carter (1991) 'Community and Conflict: the Alexandra Rebellion of 1986', *Journal of Southern African Studies*, 18, 1.

24 On these experiences see (*Daily Dispatch* 29 January 1990 (in Buffalo Flats) and *Daily Dispatch* 6 April 1990 (in East London).

25 On these incidents see *Business Day* 23 March 1990, *Daily Dispatch* 11 August 1990, *E.P. Herald* 8 August 1990, and *Cape Times* 22 March 1990.

26 On these disputes, see variously the *Weekly Mail* 11 December 1987, 14 November 1988 and 19 November 1987, and Fine (1989).

27 For an account of the way black police officers in the United States adapt to the dominant (white) police culture, see Cashmore (1991) and Chapter Five (passim).

28 For example, complainants had only 90 days to seek redress not 180 days as in the SAP.

29 With a remarkable 'mea culpa' lament at the Graaf Reciret. Conference on Affirmative Action, October 1991.

30 On W.H.A.M., see for example Boraine (1988). There was one other, albeit numerically small, form of surrogate policing. Captain Dirk Coetzee in his autobiographical account of membership of the Security Police, recounts arranging for askaris – former A.N.C. guerillas who had been captured and 'turned' – to be enrolled as SAP officers.

5 An orthodox solution – doing it the Western way

1 The Goldstone Commission was set up by the South African government, with a wide-ranging mandate and unspecified powers after the Boipatong massacre of April 1992.

2 For a summary of these arguments see Brogden *et al.* (1988). For a recent summary of the North American evidence, see Berg (1992).

3 Women account for about 5 per cent of the total complement, with only a token few reaching higher ranks.

4 See Walker (1985) for a discussion of the ineffectiveness of such affirmative action programmes in American police forces. For an account of a black SAP officer see the story of Lieutenant Colonel Tshabalala in *Criminal Justice International* 8,6, 1992:

> In the 1950s, blacks with aspiration became teachers, nurses or policemen. The jobs offered respect and some immunity from 'influx controls'. . . . . what started as a job has become a calling. Colonel Tshabalala dutifully defends his institution.
>
> (1992: 11–12).

5 For a summary of the British approaches, see Brogden *et al.* 1988.

6 See, among several examples, *Minutes of Exploratory Conference relating to the Launching of an Anti-Crime Forum for the Ibhayi Area, Port Elizabeth*, 3 March 1991.

7 Interview with Chief Jim Harding of the Halton Regional Police.

8 See the *Proposed Submission of the ANC on Interim Control of the Police*, 1992.

9 The limitations of the British schemes include; detainees cannot be visited if they are perceived by the station sergeant to be drunk and incapable, a possible physical threat to the safety of the Visitor, or (if a juvenile) without permission of the parents. The scope of monitoring is strictly limited to welfare considerations and general custodial requirements. It has nothing to do with the validity of the rationale for detention. On this, see Kemp and Morgan (1990).

10 For opposing views on reinstating lay participation in the South African criminal justice process, sees Sachs (1975) and Steyn (1971).

11 Including Business and Mobile Watch Schemes, Block Parents, and Crime Stoppers.

12 Davis in Los Angeles provides the ultimate view of NWS taken to the extremes in the defence of social privilege. Personal interaction at the IDASA Conference 'Policing in South Africa in the 1990s' vividly demonstrated the proximity between senior Watch members and the Reserve Police.

13 Yach's proposals on professionalizing the SAP include making explicit appropriate standards of behaviour (backed up by legal sanctions), improved managerial training for senior officers, and training programmes committed to consultation and participation including police involvement in victim support (*Cape Times* 27 June 1991).

14 For a detailed discussion of some of the problems with police professionalization, see Berg (1992).

15 Police professionalism has a major implication for accountability. After all
    is said and done the answer to the problem of police accountability turns
    out to be 'trust the police' or at least the abstract knowledge that defines
    them as professionals. One implication of such an approach is evident in
    the important enquiry into high-level corruption in the Queensland
    Government and Police, as illustrated in the reply of the culpable former
    Premier, Sir Joh Bjelke-Petersen, in testimony before the Fitzgerald
    Royal Commission into Corruption.

> Counsel assisting the inquiry, Mr Douglas Drummond QC, suggested
> to Sir Joh that by taking the police force's side in all matters, resisting
> calls for inquiries into alleged brutality and by using it as a political
> tool in such matters as street marches, he might also have helped
> create a climate in which corruption was likely to flourish.
> Sir Joh said: 'I can't accept that at all. . . . When you have top men
> in the department and they say it's not true, naturally you believe it.
> You have to believe it or otherwise you get into a very confused
> position yourself'.

> (cited in Freckelton 1991: 63)

16 For a clear account of the importance of experiential training to police
    professionalism, see Bayley and Bittner (1989). For an excellent recent
    discussion of the general problem of relating rules to police rank-and-file
    culture, see Goldsmith (1990).
17 A curious by-product of this concern with the objectivity of police
    recording technology is the SAP radio operator who claimed that the
    tapes which might provide conclusive evidence of the lack of SAP
    involvement in the Boipatong massacre, had been accidentally erased –
    Independent 12 August 1992.
18 See the discussion of this reversal of accusatorial process in relation to
    stop-and-search powers in Brogden (1984).
19 A further complication in the assumption of a division of functions in the
    South African criminal justice process is a consequence of the relative
    proximity between the prosecutor and the magistrate, as noted by the
    Hoexter Commission – see Fernandez (1992).
20 In which system, ironically, until the beginning of the twentieth century, the
    magistrate, not the police, possessed the primary interrogative powers.
21 For example, Yach, as reported in *Cape Times*, 27 June 1991.
22 Inevitably, the South African Police, like state police everywhere,
    creatively manipulate the crime clearance rate. In the words of
    ex-Lieutenant Mike Reddy, station commanders continually artificially
    construct the rates recorded to demonstrate that 'crime is under control'
    (*Star* 26 March 1991).
23 Generally, on the manufacture of recorded criminal statistics in South
    Africa, see Van Zyl Smit (1977).
24 A theme that dominated the 'National forum on international and
    domestic monitoring of the violence in South Africa' convened by
    IDASA 23 July 1992. It was attended by monitoring groups from across
    the country to develop proposals for the inclusion of an international

presence in monitoring in South Africa. The UN-sponsored Cyrus
Vance mission to South Africa has endorsed these and similar
recommendations.
25 Both the UN and the Commonwealth have agreed to provide a small
   number of monitors to work with local monitoring groups to monitor
   'the violence'. The first steps in this regard were taken immediately after
   the Vance visit, when UN-sponsored international monitors observed
   the 'mass action' called by the ANC.

6 Processes of ordering in the townships

1 We are grateful to the Chief of the Canadian Halton Regional Police for
   this characterization.
2 Richard Ericson (1992) has captured this vision well, in a post-Gulf War
   metaphor, as 'General Schwarzkopf policing'. For evidence of the pre-
   valence of this military imagery one need only look at any of the highly
   rated 'police shows' on Western television in which well-armed police
   fight against equally well-armed crooks.
3 Or more commonly a crime 'cleared-up' in which the state police claim
   a crime has been solved though the identification of a presumed offender
   but no conviction is actively sought.
4 Recorded crime rates are of course notorious for the contrivances that go
   into their construction. They contain little 'hard' evidence from which
   to draw comparative conclusions. Even if they contained relatively more
   than a minor degree of accuracy, the police–crime relationship in
   Western societies suggests that the exponential increase in such police
   forces since the war has been accompanied (with one major exception,
   Japan) with a disproportionate increase in recorded crime.
5 An incident that represented a cathartic televisual reaction of black
   people in Los Angeles, as part of the riots of May 1991.
6 See also Heald on Ugandan self-policing in Johnston (1992).
7 Primarily (as we noted in Chapter Four) in practices relating to Pass and
   liquor offences.
8 Under the Black Administration Act 38, 1927.
9 As in Spence's (1982), admittedly limited, Chilean example.
10 For a critical discussion of this theme, see Brogden and Graham (1988).
11 Freed (1963) noted the propensity of street gangs in Johannesburg to
   adopt ordering processes with regard to their members, in order to
   enforce internal discipline. Haysom (1981) has documented the practice
   of gangs within the South African prison system conducting various
   'policing' functions among other inmates. See Lodge (1983) for an
   account of the origin of the gangs in the Rand townships. A case study
   of the 'Russian' gang on the Rand, where they have been used as
   vigilantes hired by Soweto Councillors to break a rent boycott, suggests
   a rather more complex history. While in the West Rand, there is a long
   tradition of the 'Russians' being used against the young Comrades, the
   relationship between them and the police is a problematic one. They
   originated as a group of migrant workers who originally coalesced for

protection against city youth. The AmaRasheeya, or Russians, historically regarded collaboration with the police as deviating from the true
protective aims of gang. Despite evidence that they may have been used
by the police – for example, to stir up faction fighting in Vaal Reefs Gold
Mine in 1986 – their cooperation with the objectives of the state police
appears to have been conditional rather than absolute. While used by the
SAP and by the Municipal Councils, they were not simply a creation of
either body and loyalties could be conditional and transitory.

12   Qwelane (*Star* 7 July 1991) illustrates such a Makgotla practice where a
daughter was accused of disobeying her father. Her only defence, as the
accused, was to attempt to prove that her father was lying. That defence,
the only possible tactic, entailed breaching a different community norm
– criticizing a parent. Sjambok strokes were the normal mode of punishment for such offences.

13   For example, the Sophiatown Night Watch, the Christmas Watchmen
and the Bangalalas of the Western Native Township.

14   The social history of state policing has of course (Brogden 1991b) always
committed it to that regulatory, public order, rather than crime control
role, to varying degrees.

15   Paradoxically, this intent reflects the terminology and intent of section 29
of the Bantu (Urban Areas) Consolidation Act permitting a state police
officer to arrest without warrant in an urban area any African who he has
reason to believe is an 'idle or undesirable person' and to bring him
before a Bantu Affairs Commissioner who 'shall require such Bantu to
give a good and satisfactory account of himself'.

16   In this approach, it adopted the position eschewed by writers commenting on similar situations where the state police have been delegitimated and the alternative structures viewed as proto-revolutionary (West
1987).

17   A comment on urban courts in the copperbelt of Zambia seems apposite:

> Litigants in an Urban (customary) Court rarely speak about the law;
> they address themselves to the 'facts', leaving it to the Court to decide
> whether the 'facts' disclose a cause of action and what the appropriate
> action should be . . . the customary court is concerned with social
> relationships rather than right-and-duty bearing units which form the
> core of English legal procedure.
>
> (Smith 1968: 214)

18   See the summary of criticisms of informal justice practices in Mathews
(1988), of popular justice in Fitzpatrick (1992), and generally Abel
(1982).

19   See, for example, the historical evidence in Hay and Snyder (1989) on
faults in the private prosecution process. As Fernandez (1992) has noted,
the literature on prosecution practices in South Africa is notable only by
its absence. There is no academic research into police influence on the
prosecution process. An early insightful account of practices outside the
urban centres is provided by Burger (1943). Burger notes the pressure on
the police Sergeant prosecutor (one of whose subordinates may have
investigated the crime and made the arrest) to secure a conviction. Burger

also uniquely characterizes (in a comment which reflects much more recent analyses of court-room language in Western societies) the different discourses to which the accused is subject in the Court:

> the difficulties of interpreting from a European to a Bantu language can hardly be exaggerated: it is not merely a difference in language, but in fine shades of meaning that have developed from entirely different social environments. A literally correct interpretation may convey the exact opposite of what was intended.
>
> (1943: 154)

20 Most studies of self-policing and People's Courts have concentrated on settled townships. Sapire (1992) however, has provided a unique picture of a complex informal criminal justice process operating in the physically more distressed squatter settlements of the PWV area.
21 Although one study is attempting a careful planning and monitoring – see Centre of Applied Legal Studies (1991) 'Working Document No.1' Community Dispute Resolution Committee. But see the critique of the development in Nina (1992).

7 Towards a dual system of policing

1 See, for example, Braithwaite 1989; Goldstein 1979, 1987, 1990; Eck and Spelman 1987a.
2 In the British versions of this story, John Alderson, the former Chief Constable of Devon and Cornwall, who advocated community policing about the same time as Goldstein began developing his ideas, is frequently credited as the principle source for the emerging problem-solving orientation. Alderson outlined his conception of community-policing in 'A Community Police Order' as follows:

> Community policing described a style of day-to-day policing in residential areas in which the public and other social agencies take part by helping to prevent crime and in particular juvenile delinquency through social as opposed to legal action.
>
> (Alderson 1979)

3 See also Skogan (1990). For a generally excellent discussion of the relationship between problem-solving policing and the policing of communities, see Friedmann (1992). However, Friedmann differs in his arguments on self-policing. In our view, his denial of the possibilities of dual policing – including do-it-yourself schemes – is based on two faults. Unlike Johnston (1992), he underestimates the extent of self-policing schemes that have historically existed in local communities. Second, he fails to acknowledge the trend to private policing and security schemes in middle and upper class communities (as demonstrated by Davis (1990)).
4 Goldstein's article triggered a decade of debate and experiments over the implications of his prescriptions – see Klockars and Mastrofski (1991: 478) and Sherman (1992: 691).
5 See Spitzer and Scull (1977); Shearing and Stenning (1983); and South (1988).

6 In using the term 'privatization', as we state in the Notes to Chapter One, we are clearly not adopting the typical Western conception of the term that has in practice reduced it to meaning the disposal of state monopolies to private companies, who will conduct the activity for a profit. Our use of the term, while encompassing that notion, is primarily concerned with the way state activities may be returned to civil society for 'private' individuals to reclaim their right to participate directly in governance.

7 The most obvious example of an alternative to the use of force as the primary state police resource lies in the considerable literature that suggests that women police officers may bring to problem situations quite different resources from that of the traditional masculine resource of physical force; see, for example, Brogden *et al.* (1988: 116–19).

8 Although we again use the conventional term 'accountability' as a short-hand for democratic restraint of state policing, we go beyond the orthodox meaning. 'Accountability by explanation' (Marshall 1984) is simply insufficient. It is that police officers who do not follow the dictates of the conception of *public justice* (to which we refer later in this chapter) are formally sanctioned for their actions through similar procedures that are applied to many other officials of the State. The idea that policing is a special case, as compared to other state agencies, has always been suspect. In our conception of policing as a community resource – like education and welfare – procedures have to be established in the new South Africa by which state police officers are made directly liable for their actions and inactions.

9 We do not want to overstate the effectiveness of other state forces at bandit-catching. The primacy of the public order – as opposed to crime-fighting role – of state police forces is as evident in the West as elsewhere. But all things are relative. For the most part, Western police forces attempt to follow through their crime-fighting rhetoric with a relative effectiveness in relation to particular groups of offences.

10 Former editor of the *Rand Daily Mail*, and one of South Africa's foremost political commentators, in an editorial commenting on a letter he received from the General in charge of the SAP's Internal Stability Unit defending their tactics at Boipatang. (Sparks was present at Boipatong during President de Klerk's post-massacre visit.) The sinecured 'General Staff' are as culpable as any group in South Africa for the appalling suffering of recent years. In a revengeful society, many of them would be arraigned before a Nuremberg-style tribunal. In South Africa, where 'reconciliation' made possible through a general amnesty seems more likely, the decision to retire nearly a quarter of the general staff (August 1992) can only be a preliminary step. It will be important to ensure that any members of the SAP who do not commit themselves to community protection should be disposed of in the most economic form possible.

11 See the Goldstone Commission Press Releases 22 July 1992.

12 See Ayers and Braithwaite's (1992) discussion of 'tripartism' in the regulatory arena.

Bibliography

Abel, R.L. (1982) 'Western Courts in Non-Western Settings: Patterns of Court use in Colonial and Neo-colonial Africa', in R.L. Abel (ed.) *The Politics of Informal Justice*, London: Academic Press.

Abrahams, R. (1987) 'Sungusungu: Village Vigilante Groups in Tanzania', *African Affairs*, 86 (343): 179–96.

Alderson, J. (1979) *Policing Freedom*, Plymouth: McDonald and Evans.

Allison, J. (1990) 'In Search of Revolutionary Justice' *International Journal of the Sociology of Law* 18: 409–28.

Amnesty International (1986) *South Africa: Imprisonment under the Pass Laws*, London.

—— (1992) *South Africa: State of Fear; Security force complicity in torture and killings 1990–1992*, New York.

Anderson, D.M. and Killingray, D. (1991) (eds) *Policing the Empire*, Manchester: Manchester University Press.

Ayers, I. and Braithwaite, J. (1992) *Responsive Regulation: Transcending the Deregulation Debate*, Oxford: Oxford University Press.

Balbus, I. (1978) 'Commodity Form and Legal Form: An Essay on the Relative Autonomy of Law', in C.E. Reasons and R.M. Rich (eds) *The Sociology of Law*, Toronto: Butterworths.

Bapela, M.S.W. (1987) *The People's Courts in a Customary Law Perspective*, mimeo., Pretoria: UNISA.

Barak, A. (ed.) (1990) *Crimes by the Capitalist State*, Albany: State University of New York Press.

Bayley, D.H. (1985) *Patterns of Policing: A Comparative International Analysis*, New Brunswick, New Jersey: Rutgers University Press.

—— (1991) *Policing Democracy*, New Brunswick, New Jersey: mimeo.

Bayley, D.H. and Bittner, E. (1989) 'Learning the skills of policing', in R.G. Dunham and G.P. Alpert (eds) *Critical Issues in Policing: Contemporary Readings*, Prospect Heights, Il.: Waveland Press.

Baynham, S. (1990) 'Security Strategies for a Future South Africa', *Modern African Studies*, 28 (3): 401–30.

Bennet, T.W. and Scholtz, W.M (1979) *C.I.L.S.A.*, 12; 288–301.

Bennett, T. (1989) *An Evaluation of Two Neighbourhood Watch Schemes*, Cambridge: Institute of Criminology.

—— (1989) 'The Neighbourhood Watch Experiment', in R. Morgan and D.J. Smith (eds) *Coming to Terms with Policing*, London: Routledge.

Benyon, J. and Bourn, C. (eds) (1986) *The Police: Powers, Procedures, and Proprieties*, Oxford: Pergamon.

Berg, B.L. (1992) *Law Enforcement*, London: Allyn & Bacon.

Bindman, G. (ed.) (1988) *South African: Human Rights and the Rule of Law*, London: International Commission of Jurists, Pinter Publishers.

Bittner, E. (1980) *The Functions of Police in Modern Society*, Cambridge, Mass.: Olegeschlager, Gunn, and Haine.

Bohme, G. and Stehr, N. (eds) (1986) *The Knowledge Society*, Sociology of Science Yearbook, Vol. 10, Dordrecht: Reidel.

Boraine, A. (1988) 'Wham, Sham, or Scam – Security Management, Upgrading and Resistance in a South African Township', unpublished African Studies seminar paper, University of Cape Town.

—— (1989a) 'Grassroots Intervention in South African Black Townships: New Trends in Policing and Security Management', paper given at the *Conference on Towards Justice?* Crime and State Control in South Africa, University of Cape Town, May.

—— (1989b) 'The Militarisation of Urban Control: the Security Management System in Mamelodi, 1986–88' in J.A. Cock and L. Nathan (eds) *War and Society: the Militarisation of South Africa*, Cape Town: Gordon Phillip.

Bouman, M. (1987) 'A Note on Chiefly and National Policing in Botswana', *Journal of Legal Pluralism*, 275–99.

Braithwaite, J. (1989) *Crime, Shame and Reintegration*, Cambridge: Cambridge University Press.

Braithwaite, J. and Brabosky, P. (eds) (1992) *The Future of Regulatory Enforcement*, Canberra: Australian Institute of Criminology.

Braithwaite. J. and Pettit, I., (1990) *Not Just Deserts: A Republican Theory of Criminal Justice*, Oxford: Oxford University Press.

Brewer, J.D. (1990) *Inside the R.U.C.*, Cambridge: Clarendon Press.

Brewer, J.D., Guelke, A., Hulme, I., Moxon-Browne, E. and Wilford, R. (eds) (1988) *The Police, Public Order, and the State*, London: Macmillan.

Brogden, M. E. (1982) *The Police: Autonomy and Consent*, London: Academic Press.

—— (1984) 'From Henry III to Liverpool 8: The Complex Unity of Police Street Powers' *International Journal of the Sociology of Law*, 12.4.

—— (1987a) 'The Emergence of the Police – the Colonial Dimension', *British Journal of Criminology*, 27 (1): 4–14.

—— (1987b) 'An Act to Colonise the Internal Lands of the Island' *International Journal of the Sociology of Law*, 15, 2.

—— (1989) 'The Origins of the South African Police: Institutionalist Versus Structuralist Approaches', *Acta Juridica*, Cape Town: Juta & Co.

—— (1991a) 'The Rise and Fall of the Western Metis in the Criminal Justice Process', in S.W.Corrigan and L. J. Barkwell (eds) *The Struggle for Recognition: Canadian Justice and the Metis Nation*, Winnipeg: Pemmican Publishers.

—— (1991b) *On the Mersey Beat*, Oxford: Oxford University Press.

Brogden, M.E. and Graham, D. (1988) 'Police Education: the Hidden

Curricula', in R. Fieldhouse (ed.) *The Political Education of State Servants*, Manchester: Manchester University Press.

Brogden, M.E., Jefferson, T., and Walklate (1988) *Introducing Policework*, London: Unwin Hyman.

Budlender, G. (1988) 'Law and Lawlessness in South Africa', *South African Journal of Human Rights*, 4: 303.

Bull, R. and Horncastle, P. (1986) *Metropolitan Police Recruit Training: an Independent Evaluation*, London: Police Foundation.

Burchell, G., Gordon, C. and Miller, P. (eds) (1991) *The Foucault Effect: Studies in Governmentality*, London: Harvester Wheatsheaf.

Burger, J. (1943) *The Black Man's Burden*, London: Gollancz.

Burman, S.B., and Harrell-Bond, B.E. (eds) (1979) *The Imposition of Law*, London: Academic.

Cain, M. (1979) 'Trends in the Sociology of Police Work' *International Journal of the Sociology of Law*, 7 (2): 143–67.

Carriere, K.D. and Ericson, R.V. (1989) *Crime Stoppers: A Study in the Organisation of Community Policing*, Toronto: University of Toronto, Institute of Criminology.

Carter, C. (1991) 'Community and Conflict: the Alexandra Rebellion of 1986', *Journal of Southern African Studies*, 18, 1.

Cashmore, E. (1991) 'Black Cops Inc.' in E. Cashmore and E. McLaughlin (eds) *Out of Order: Policing Black People*, London: Routledge.

Catholic Institute for International Relations (1988) *Now Everyone is Afraid: the Changing Face of Policing in South Africa*, Cape Town.

Cawthra, G. (1986) *Brutal Force*, London: International Defence and Aid Fund.

—— (1992) *South Africa's Police: From Police State to Democratic Policing?* London: Catholic Institute for International Relations.

Centre of Applied Legal Studies (1991) 'Working Document No.1' Community Dispute Resolution Committee.

Chanock, M. (1987) *Law, Custom, and Social Order*, Cambridge: Cambridge University Press.

Clarke, M.J. (1989) 'Citizenship, community, and the management of crime', *British Journal of Criminology*, 27 (1): 384–400.

Cobbett, W. and Cohen, R. (eds) (1988) *State, Resistance and Change in South Africa*, London: James Currey.

Cock, J.A. and Nathan, L. (eds) (1989) *War and Society: the Militarisation of South Africa*, Cape Town: David Phillip.

Cole, J. (1987) *The Politics of Reform and Repression*, Johannesburg: Ravan Press.

Collins, S. (1992) *Police Deviance in the Western Cape Taxi War*, Cape Town: mimeo.

Comaroff, J.L. and Roberts, S. (1981) *Rules and Processes – the Cultural Logic of Disputes in an African Context*, Chicago: University of Chicago Press.

Connelly, W.E. (1987) *Politics and Ambiguity*, Madison: University of Wisconsin Press.

Corder, H. (1983) 'A Fragile Plant: the Judicial Branch of the Government and the Hoexter Report' in D.J. Van Vuuren, N.E. Wiehahn, J.A.

Lombard and N.J. Rhoodie (eds) *South Africa: A Plural Society in Transition*, Durban: Butterworths.

Corrigan, S.W. and Barkwell, L.J. (eds) (1991) *The Struggle for Recognition: Canadian Justice and the Metis Nation*, Winnipeg: Pemmican Publishing.

Critchley, T. (1979) *A History of Police in England and Wales* (2nd edn), London: Constable.

Cumberbatch, W.G. (1984) 'Community Policing in Britain' in D.J. Miller, D.E. Blackman and A.J. Chapman (eds) *Psychology and Law*, London: John Wiley.

Dahrendorf, R. (1985) *Law and Order*, London: Steven & Co.

Davis, D. (1990) *City of Quartz*, London: Vintage.

DeWitt, General H.G. (1988) 'Policing the Changing Society' in *SAP – Quo Vadis?*, International Symposium on Policing, Pretoria: UNISA.

Dendy, M. (1989) 'When the Force Frolics: A South African History of State Liability for the Delicts of the Police', *Acta Juridica*, 20–43.

Dipennaar, M. (1988) *The History of the South African Police*, 1913–1988, Silverton: Promedia.

Dixon, D., Coleman, C. and Bottomley, K. (1990) 'Consent and the Legal Regulation of Policing', *Journal of Law and Society* 17 (3): 345–59.

Doob, A.N. and Greenspan, E.L. (eds) (1984) *Perspectives in Criminal Law: Essays in Honour of John Ll.J. Edwards*, Toronto: Canada Law Book.

Dugal, N.K. (ed.) (1981) *Towards a New Legal System for Independent Namibia*, UN Institute for Namibia.

Dugard, J. (1978) *Human Rights and the South African Legal Order*, Princeton: Princeton University Press.

Duncan, P. (1964) *South Africa's Rule of Violence*, London: Methuen.

Dunham, R.G. and Alpert, G.P. (eds) (1989) *Critical Issues in Policing*, Prospect Heights, Il.: Waveland Press.

Du Preez, G.T. (1988) 'The Partnership in Policing: Fact or Fiction', in *SAP – Quo Vadis?*, International Symposium on Policing, Pretoria: UNISA.

Du Preez, J.A. (1982) 'Ideological Crimes of Violence in South Africa' in J. Van der Westhuizen (ed.) *Crimes of Violence in South Africa*, Pretoria: UNISA.

Eck, J.E. and Spelman, W. (1987) 'Who Ya Gonna Call? The Police as Problem-Busters', *Crime and Delinquency* 33 (1, January): 31–52.

——— (1989) 'Problem-Solving: Problem-oriented Policing in Newport News' in R.G. Dunham and G.P. Alpert (eds) *Critical Issues in Policing*, Prospect Heights, Il.: Waveland Press.

Ehrlich-Martin, S. (1980) *Breaking and Entering: Policewoman on Patrol*, Berkeley: University of California Press.

Enloe, C.H. (1980) *Ethnic Soldiers: State Security in Divided Societies*, Athens: University of Georgia Press.

Ericson, R. (1981) 'Rules for police deviance' in C.D. Shearing (ed.) *Organisational Police Deviance*, Toronto: Butterworths.

——— (1982) *Reproducing Order: A Study of Police Patrol Work*, Toronto: University of Toronto Press.

Ericson, R. V. (1992) *The Division of Expert Knowledge in Policing and Security*, mimeo, Toronto: University of Toronto, Centre of Criminology.

Ericson, R.V. and Shearing, C.D. (1986) 'The Scientification of Police

Work' in G. Bohme and N. Stehr (eds) *The Knowledge Society*, Sociology of Science Yearbook, Vol. 10, Dordrecht: Reidel.

Farson, A.S. (1990) 'Old Wine in New Bottles and Fancy Labels: the Re-discovery of Organisational Culture in the Control of Intelligence' in G. Barak (ed.) *Crimes by the Capitalist State*, Albany: State University of New York Press.

Fernandez, L. (1991) *Police Abuses of Non-Political Criminal Suspects: A Survey of Practices in the Cape Peninsula Area*, Cape Town: University of Cape Town, Institute of Criminology.

—— (1992) *Profile of a Vague Figure: The South African Public Prosecutor*, Cape Town: University of Cape Town, Institute of Criminology.

Fieldhouse, R. (ed.) (1988) *The Political Education of State Servants*, Manchester: Manchester University Press.

Fine, B. (ed.) (1979) *Capitalism and the Rule of Law*, London: Hutchinson.

Fine, D. (1989) 'Kitskonstabels: A Case Study in Black on Black Policing', *Acta Juridica*, Cape Town: Juta & Co.

Fine, D. and Hansson, D. (1990) 'Community Responses to Police Abuse of Power: Coping with the Kitskonstabels', in D. Hansson and D. Van Zyl Smit (eds) *Towards Justice: Crime and State Control in South Africa*, Cape Town: Oxford University Press.

Fitzpatrick, P. (1992) 'The Impossibility of Popular Justice', *Social and Legal Studies*, 1: 199–215.

Foster, D. and Luyt, C. (1986) 'The Blue Man's Burden: Policing the Police in South Africa', *South African Journal of Human Rights*.

Foster, D., Davis, D., and Sandler, D. (1987) *Detention and Torture in South Africa*, Cape Town: David Phillip.

Foucault, M. (1979) *Discipline and Punish*, Harmondsworth: Penguin.

—— (1986) 'Space, Knowledge and Power' in *The Foucault Reader*, (eds) H. Dreyfus and P. Rabinow, London: Harmondsworth.

Frankel, P.H. (1980) 'South Africa: The Politics of Police Control', *Comparative Politics* 12 (4): 481–9.

—— (1984) *Pretoria's Praetorians: Civil-Military Relations in South Africa*, Cambridge: Cambridge University Press.

Franklin (1935) 'The Native and the Administration of Justice', *South African Outlook*, August: 168–70.

Freckelton, I. (1991) 'Shooting the Messenger: The Trial and Execution of the Victorian Police Complaints Authority', in A.J. Goldsmith (ed.) *Complaints Against the Police: The Trend to External Review*, Oxford: Clarendon Press: 63–114.

Freed, L.F. (1963) *Crime in South Africa: an Integralist Approach*, Cape Town: Juta & Co.

Friedland, M.L. (ed.) (1990) *Securing Compliance: Seven Case Studies*, Toronto: University of Toronto Press.

Friedmann, R.R. (1992) *Community Policing: Comparative Perspectives and Prospects*, New York: Harvester.

Frontline (1986) 'The Rocky Rise of Peoples' Power', Christmas.

Galanter, M. (1981) 'Justice in Many Rooms: Courts, Private Ordering, and Indigenous Law', *Journal of Legal Pluralism*, 19: 1–47.

Gardbaum, S.A. (1992) 'Law Politics and the Claims of Community' *Michigan Law Review*, 90(4): 685–760.

Gelhorn, W. (1966) *Ombudsman and Others*, Cambridge, Mass.: Harvard University Press.

Giddens, A. (1991) *Modernity and Self-Identity: Self and Society in the Late Modern Age*, Cambridge: Polity Press.

Goldsmith, A. (1990) 'Taking Police Culture Seriously: Police Discretion and the Limits of the Law', *Policing and Society*, 1: 91–114.

—— (ed.) (1991) *Complaints Against the Police: The Trend to External Review*, Oxford: Clarendon Press.

Goldstein, H, (1979) 'Improving Policing: A Problem-oriented Approach' *Crime and Delinquency*, 25: 236–58.

—— (1987) 'Towards Community-oriented Policing: Potential Base Requirements and Threshold Questions', *Crime and Delinquency*, 33: 6–30.

—— (1990) *Problem-Oriented Policing*, New York: McGraw-Hill.

Goodhew, D. (1991) 'Between the Devil and the Deep Blue Sea: Crime and policing in the Western Areas of Johannesburg c.1930–1962', paper given at History Workshop *Structure and Experience in the Making of Apartheid*, University of Witwatersrand.

Gordon, C. (1991) 'Governmental Rationality: an Introduction', in G. Burchell, C. Gordon and P. Miller (eds) *The Foucault Effect: Studies in Governmentality*, London: Harvester Wheatsheaf.

Grant, E. (1989) 'Private Policing', *Acta Juridica*, Cape Town: Juta & Co.

Grundy, K.W. (1983) *Soldiers without Politics – Blacks in the South African Armed Forces*, Berkeley: University of California Press.

—— (1988) *The Militarization of South African Politics*, London: Oxford University Press.

Hansson. D. (1989) 'Trigger-happy? An Evaluation of Fatal Police Shootings in the Greater Cape Town Area from 1984 to 1986', *Acta Juridica*, Cape Town: Juta & Co.

Hansson, D. and Van Zyl Smit, D. (eds) (1990) *Towards Justice? Crime and state control in South Africa*, Cape Town: Oxford University Press.

Harcourt, A.B. (ed.) (1969) *Swift's Law on Criminal Procedure*, Durban: Butterworths.

Harms, L.T.C. (1990) *Report of the Committee of Inquiry into Certain Alleged Murders*, Pretoria: Government Printers.

Havemann, P. (1988) 'The Indigenisation of Social Control in Canada' in B. Morse and G. R. Woodman (eds) *Indigenous Law and State Law*, Dordrecht: Foris.

Hay, D. and Snyder, S. (1989) *Policing and Prosecution, 1750–1850*, Oxford: Clarendon Press.

Hay, M.J. and Wright, M. (eds) *African Women and the Law: Historical Perspectives*, Boston: Boston University Press.

Haysom, N. (1981) *Towards an Understanding of Prison Gangs*, Cape Town: Institute of Criminology.

—— (1986) *Mabangalala; The Rise of Right-Wing Vigilantes in South Africa*, Johannesburg: Centre for Applied Legal Studies, University of the Witwatersrand.

—— (1987) 'License to Kill; the SAP and the Use of Deadly Force', *South African Journal of Human Rights* 2: 3–27.

—— (1989a) 'Vigilantes and Militarisation of South Africa' in J. Cock and L. Nathan (eds) *War and Society: The Militarisation of South Africa*, Cape Town: David Philips.

—— (1989b) 'Policing the Police: A Comparative Survey of Police Control Mechanisms in the U.S., S.A., and the U.K.', *Acta Juridica*, Cape Town: Juta & Co.

—— (1990) 'Vigilantism and the Policing of African Townships' in D. Van Zyl Smit and D. Hansson (eds) *Towards Justice*, Cape Town: Oxford University Press.

Heald, S. (1986) 'Mafias in Africa: the Rise of Drinking Companies and Vigilante Groups in Bugisu District, Uganda', *Africa* 56 (4): 446–66.

Heymans, C. and Totemeyer, G. (1990) *Government by the People*, Cape Town: Juta & Co.

Hill, R. (1987) *The History of Policing in New Zealand*, Vols I, II, Wellington: GP Books.

Hindson, D. (1988) *Pass Controls and the Urban African Proletariat*, Johannesburg: Ravan Press.

Hochschild, A. (1991) *The Mirror at Midnight*, London: Collins.

Hund, J. and Kotu-Rammopo, M. (1983) 'Justice in a South African Township: the Sociology of Makgotla', *Journal of Comparative Justice of International Law in South Africa*, XVI, July.

Hund, J. and Van der Merwe, H.W. (1986) *Legal Ideology and Politics in South Africa*, Cape Town: University of Cape Town, Centre for Inter-group Studies.

Isaacman, B. and Isaacman, A. (1982) 'A Socialist Legal System in the Making: Mozambique before and after Independence' in R.Abel (ed.) *The Politics of International Justice*, London: Academic Press.

Jackson, R.L. (ed.) (1987) *Security – A National Strategy: the Integration of Security in the Public and Private Sectors*, Cape Town: Lex Patria.

Jaffee, G. (1986) 'Beyond the Cannon of Mamelodi' *Work in Progress* 41, April.

Jefferson, T. (1990 *The Case Against Para-Military Policing*. London: Open University Press.

Jefferson, T., and Grimshaw, R. (1984) *Interpreting Policework*, London: Unwin Hyman.

Jefferson,T., McLaughlin, E., & Robertson, L. (1988) 'Monitoring the Moni- tors: Accountability, Democracy, and Policewatching in Britain, *Contemporary Crises*, 12 (2).

Johnston, L. (1992) *The Rebirth of Private Policing*, London: Routledge.

Jones, S. & Joss, R. (1985) 'Do Police Officers Survive their Training?' *Policing*, 1 (4).

Kahanovitz, S. (1988) *Discovering South African Police Procedures*, mimeo, Cape Town: Legal Resources Centre.

Kanneymeyer, D.D.V. (1985) *Report of the Commission Appointed to Inquire into the Incident which occurred on 21st March 1985 at Uitenhage*, Pretoria: Government Printer.

Kemp, C. and Morgan, R. (1990) *Lay Visitors to Police Stations: Report to the Home Office*, Bristol: Bath and Bristol Centre for Criminal Justice.

Kinsey, R., Lea, J. and Young, J. (1986) *Losing the Fight Against Crime*, Oxford: Blackwell.

Klockars, C.B. (1985) *The Idea of Police*, Beverley Hills: Sage.

Klockars, C.B. and Mastrofski, S.D. (1991) (eds) *Thinking about Police*, New York: McGraw-Hill.

Landsdown, C. (1937) *Report of the Police Commission of Inquiry*, Pretoria: Government Printer.

Laurence, P. (1990) *Death Squads: Apartheid's Secret Weapon*, London: Penguin Books.

Lawyers Commission for Human Rights (1988) *The War Against Children: South Africa's Youngest Victims*, New York.

Leonard, R. (1984) *South Africa at War: White Power and the Crisis in Southern Africa*, Westport: Lawrence Hill & Co.

Lipson, L. and Wheller, S. (eds) (1986) *Law and the Social Sciences*, New York: Russell Sage Foundation.

Llewellyn, K.N. and Hoebel, E.A. (1941) *The Cheyenne Way*, Norman: Univerisity of Oklahoma Press.

Lodge, T. (1983) *Black Politics in South Africa since 1945*, London: Longman.

—— (1988) 'The U.D.F.: Leadership and Ideology' in J.D. Brewer, A. Guelke, I. Hulme, E. Moxon-Browne and R. Wilford (eds), *The Police, Public Order, and the State*, London: Macmillan.

Lustgarten, L. (1986) *The Governance of the Police*, London: Sweet & Maxwell.

Macauley, S. (1986) 'Private government', in L. Lipson and S. Wheeler (eds) *Law and the Social Sciences*. New York: Russell Sage Foundation.

McBarnet, D. (1981) *Conviction*, London: Macmillan.

McConville, M. & Baldwin, J. (1981) *Courts, Prosecutions and Convictions*, London: Oxford University Press.

McConville, M. Sanders, A. and Leng, R. (1991) *The Case for the Prosecution*, London: Routledge.

McConville, M. and Shepherd, D.(1992) *Watching the Police, Watching the Communities*, London: Routledge.

McNally, N.J.(1988) 'Law in a changing society: A view from North of the Limpopo' *South African Law Journal*, (105)

Maduna, P. (1990) 'The need to re-structure the South African legal system', paper given at *Conference on Para-legals in a Changing South Africa at University of Cape Town*, July.

Makamure, K. (1985) 'A comparative study of Comrades' courts under Socialist legal systems and Zimbabwe Village Courts', *Zimbabwe Law Review*, 3.

Manganyi, N.C. and du Toit, A. (eds) (1990) *Political Violence and the Struggle in South Africa*, London: Macmillan.

Manning, P (1977) *Police Work: The Social Organization of Policing*, Cambridge, Mass.: MIT.

Marais, E., (1991) *Police–Community Relations in the Natal Conflict*, Association of Sociologists of Southern Africa Conference paper, University of Cape Town.

—— (1992a) *Policing the Periphery: Police and Society in South Africa's Homelands*, Association of Sociologists of Southern Africa, Pretoria.

—— (1992b) *Proposal for International and Local monitoring in the transition*, paper presented at the IDASA Monitoring Conference, Pretoria.

Marais, E. and Rauch, J. (1991) 'Policing the Accord', *Work in Progress*, Nov/Dec.

—— (1992) *Policing South Africa: Reform and Prospects*, Johannesburg: Project for the Study of Violence, IDASA.

Marenin, O. (1982) 'Parking Tickets and Class Oppression', *Contemporary Crisis*, 2.

—— (1992) 'Policing the Last Frontier', *Policing and Society*.

Marshall, G. (1965) *Police and Government*, Methuen: London.

—— (1984) *Constitutional Conventions* Oxford: Oxford University Press.

Mathews, A.S. (1971) *Law and Order in South Africa*, Cape Town: Juta & Co.

—— (1986) *Freedom, State Security and the Rule of Law*, Kenwyn: Juta & Co.

Mathews, R. (1988) *Informal Justice*, London: Sage.

—— (1991) *The Policing of the Conflict in Greater Pietermaritzburg*, University of Natal, Centre of Criminal Justice.

Mayet, H.R. (1976) *The Role and Image of the SAP in Society from the Point of View of the Coloured People*, M.A. Thesis, Pretoria: UNISA.

Merry, S.E. (1991) 'Law and Colonialism', *Law and Society Review*, 25 (4).

Miller, D.J., Blackman, D.E. and Chapman, A.J. (eds) (1984) *Psychology and Law*, London: John Wiley.

Milton, J.R.L. (1967) 'The Vicarious Liability of the State for the Delicts of the police' *South African Law Journal*, 93.

Mnguni, J.H. (1988) *Three Hundred Years*, Cumberwood: APUDSA.

Moore, S.F. (1992) 'Treating law as knowledge: Telling Colonial Officers what to say to Africans about "their own" Native Courts', *Law and Society Review* 26 (1).

Morgan, R. (1987) *Police Accountability: the Implantation of Local Consultative Committees*, paper given at the Socio-Legal Conference, University of Sheffield, March.

—— (1987) 'Police accountability: developing the local infrastructure', *British Journal of Criminology*, 27 (1): 87–96.

Morgan, R. and Smith, D.J. (eds) (1989) *Coming to Terms with Policing*, London: Routledge.

Morse, B. and Woodman, G.R. (eds) (1988) *Indigenous Law and State Law*, Dordrecht: Foris.

Moses, J. (1990) *Peoples Courts and Peoples Justice*, Ll.b. thesis, Cape Town: University of Cape Town, Institute of Criminology.

Moss, G. (1987) 'State Moves against Peoples' Courts' *Work in Progress* 46, February.

Mott, J. (1979) Control of African Mobility: 16, *Labour Law Essays*: 16.

Mqeke, R.B. (1986) 'The History of the Recognition of Indigenous law in Ciskei', *Transkei Law Journal*.

Mwansa, K.T. (1986) 'The Status of African Customary Law and Justice under the Received English Criminal Law in Zambia', *Zimbabwe Law Review*, 4.

Nathan, L. (1989) 'Troops in the Townships, 1984–1987' in J.A. Cock and L. Nathan (eds), *War and Society: the Militarisation of South Africa*, Cape Town: David Phillips.

Nathan, L. (1990) *Marching to a Different Drum – Formation of the Namibian Police and Defence Force*, University of the Western Cape.

Ndabandaba, G.L. (1987) *Crimes of Violence in South African Townships*, Durban: Butterworths.

Ndaki, B.F. (1981) 'What is to be said for Makgotla?' in A.J.G.M. Sanders (ed.) *Southern Africa in Need of Law Reform*, Johannesburg: University of South Africa.

Ngcokvane, C. (1989) *Demons of Apartheid*, Braamfontein: Skotaville Publishers.

Niederhoffer, A.(1967) *Behind the Shield*, New York: Doubleday.

Nina, D. (1992) *Popular Justice in a 'New South Africa': from Peoples Courts to Community Courts in Alexandra*, Centre for Applied Legal Studies, University of Witwatersrand, Occasional Paper 15.

Omar, Dullah (1990) 'An Overview of State Lawlessness in South Africa', in D. Hansson and D. Van Zyl Smit (eds), *Towards Justice? Crime and State Control in South Africa*. Cape Town: Oxford University Press.

Panel, Testimony of Multinational (1992) *Lawful Control of Demonstrations in the Republic of South Africa for the Commission of Inquiry regarding the Prevention of Public Violence and Intimidation*, Cape Town: Government Printer.

Pauw J, (1991) *In the Heart of the Whore*, Pretoria: Southern Book Publishers, Halfway House.

Pettit, P. (1990) 'Liberty in the Republic', *John Curtin Memorial Lecture*, Canberra: Australian National University.

Pheto, M. (1983) *And Night Fell*, London: Allison & Busby.

Philips, K. (1989) 'The Private Sector and the Security Establishment', in J. Cock and L. Nathan (eds) *War and Society: The Militarisation of South Africa*, Cape Town: David Phillip.

Piliavin, I. and Briar, S. (1964) 'Police Encounters with Juveniles', *American Journal of Sociology*, 70: 206–14.

Pinnock, D. (1982) *Towards an Understanding of the Structure Function and Cause of Gang Formation in Capetown*, Master's dissertation, Cape Town: Univerisity of Cape Town, Institute of Criminology.

Pinnock, D. (1984) *The Brotherhoods: Street Gangs and State Control*, Cape Town: David Phillip.

Posel, D. (1984) 'Language, legitimation and control: the South African state after 1978', *Social Dynamics*, 10(1): 1–16.

—— (1989) 'A Battlefield of Perceptions': State Discourses on Political Violence, 1985–1988', in J. Cock and L. Nathan (eds) *War and Society: the Militarisation of South Africa*, Cape Town: David Philip.

Pothol, C.P. and Dale, R. (eds) (1972) *South Africa: Abuse in Perspective*, New York: Free Press.

Price, R.M. (1991) *The Apartheid State in Crisis*, Oxford: Oxford University Press.

Prinsloo, M.W, (1987) 'Re-statement of Indigenous law' *C.I.L.S.A.*, XX.

Prior, A. (1988) '*The South African Police and the National Security System*' unpublished paper, Cape Town: University of Cape Town, Institute of Criminology.

Punch, M. (1979) *Policing the Inner City*, London: Macmillan.

Qwelane, J (1991) *Star* 7 July.

Rabie, P.J. (1981) *Report of the Commission of Inquiry into Security Legislation*, Pretoria: Government Printer.

Ramahapu, T.V. (1981) 'The Controlling Mechanisms of the Mine Compound System in South Africa' *Institute of Labour Studies*, Maseru Discussion Paper No.1.

Randall, P. (1972) *Law, Justice, and Society*, Report of the Legal Commission on the Study Project on Christianity in Apartheid Society, Johannesburg.

Rauch, J. (1988) *A Preliminary Investigation into the Origins, Structure, and Operation of the Neighbourhood Watch System in the 'White' Suburbs of Cape Town*, unpublished B.Soc.Sc (Hons) dissertation, University of Cape Town.

—— (1991a) *The Challenges for Policing in the New South Africa: Policing the Violence*, paper presented to the American Society of Criminal Conference, San Francisco.

—— (1991b) '*Deconstructing the SAP*' paper presented the Association of Sociologists of Southern Africa Conference, University of Cape Town.

—— (1992a) 'South African Police Basic Training: a Preliminary Assessment' *Project for the Study of Violence*, Seminar Paper 4. University of the Witwatersrand.

—— (1992b) *A preliminary assessment of the impact of the Peace Accord Code of Conduct on Police Behaviour*, Policing Research Project, University of Witwatersrand.

Reasons, C.E. and Rich, R.M. (eds) (1978) *The Sociology of Law*, Toronto: Butterworths.

Reiner, R. (1985) *The Politics of the Police*, Brighton: Harvester.

Roberts, S. (1984) 'Some Notes on Customary African Law', *Journal of African Law* 1–5.

Rorty, R. (1979) *Philosophy and the Mirror of Nature*, Princeton: Princeton University Press.

—— (1992) 'The Intellectuals at the End of Socialism', *Harper's Magazine*, Spring.

Rose, N. (1989) *Governing the Soul: The Shaping of the Private Self*, London: Routledge.

Sachs, A. (1973) *Justice in South Africa*, London: Chatto Heinemann.

—— (1975) 'The Instruments of Domination in South Africa', in L. Thompson and J. Butler (eds) *Change in Contemporary South Africa*, Berkeley: University of California Press.

—— (1985) 'The Two Dimensions of Socialist Legality: Recent Experience in Mozambique', *International Journal of the Sociology of Law*, 2, May.

—— (1987) *Towards a Bill of Rights in a Democratic South Africa*, mimeo, Maputo, Mozambique.

Safro, W. (1990) *Special report on Violence against Black Town Councillors and Policemen*, South African Institute of Race Relations, December.

Sanders, A.J.G.M. (ed.) (1981) *Southern Africa in Need of Law Reform*, Johannesburg: University of South Africa.

—— (1985) 'Legal Dualism in Lesotho, Botswana, and Swaziland: a General Survey', *Lesotho Law Journal*, 1 (1).

Santos, B. (1977) 'The Law of the Oppressed: the Construction and Reproduction of Legality in Pasargada' *Law and Society Review* 12 (1).

―― (1979) 'Popular Justice, Dual Power, and Socialist Strategy', in B. Fine (ed.) *Capitalism and the Rule of Law*, London: Hutchinson.

―― (1984) 'From Customary law to Popular Justice', *Journal of African Law*, 28 (1/2)

―― (1992) 'State, Law and community in the World System: an Introduction' *Social and Legal Studies*, 1(20): 131–41.

Schalkwyk, P.J. (1987) 'Security and the Defense Force: the National Key Points Experience', in R.L. Jackson (ed.) *Security – A National Strategy: the Integration of Security in the Public and Private Sector*, Cape Town: Lex Patria.

Scharf, W. (1988) 'Peoples Justice' *Sash*, March.

―― (1989) 'Community Policing in South Africa', *Acta Juridica* Cape Town: Juta & Co.

―― (1990) 'The Resurgence of Urban Street Gangs and Community Responses in Cape Town during the late Eighties', in D. Hansson and D. Van Zyl Smit (eds) *Towards Justice? Crime and State Control in South Africa*, Cape Town: Oxford University Press.

Scharf, W. and Nbcokoto,B. (1990c) 'Images of Punishment in the Peoples' Courts of Cape Town – from Pre-figurative Justice to Populist Justice', in N.C. Manganyi and A. du Toit (eds) *Political Violence and the Struggle in South Africa*, London: Macmillan.

Schlemmer, L. (1987) 'The role of Blacks in Politics and Change in South Africa' in D.J. Van Vuuren *et al. South Africa in Transition*, Durban: Butterworths.

Seegers, A. (1990) 'Extending the Security Network to the Local Level' in C. Heymans and G. Totemeyer (eds) *Government by the People*, Johannesburg: Juta & Co.

Seekings, J. (1989) 'Peoples Courts in the Pretoria-Witwatersrand region in 1986', *South African Review*, 5.

Selvan, (1984) 'Limitation of Actions of the Police – the Case for Reform', *Lawyers for Human Rights Bulletin*, 3, January.

Shank, G. (1991) 'Introduction to South Africa in Transition' *Social Justice*, 18: 1–2.

Shearing, C.D. (1981a) 'Subterranean Processes in the Maintenance of Power: an Examination of the Mechanisms of Coordinating Police Action', *Canadian Review of Sociology and Anthropology*, 18(3).

―― (1981b) 'Introduction', in C.D. Shearing (ed.) *Organisational Police Deviance: its Structure and Control*, Toronto: Butterworths.

―― (1986) 'Policing South Africa: Reflections on Botha's reforms' *Canadian Journal of Sociology* 11 (3, Summer): 293–307.

―― (1990a) *Post-Complaint Management: The Impact of Complaints Procedures on Police Discipline*, Discussion Paper: Royal Canadian Mounted Police External Review Committee, Ottawa: Minister of Supply and Services, Canada.

―― (1990b) 'Review of G.L. Ndabandaba's *Crimes Violence in Black Townships*', *British Journal of Criminology*, 30(2): 251, 253.

―― (1991) 'Policing the police: the Ombudsman Solution', *Indicator S.A.*, 8(4): 11–14.

―― (1992a) 'A Constitutive Conception of Regulation' in J. Braithwaite and P. Brabosky (eds) *The Future of Regulatory Enforcement*, Canberra: Australian Institute of Criminology.

—— (1992b) 'Affirmative Action: The Case of the South African Police' *Proceedings of the Conference on Affirmative Action in a New South Africa*, Port Elizabeth, South Africa.

—— (1992c) *Reflections on Police Management*, Discussion paper: Royal Canadian Mounted Police External Review Committee, Ottawa: Ministry of Supply and Services.

—— (1992d) 'Conceptions of Policing: the Relationship Between its Public and Private Forms' in M. Tonry and N. Morris (eds) *Modern Policing*, Chicago: University of Chicago Press.

Shearing, C.D. and Mzamane, M. (1992) *Community Voices on Policing in Transition*, Belleville: Community Law Centre, University of the Western Cape.

Shearing, C.D., and Stenning, P.C. (1983) 'Private Security – implications for social control', *Social Problems* 30 (5): 493–506.

—— (1984) 'From the Panopticon to Disney World: The development of discipline' in A.N. Doob and E.L. Greenspan (eds), *Perspectives in Criminal Law: Essays in Honour of John Ll. J. Edwards*, Toronto: Canada Law Book.

—— (1987) *Private Policing*, California: Sage.

Shearing, C.D., Stenning, P., Addario, S.M. and Condon, M. (1990) 'Controlling Interests: Two Conceptions of Ordering Financial Markets' in M. L. Friedland (ed.) *Securing Compliance: Seven Case Studies*, Toronto: University of Toronto Press.

Sherman L.W. (1992) Book Review, *The Journal of Criminal Law and Criminology*, 82(3): 690–707.

Simons, J. (1934) 'European Civilisation and African Crime', *The African Observer*, 2(2): 20–7.

—— (1956) 'Passes and Police', *Africa South*, Spring.

—— (1991) 'South Africa's Common Society', University of Cape Town, African Studies School Seminar.

Skogan, W. G. (1990) *Disorder and Decline: Crime and the Spiral of Decay in American Neighborhoods*, New York: The Free Press, 1990.

Skolnick, J. (1966) *Justice Without Trial*, New York: Wiley.

Sloth-Nielsen, J.A. (1987) *Lwandle: Criminalisation of a Community*, Ll.M dissertation, University of Cape Town.

Smit, B.F. (1988) 'National Police: Pipedream or Reality?' *International Symposium on Police* Pretoria: UNISA.

Smith, D.N. (1968) 'Native Courts of Northern Nigeria: Techniques for Institutional Development', *B.U.L. Review* 49.

—— (1972) 'Man and Law in Urban Africa: A Role for Customary Courts in the Urbanisation Process', *American Journal of Comparative Law*, 20: 223–46.

South African Institute of Race Relations (1949) *Race Relations in South Africa*, Cape Town: Oxford University Press.

South, N. (1988) *Policing for Profit*, London: Sage.

Sparrow, M.K., Moore, M.H. and Kennedy, D.M. (1990) *Beyond 911: A New Era for Policing New York*, New York: Basic Books.

Spelman, W. (1983) 'Reactions to Crime in Atlanta and Chicago: A Policy-oriented Re-analysis' *Final Report to the National Institute of Justice*, Cambridge: Harvard Law School.

Spence, J. (1982) 'Institutionalizing Neighbourhood Courts: two Chilean Experiences' in R. Abel (ed.) *The Politics of Informal Justice*, London: Academic Press.

Spitzer, S. and Scull, A. (1977) 'Privatization and Capitalist Development: the Case of the Private Police,' *Social Problems* 25(1): 18–29.

Stenning, P.C. (1981) *Legal Status of the Police*, A Study Paper prepared for the Law Reform Commission of Canada. Ottawa: Minister of Supply and Services.

Stenning, P.C. and Shearing, C.D. (1980) 'The Quiet Revolution: the Nature, Development and General Legal Implications of Private Security in Canada', *Criminal Law Quarterly* 22: 220–48.

Stenning, P.C. and Shearing, C.D. (1987) *Private Policing*, Beverley Hills: Sage.

Steyn, J.H. (1971) 'Public Participation in the Prevention of Crime', *South African Law Journal*.

Steytler, N. C. (1987) 'An Unruly Trojan Horse – the Use of Force by the Police in Times of Unrest', *South African C.C.* 11: 161.

—— (1989) 'Policing "Unrest": the Restoring of Authority', *Acta Juridica*, Cape Town: Juta & Co.

—— (1990) 'Policing Political Opponents: Death Squads and Cop Culture' in D. Van zyl Smit and D. Hannson (eds) *Towards Justice*, Cape Town: Oxford University Press.

Storch, R. (1975) 'The Plague of the Blue Locusts', *International Review of Social History*, 20: 61–90.

Strauss, S.A. (1975) 'The Development of the Law of Criminal Procedure since Union', *Acta Juridica*, Cape Town: Juta & Co.

Sutcliffe, R. (1988) *The Tightening Noose: Violence against the Anti-Apartheid Organisations*, unpublished paper, Durban: Association of Sociologists of Southern Africa.

Suttner, R.S. (1968) 'Towards Judicial and Legal Integration in South Africa' *South African Law Journal*, LXXXV.

—— (1986) 'Popular Justice in South Africa Today', paper delivered at the conference on *Law in a state of Emergency*, University of Cape Town, 1–27.

Swilling, M. (1988) 'The United Democratic Front and the Township Revolt' in W. Cobbett and R. Cohen (eds) *State, Resistance and Change in South Africa*, London: James Currey.

Swilling, M. and Phillips, M. (1989) 'State Power in the 1980s: From "Total Strategy" to "Counter-revolutionary Warfare"' in J.A. Cock and L. Nathan (eds) *War and Society: the Militarisation of South Africa*, Cape Town: David Phillip.

Tanzer, E.G. (1988) *Botha's Dogs* Ll.b thesis, University of Cape Town, Institute of Criminology.

Thompson, J. (1992) 'Rorty's Vision', Letter, *Harper's Magazine*, August.

Thompson, L. and Butler, J. (eds) (1975) *Change in Contemporary South Africa*, Berkeley: University of California Press.

Tonry, M. and Morris, N. (eds) (1992) *Modern Policing*, Chicago: University of Chicago Press.

Trojanowicz R. and Bucqueroux, B. (1990) *Community Policing: A Contemporary Perspective*, Ohio: Anderson Publishing Co.

Turk, A. (1981) 'The meaning of criminality in South Africa' *International Journal of the Sociology of Law*, 9, 123–55.

—— (1987) 'Popular justice and the politics of informalism', in P.C. Stenning and C.D. Shearing (eds) *Private Policing*, Beverley Hills: Sage.

UMAC (Urban Monitoring and Awareness Committee) (1992) *Proposal and Motivation for the Formation of a National Monitoring Trust in South Africa*, paper presented to the National Forum on International and Domestic Monitoring of Violence in South Africa, 23 July, Pretoria.

UNISA, Criminology (1983): *Only guide for KRM100-5*, Pretoria: University of South Africa.

University of Witwatersrand Centre of Applied Legal Studies (1991) *Community Dispute Resolution Committee Working Document*, No 1.

Van Heerden, T. (1982) *Introduction to Police Science*, Pretoria: UNISA.

Van der Merwe, S.E. (1981) 'Accusatorial and Inquisitorial Procedures and Restricted and Free Systems of Evidence', in A.J.G.M. Sanders (ed.) *Southern Africa in Need of Law Reform*, Johannesburg: University of South Africa.

Van der Spuy, E. (1988) 'Policing the Eighties: Servamus or Servimus?' unpublished paper, Durban: Association of Sociologists of Southern Africa.

—— (1989) 'Literature on the Police in South Africa: An Historical Perspective' *Acta Juridica*, Cape Town: Juta & Co.

—— (1990) 'Political Discourse and the History of the South African Police' in D. Van Zyl Smit and D. Hansson (eds) *Towards Justice*, Cape Town: Oxford University Press.

Van der Westhuizon, J. (ed.) (1982) *Crimes of Violence in South Africa*, Pretoria: UNISA.

Van Niekerk, B. (1972) 'The police in apartheid society' in *Law Justice and Society*, Report of the Spro-cas Legal Commission.

Van Niekerk, G.J. (1986) *A Comparative Study of Indigenous Law in the Administration of Criminal Justice in Southern Africa*, Ll.b thesis, Pretoria: University of South Africa.

Van Vuuren, D.J., Wiehahn, N.E., Lombard, J.A. and Rhoodie, N.J. (eds) (1983) *South Africa: A Plural Society in Transition*, Durban: Butterworths.

Van Zyl Smit, D (1977) 'Die Hantering van Amptelike Misdaadstatistiek in die Suid-Afrikaanse Kriminologie', *South African Journal of Criminal Law and Criminology*, 1: 123–34.

—— (1990) 'Contextualising Criminology in Contemporary South Africa' in D. Van Zyl Smit and D. Hansson, (eds) *Towards Justice*, Cape Town: Oxford University Press.

Van Zyl Smit, D. and Hansson, D. (eds) (1990) *Towards Justice*, Cape Town: Oxford University Press.

Verskin, M. (1976) 'Vagueness in South African Subordinate Legislation', *South African Law Journal* 93.

Waddington, P. (1991) *Testimony of the Multi-National Panel regarding Lawful Control on Demonstrations in the Republic of South Africa Before the Commission of Inquiry regarding the Prevention of Public Violence and Intimidation*, Cape Town: Government Printer.

—— (1992a) Executive Summary, *Report of the Inquiry into the Police Response to, and Investigation of Events in Boipatong on 17th June 1992*, submitted to the Commission of Inquiry Regarding the Prevention of Public Violence and Intimidation, Cape Town: Government Printer.

—— (1992b) *Report of the Inquiry into the Police Response to, and Investigation of, Event in Boipatong on 17th June 1992*, submitted to the Commission of Inquiry Regarding the Prevention of Public Violence and Intimidation, Cape Town: Government Printer.

Walker, S. (1985) 'Racial Minority and Female Employment in Policing: The Implications of "Glacial" Change', *Crime and Delinquency* 31: 555–72.

Walklate, S. (1986) *The Merseyside Lay Visiting Scheme*, Liverpool: Merseyside County Council.

Weitzer, R. (1990) 'Police in Need of a New Ethos', *Democracy in Action, IDASA Bulletin*, September–October.

—— (1992) 'Northern Ireland's Police Liaison Committees', *Policing and Society*, 2: 233–43.

Weitzer, R. & Repetti, (undated) *Police Killings in South Africa, Criminal Cases, 1986–9*.

Wells, J. (1982) 'Passes and Bypasses: Freedom of Movement for African Women under the Urban Areas Act of South Africa', in M.J. Hay and M. Wright (eds) *African Women and the Law: Historical Perspectives*, Boston: Boston University Press.

West, W.G. (1987) 'Vigilancia Revolucionaria: A Nicaraguan resolution to Public and Private Policing', in P.C. Stenning and C.D. Shearing (eds) *Private Policing*, Beverley Hills: Sage.

White, J.B. (1984) *When Words Lose Their Meaning: Constitutions and Reconstitutions of Language, Character and Community*, Chicago: University of Chicago Press.

Wilson, J.Q. and Kelling, G. (1982) 'Broken Windows', *The Atlantic Monthly*, February: 29–38.

—— (1989) 'Making Neighbourhoods Safe,' *The Atlantic Monthly*, February: 46–52.

Worrall, D.J.C. (1972) 'Afrikaner Nationalism: A Contemporary Analysis' in C.P. Pothol and R. Dale (eds) *South Africa: Abuse in Perspective*, New York: Free Press.

Name index

Abel, R.L. 162, 208
Abrahams, R. 137
Alderson, J. 209
Allison, J. 164
Amnesty International 23, 26, 32, 38, 66
Anderson, D.M. 194
Ayers, I. 10, 210

Balbus, I. 5
Bapela, M.S.W. 141
Bayley, D.H. 2, 206
Baynham, 70
Bennett, T. 106
Benyon, J. 109
Berg, B.L. 103, 205
Biko, Steve 34, 124
Bindman, G. 30, 37
Bittner, E. 101, 206
Boesak, Desmond 45
Boraine, A. 159, 203
Bouman, M. 136-7
Braithwaite, J. 1, 10, 134, 155, 167, 175, 183, 210
Brewer, J. 33, 71, 192
Brogden, M.E. 3-4, 9, 30, 76, 104, 136, 167, 195, 205, 208, 210
Bucqueroux, B. 132
Budlender, G. 18-19
Bull, R. 102

Cain, M.E. 194, 201
Calitz, General Jacobus 93
Carriere, K. 131

Cashmore, E. 100-1
Cawthra, G. 17, 24-5, 77, 194, 198
Chanock, M. 134
Collins, S. 23, 121
Commissions, Lange 65; Cillie 197; Lansdown 17, 42-3, 61-2, 64, 76; Goldstone 40, 94, 95, 123, 176, 182, 186, 188-9, 205, 210; Harms 37; Hoexter 184, 202, 206; Kannemeyer 19, 35; Parsons 201; Rabine 28
Connelly, W.E. 123
Corder, H. 185
Critchley, T. 189-90
Cumberbatch, W.G. 132

Dahrendorf, R. 162
Davis, D. 63, 86
De Klerk 24, 26, 124, 176, 210
Denning, Lord 126
Dendy, M. 198
DeWitt, H.G. 4, 17, 76, 81
Dipennaar, M. 49, 53
Dixon, D. 110
Dugal, N.K. 141
Dugard, J. 139
Du Preez, G.T. 8, 66

Eck, J.E. 168-9, 209
Ehrlich-Martin, S. 180
Ericson, R. 42, 46, 54-5, 110, 119, 131, 185, 207

Fernandez, L. 20-2, 32-3, 44, 59,

62–3, 115, 159, 206
Fine, D. 82, 84, 204
Fitzpatrick, P. 140, 167, 175
Foster, D. 20, 27, 34–5
Foucault, M. vi, 119, 133
Frankel, P.H. 36, 76, 192
Franklin, P. 20, 195
Freckelton, I. 206
Freed, L.F. 203, 207
Friedmann, R.R. 123, 209

Gardbaum, S.A. 167
Gelhorn, W. 121
Giddens, A. 123, 184
Gluckmann, Dr. J. 22, 124
Goldsmith, A. 201
Goldstein, H. 168, 209
Goodhew, D. 44, 99, 146–7
Goosen, Pieter 34
Grant, E. 72–3, 181, 188, 204
Grundy, K.W. 76–7

Hansson, D. 186
Harcourt, A.B. 114
Haysom, N. 27–8, 33, 62, 85, 86, 88, 111, 198
Hindson, D. 63–4
Hochschild, A. 196
Hoebel, E.A. 126
Horak, Lieutenant-Colonel 34
Hund, J. 138, 154

Isaacman, B. 139

Johnston, L. 4, 19, 106, 134, 167, 185–6, 189, 205, 209
Jones, S. 102
Joss, R. 102
Jefferson, T. 3, 27, 119, 180

Kahanowitz, S. 29
Kemp, C. 205
Kinsey, R. 107, 117
Klockars, C.B. 194, 209
Kotu-Rammopo, M. 138, 154
Kruger, Minister 41, 50

Laurence, P. 25
Lawyers Commission for Human

Rights 29, 35
Le Roux Report 38
Llewellyn, K.N. 126, 216

McBarnet, D. 200
McConville, M. 5, 32, 110, 111, 114, 197, 200
McNally, N.J. 135
Mabitsa, Whitey 39
Makamure, K. 152
Malan, General Magnus 71
Mandela, Nelson 24
Manning, P. 47
Marais, E. 39, 119, 121, 129
Marenin, O. 166, 184, 194
Marshall, G. 210
Mastrofski, S.D. 209
Mathews, T. 32, 118, 179
Merry, S.E. 138, 139
Milton, J.R. 198
Mnguni, J.H. 60
Moore, S.F. 137–8
Morgan, R. 104, 179, 205
Moses, J. 142, 148, 157
Mott, J. 62
Mwansa, K.T. 136
Mzamane, M. 7, 23, 38, 44–5, 80, 118, 147, 159

Nathan, L. 104, 195
Ngcokvane, C. 51
Niederhoffer, A. 108
Nina, D. 181–2, 209

Pauw, J. 25
Perlman, John 38
Pettit, P. 1–2
Pheto, M. 63
Pinnock, D. 8, 19
Philips, K. 72–3
Posel, D. 54–5, 203
Price, R.M. 148, 150–2, 163
Prinsloo, M.W. 142
Prior, A. 51, 202

Ramahapu, T.V. 71
Randall, P. 64
Rauch, J. 39, 47, 57, 76, 80, 99–100, 103, 106, 109, 204

Reiner, R. 42, 167
Rhodes, Cecil 60
Rockman, Lieutenant 33, 78–9
Rose, N. 46, 119
Rose-Innes, Judge 34

Sachs, A. 17, 68, 71, 76, 165, 193,
    202
Sanders, A.J.G.M. 143
Santos, B. 162, 172–3, 184–5
Schalkwyk, P.J. 71
Scharf, W. 72, 150, 153, 155–7,
    163–5
Schalkwyk, Ockert van 34
Scull, A. 209
Seekings, J. 148, 157
Selvan, K. 37
Shank, G. 70
Shearing, C.D. 4–5, 7, 10, 15–16,
    23, 25, 38, 42, 44–7, 54–5, 72,
    80, 109, 112, 118–19, 122, 127,
    147, 159, 172, 174, 178, 201,
    203, 209
Sherman, L.W. 168, 209
Simons, J. 195
Skogan, W.G. 168, 209
Sloth-Nielsen, J.A. 203
Smit, B. 36, 157
Smith, D.N. 208
South African Institute of Race
    Relations 19–20, 44, 67
South, N. 9, 189, 209
Sparks, Allistair 177, 210
Spelman, W. 168–9, 209
Spence, J. 145–6, 152, 207

Spitzer, S. 209
Stenning, P. 4–5, 172
Steyn, J.H. 205
Steytler, N. 16, 19, 22, 42, 197
Suttner, R.S. 135, 139, 144
Swilling, M. 151

Tanzer, E.G. 83–5
Trojanowicz, R. 132
Turk, A. 66, 162, 201
Tutu, Archbishop 7, 45

Van den Eyck, Commissioner 43
Van der Merwe, Commissioner 43,
    48
Van der Spuy, E. 46–7, 53–4
Van Heerden, T. 3, 48, 58
Van Niekerk, G.J. 138–9
Van Zyl Smit, D. 203, 206
Viljoen, Acting Judge 34
Vlok, A. 53, 56, 78, 193
Vollmer, 108
Vorster, H. 23, 46, 48

Waddington, P. 95, 176–7
Walker, S. 205
Walklate, S. 3, 105
Wondrag, Brigadier 83
Weitzer, R. 36, 178–81, 195, 200
Wells, J. 202
West, G. 207
Wilson, J.Q. 168
Worrall, D. 52

Yach, Diana 108

Subject index

accountability 7, 10, 16, 26–40, 108, 208; democratic 36, 119, 156; internal 33, 199; legal 197–8; orthodox reform of 124–9; political 36–7, 40, 127–8; visibility and 129

Acts; Bantu (Urban Area) Consolidation Act 113, 208, Black Administration Act 138, 207; Black Local Authority 81; Criminal Procedure 113–14, 199; Internal Security Act 28, 30–2, 67; National Key Points 71; Police Acts 37, 192; Police Third Amendment 82; Security Officers 72

affirmative action 55, 93, 99, 101, 205

Afrikaans Cultural Association 47

Alexandra 87, 148, 151, 164, 181

Amnesty International 121

African National Congress 24, 52, 65, 80, 124, 151, 184, 189, 194, 207; and police reform 194–5

Anglo–American policing 95

Angola 194

apartheid 1, 5–8, 15–16, 28, 41, 46, 57, 60, 132, 196

Atteridgeville 151–2, 158

Attorney-General 39, 198–9

bandit-catching policing 166–71, 210; critique of 168–71, 177–80

Bantu Affairs Board 113; Commissioner of 113; Courts 137–40, 184–5

Behavioural Science, Institute of 55

Bill of Rights 193–4

Black Sash 120–1

Boipatong 18, 206, 210; and failings of SAP 176–8

Boputhatswana 89, 201

Botswana 136–7

British police 94, 126

Canada 94, 105, 126

Carltonville 39

Casspir 9, 44, 72, 79, 87, 194, 202

Cape 20, 76; Eastern 20, 81, 86, 151; Western 88, 147, 196

Cape Town 19, 22, 23, 33, 34

Centre for Criminal Justice 118

Certified Community Monitors 195

child police 200–1

children 30, 33

Chile, self-policing in 145–6

Ciskei 66, 86, 189

Civic Associations 83, 160, 163; and policing 133, 150, 153

civil policing 170–91, 209–10

Committee on Police Standards and Codes of Conduct 20

committees, street 8, 130, 148–53, 159; origins of 150; problems with 163; varied functions 150

communism 15, 52, 53–4, 93

communities, changes in state policing with 171–6

Community Guards 81; history on Rand 146, 207
community-ordering systems 134, 141
Community Policing 131, 166, 209
complaint system 119
COSATU 86, 189
crime 54, 67, 70, 117; manipulation of figures 206; police reaction to 118; and street committees 152–3
crime rates 117–18
criminology 7, 192, 203
Crown Prosecution Service 116
Codes of Practice 108–10
colonialism 1, 3
Commission of Jurists, International 121
Commissioner of Police 36
common law 95, 112–14, 115–16, 125, 138, 196; and citizen powers 199
Community Forums 103–5, 195
Community Councillors 157, 164
confessions 29
courts, state 33, 113–14, 115, 156
Crime-combatting and Investigating Department 194
Cradock 19
Crime-Stoppers 131
criminal justice 3
criminal law 27–8, 31
Crossroads 87–8
culture, police 17, 41–58, 77–8, 80, 99–107, 178; as obstacle 96, 98; religious 45–8
cultural colonialism 98–103
culturalist devices 96–107; limitations of 122–4
cultural movements 142
customary African law 134–6, 137, 140–1, 143, 164; court process 135–6, 154, 208

deaths-in-custody 22, 35, 124, 196–7
democracies, liberal and Western 3, 9, 93
democratic policing 95, 123–4
demonstrations 18, 30, 182, 189

detention 29–32
discourse, legal 54; political 46, 52–4; religious 46–51; scientific 54–7
Dispute Resolution Committees, Local 104, 120
District Attorney 116
dominion 1, 2, 3, 5, 6, 10, 181, 191
dual policing 165–91
Durban 80
Dutch Reformed Church 51

Elsies River 18, 34
Emergency, State of 18, 28, 30, 37, 49, 52, 53, 71, 77, 143, 152, 157, 159, 161, 200
Examining Magistrate 115–17

fingerprint science 55
frankpledge 190

gangs 142, 207–8
gendarmerie 33, 95
Graafwater 153, 158
Grahamstown 19
Groenwold 201
Gugeletu 147, 164

Heidelburg 81
homelands 16, 89
hostel dwellers 176

IDASA 19, 203
incorporatist devices 98, 103–7
informal courts 141
Inkatha Freedom Party 24, 56, 86–7, 184, 201
Inkathagate 193
Institute of Race Relations, South African 19
indigenous law 137
indigenous policing systems 136–7
Internal Stability Unit 177
interrogation 19–20, 29, 32
Israelites 18

Johannesburg 72, 80, 143
Judges' Rules 29, 95
judiciary 32–5

Katlehong 87–8
killings, by police 18, 19, 27–32,
    196
kitzonstabels 83–5, 143; attitude to
    84–5; training 84; salaries 83;
    violence by 84–5; brutality and
    torture by police 19, 20, 21, 22
Khayelitsha 158
Khutsong 39
KwaNdebele 201
KwaZulu 89, 201
Langa 38, 150, 153
Lay Visitors 103, 105–6, 120, 206;
    abuse of detainees 105
law, rule of 61–2
law-in-the books 112–14
laws, security 66–7
laws, segregative 65–6, 67, 71, 75
legalist devices 96–8; limitations of
    122–4

Magistrates 106, 200
Makgotla 139, 143–4, 154, 157,
    163, 165, 208
Mamelodi 147, 152, 153–5, 159,
    161, 163
Manenberg 147
methodology 192–3
Mossel Bay 149
Mozambique 139, 152
military structure 41
Minister for Law and Order 36, 40,
    118, 194
Minister of Police 19
minorities, ethnic 4
monitoring schemes 119–22, 128–9;
    in South Africa 120–1, 207

Namibia 16, 94, 122, 124, 129,
    132, 179, 195
Natal 20, 23, 24, 86, 199
National Party 16, 36, 51, 57
National Task Force 190
natural justice 137
necklacing 164
Neighbourhood Watch Schemes
    106–7, 205
New Police 145
NICRO 70

Northern Ireland 192
Nyanga 153, 155, 157, 163

ombudsman 121, 127–8, 195
Oudtschoorn 84

Pan African Congress 65
Parliament 36
Parow 19
pass laws 18, 60, 61–5, 67, 71, 202
Patrys Spoeurklub 200–1
Peace Accord 39, 104, 109, 122,
    176, 188, 200
Peoples' Courts 142–65; crime and
    149; imprisonment of members
    161; Mandela Plan 151;
    organisation 149; origins 151–2;
    outside South Africa 151–2;
    processes 144–5, 154–7;
    punishments 154–7; relation with
    State 144, 157–61; variety 149
police; Anglo-American 10;
    assistants (see kitzconstabels); as
    coercive resource 174, 187;
    autonomy 126–7; black 33,
    44–5, 69, 76–8, 100–1, 146,
    204; Chinese 76; complaints
    against 37–40, 42, 82, 152, 204;
    crime fighting 131–2; democratic
    37; definition 95, 194, 201;
    discipline 26; families 50–1;
    gendarmerie 10; guilty 26, 35; in
    Eastern Europe 2; Indian 65,
    76–7, 80; manpower 69–71,
    75–7, 203; organization 33;
    recruitment 44, 78; reform 4, 8,
    9, 10, 25, 39, 68, 70, 93,
    176–91; resignations 74; Second
    Amendment Bill 35; selection
    98–101; training 80, 94, 98,
    101–3; van 33; violence 17,
    18–40, 49, 63, 68, 77, 81–5,
    158, 176; discrediting complaints
    of 193
Police and Criminal Evidence Act
    95, 104, 108, 109, 112, 199, 206
Police, Municipal 80–3, 85–6, 143;
    killings of 82; strike 79; violence
    by 81–2

Police Judicaire 117
Police Reporting Officer 105, 195
Police Reserve 71, 107
policing, centralization of 4; and
    civil society 174–6, 179–91; and
    social justice 180; civil 5;
    community 4, 5, 181; colonial
    194; corporate 4, 171–5;
    definitions 9; dual 10;
    order-centred 130–5; popular 11,
    133; private 4, 5, 10; research on
    192; state 3, 6, 8, 10, 59,
    167–75; Western 9, 10; wives
    50–1, 75
POPCRU 78–9
popular justice 135, 139, 156
Prison Visitors 106
Pretoria 45, 64, 143
private security industry 71–3, 132,
    189, 198, 204
privatization and civil policing 5, 9,
    194
problem-solving policing 5, 10,
    167–75, 186, 195–6, 209
Procurator Fiscal 115
professionalism 56, 107–9, 132
prosecution 114–17, 163, 196

Queensland, Fitzgerald
    Commission 206

racism 9
Randburg 106
rape, forcible 70, 158
referendum 6, 7
Reserve Police Force 71
Riot Police 19, 33, 55, 59, 75, 89,
    184, 194, 201
Roman–Dutch law 198
rules, legal 8, 26, 27–9, 41, 42, 45;
    organizational 42; political 8
rule-making devices 98, 107–22;
    internal rule-making 98, 107–11;
    external rule-making 111–22
safety triangles 183–4, 188, 190
Sebokeng 54
Security Police 31, 33, 60, 80, 89,
    194
self-policing 136–7, 145–9, 158–9,

167; origins 147–8; pyramid
    relation 149
Sharpeville 18, 19, 65
shaming, integrative 134, 155
shocks, electric 20, 21
South African Broadcasting
    Corporation 202
South African Constabulary 9, 69
South African Community Party 52
South African Defence Force 56,
    71, 83, 88, 194
South African Police 4, 23, 24,
    26–7, 33, 35–6, 41–3, 47, 51,
    53, 55, 60, 62, 68, 70; chaplains
    48; Code of Honour 47–8; ethics
    course 48
South West African Police 94
Soweto 18, 30, 60, 80, 87, 130,
    148, 157, 197–8
street patrols, informal 142
suburbs, white 16

Tanzania 137–8
taxi wars 23, 121
technological recording devices
    109–11
Tembisa 87
theocratic racism 42
Thokoza 87–8
townships 16, 130; hostility to SAP
    62; ordering processes 142–65,
    161–5; policing 59–89
Transkei 66, 76
Trojan Horse 19
Transvaal 9, 64, 81, 120, 143
Tumahole 81, 88

Uitenhage 18, 148
UNISA 49, 52, 55, 74
United Democratic Front 24
United Nations 122, 129
United States 94, 106, 116

Vereeniging 143
victim surveys 117–18, 192
vigilantes 84–89, 143; origins 85;
    relationship with SAP 86–9;
    violence by 86–9
Viljoenskroon 54

Volk 42, 45, 51, 54
Voortrekker Monument 45, 47

war, Anglo–Boer 45, 51
weapons 19

women 4, 64–5, 70, 154, 202
women police 76, 78, 82, 100, 204

Zimbabwe 152
Zonkezizwe 87